Scientific Exploration and Expeditions

Volume One

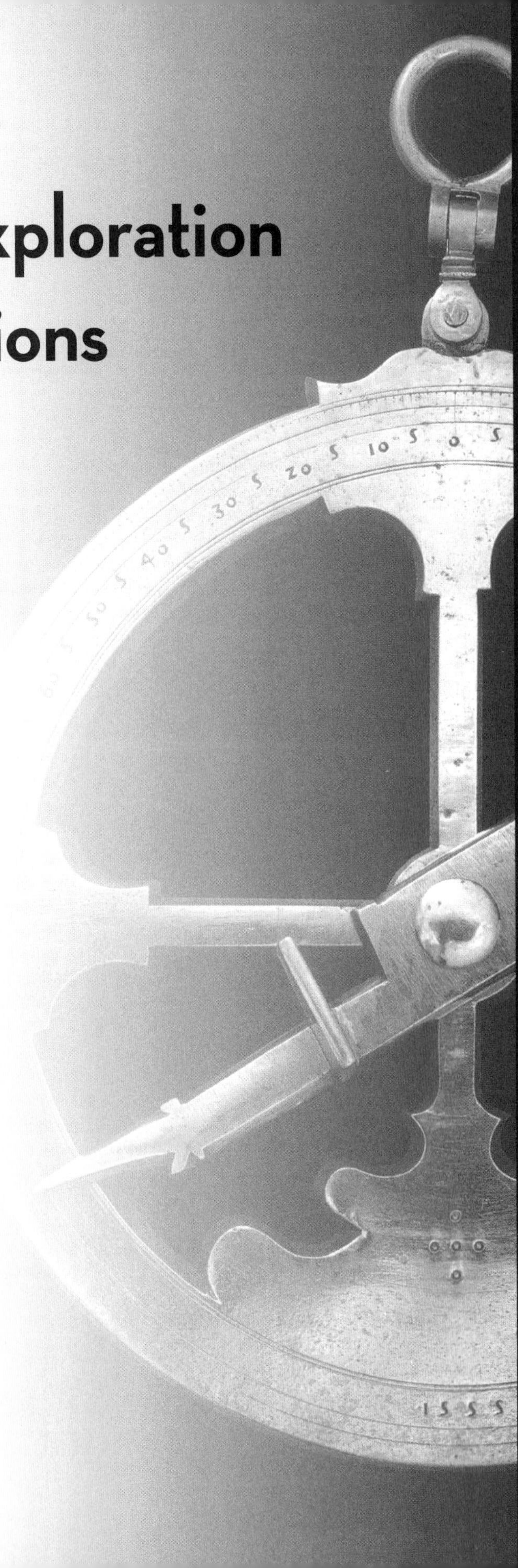

Scientific Exploration and Expeditions

From the
Age of Discovery
to the
Twenty-First Century

Volume One

Neil A. Hamilton

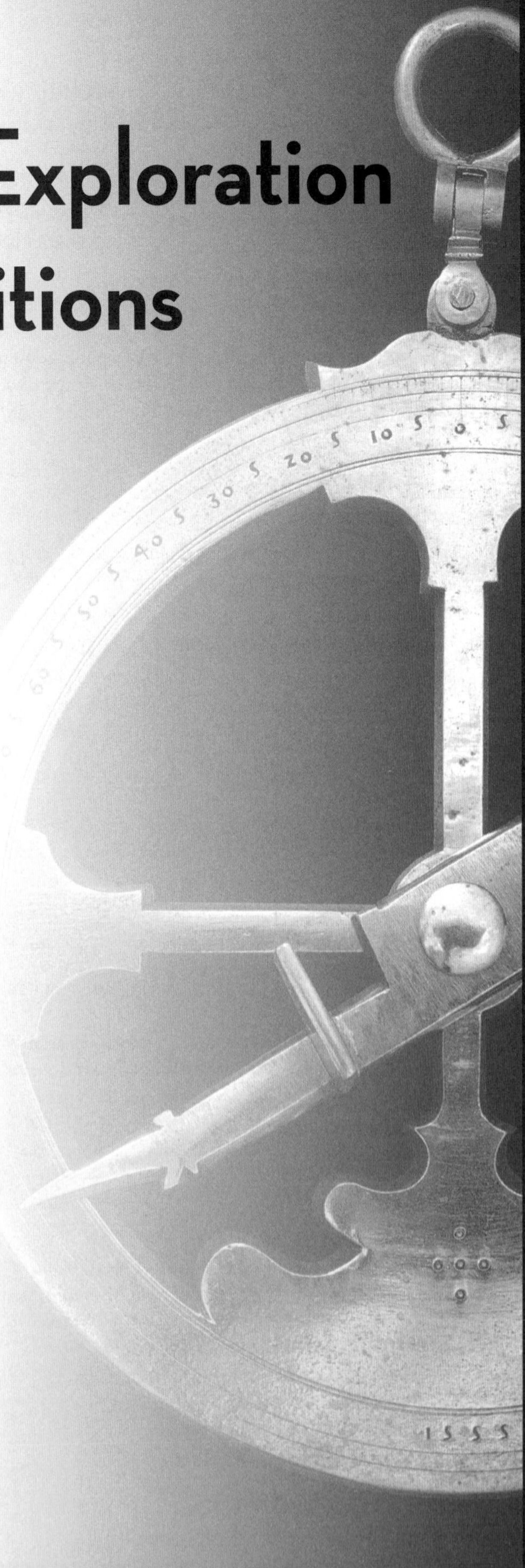

SHARPE REFERENCE
an imprint of M.E. Sharpe, Inc.

SHARPE REFERENCE
Sharpe Reference is an imprint of M.E. Sharpe, Inc.

M.E. Sharpe, Inc.
80 Business Park Drive
Armonk, NY 10504

Library of Congress Cataloging-in-Publication Data

Hamilton, Neil A., 1949–
Scientific exploration and expeditions: from the age of discovery to the twenty-first century / Neil Hamilton.
p. cm.
Includes bibliographical references and index.
ISBN 978-0-7656-8076-1 (hardcover: alk. paper)
1. Scientific expeditions—History. I. Title.

Q115.H167 2011
508—dc22 010012118

Cover Images: Science & Society Picture Library/Getty Images (background map); left to right: David Boyer/National Geographic/Getty Images; NASA/Getty Images; Granger Collection, New York; Thomas J. Abercrombie/National Geographic/Getty Images; Robert Lackenbach/Time & Life Pictures/Getty Images; Granger Collection, New York (astrolabe).

Printed and bound in the United States of America

The paper used in this publication meets the minimum requirements of American National Standard for Information Sciences Permanence of Paper for Printed Library Materials, ANSI Z 39.48.1984.

(c) 10 9 8 7 6 5 4 3 2 1

Publisher: Myron E. Sharpe
Vice President and Director of New Product Development: Donna Sanzone
Vice President and Production Director: Carmen Chetti
Executive Development Editor: Jeff Hacker
Project Manager: Laura Brengelman
Program Coordinator: Cathleen Prisco
Assistant Editor: Alison Morretta
Text Design: Patrice Sheridan
Cover Design: Jesse Sanchez

CONTENTS

List of Sidebars .... *vii*
Topic Finder .... *ix*
Introduction .... *xi*

VOLUME 1

A

African Association 3
Amazon River and Basin 5
Amundsen, Roald 8
Andrews, Roy Chapman 16
Antarctica 21
Arctic 26

B

Ballard, Robert 31
Banks, Joseph 38
Bates, Henry Walter 44
Beagle, Voyage of the 47
Bell, Gertrude 51
Bingham, Hiram 55
Bougainville, Louis-Antoine de 58
Bruce, James 61
Burton, Richard Francis 64
Byrd, Richard E. 69

C

Carter, Howard 75
Cheesman, Lucy Evelyn 78
Como Bluff, Wyoming 80
Cook, James 82
Cope, Edward Drinker 90
Cousteau, Jacques-Yves 92

D

Darwin, Charles 96
Discovery, Age of 105
Dunbar-Hunter Expedition 113

E

Earle, Sylvia 117
Everest Expeditions 120
Explorers Club 123

F

Flinders, Matthew 124

G

Gobi Desert 129

H

Hakluyt Society 131
Hanbury-Tenison, Robin,
and Marika Hanbury-Tenison 133
Hedin, Sven 135
Henson, Matthew 140
Heyerdahl, Thor 142
Horner, John R. 150
Humboldt, Alexander von 152

I

International Geophysical Year 158
International Polar Year 160

J

Jones, Albert José 162

K

Kingdon-Ward, Frank 163
Kingsley, Mary 165

L

Leakey Family 170
Lewis and Clark Expedition 175
Livingstone, David, and
Henry Morton Stanley 184

VOLUME 2

M

Mackenzie, Alexander 193
Malinowski, Bronislaw 195
Maps and Mapmaking 199
Marsh, Othniel Charles 205
Mexia, Ynes 207
Mouhot, Henri 209

N

Nansen, Fridtjof 211
National Geographic Society 216
Nordenskjöld, Adolf Erik 219

O

Oceanography, History of 222
Ostrom, John H. 229

P

Pacific Exploration 231
Park, Mungo 238
Peary, Robert E. 242
Powell Expeditions 245

R

Royal Geographical Society 250
Russian Exploration 252

S

Schliemann, Heinrich 259
Schultes, Richard 265
Schweinfurth, Georg August 267
Scoresby, William 269
Scott, Robert Falcon 272
Shackleton, Ernest 278
Society of Woman Geographers 285
Space Exploration, Manned 287
Space Exploration, Unmanned 301
Speke, John Hanning 317
Stark, Freya 321

T

Thomas, Elizabeth Marshall 324

V

Van der Post, Laurens 326

W

Wallace, Alfred Russel 331
Washburn, Bradford 336
Waterton, Charles 340
Watkins, Gino 342
Wilkes Expedition 345

Glossary *351*
Bibliography *356*
Index *I-1*

SIDEBARS

Amundsen, Roald:
Dogsleds.....11
The Wandering North Magnetic Pole.....14
Andrews, Roy Chapman: Fossil Extraction.....20
Antarctica: McMurdo Station.....24
Artic: Artic Drifting Stations.....30
Ballard, Robert:
Deep-Sea Vents.....33
Alvin.....37
Banks, Joseph: Carl Linnaeus and Modern Taxonomy.....40
Bates, Henry Walter: Mimicry.....46
Bell, Gertrude: Archaeological Digs.....54
Burton, Richard Francis: Chronometers.....67
Byrd, Richard E.: The Tin Goose.....73
Carter, Howard: The Curse of King Tut.....76
Cook, James:
The *Endeavour*.....86
The Transit of Venus.....88
Cousteau, Jacques-Yves: The *Calypso*.....94
Darwin, Charles:
Darwin's Finches Keep Evolving.....100
The Descent of Man.....103
Discovery, Age of:
Life Aboard the *Niña, Pinta,* and *Santa María*.....109
The Mariner's Astrolabe.....111
Dunbar-Hunter Expedition: Hot Springs.....115
Earle, Sylvia: The JIM Suit.....119
Flinders, Matthew: Nicolas Baudin.....126
Hedin, Sven: The Silk Road.....137
Heyerdahl, Thor:
Building the *Kon-Tiki*.....145
Pacific Ocean Currents.....149
Horner, John R.: The Question of Dinosaur Growth.....151
Humboldt, Alexander von: Humboldt's Instruments.....156
Kingsley, Mary: On African Intelligence.....168
Leakey Family: Olduvai Gorge.....173
Lewis and Clark Expedition:
Scientific Discoveries.....180
Charles Willson Peale's Museum.....182

Livingston, David, and Henry Morton Stanley:
Stanley's African Observations....190
Malinowski, Bronislaw:
The Participant Observer....197
Nansen, Fridtjof: Nansen's Instruments....214
Oceanography, History of:
The Hardy Continuous Plankton Recorder....227
Digging Into the Ocean Floor....228
Pacific Exploration:
The Pacific Floor....235
The *Trieste*....236
Park, Mungo:
Mungo Park's Escape and His Discovery of the Niger....240
Peary, Robert E.: Peary Versus Cook....244
Powell Expedition: The Grand Canyon as Geological Park....248
Russian Exploration:
Russian Explorers in Alaska....255
The Sea Bear Confronted....256
Schliemann, Heinrich: Is Agamemnon's Mask a Hoax?....263
Scott, Robert Falcon: The *Terra Nova*....275
Shackleton, Ernest: The Building of the *Endurance*....282
Space Exploration, Manned:
The Lunar Lander and Experiments Package....293
Experiments on the International Space Station....300
Space Exploration, Unmanned:
Sputnik 1....303
Sojourner....314
Speke, John Hanning: Speke's Scientific Findings....320
Van der Post, Laurens: Removal of the Bushmen....327
Wallace, Alfred Russel:
Alfred Russel Wallace and the Geographical Distribution of Animals....334
Washburn, Bradford: Washburn's Camera in Space....338

TOPIC FINDER

EXPEDITIONS, PROGRAMS, PERIODS

Beagle, Voyage of the
Discovery, Age of
Dunbar-Hunter Expedition
Lewis and Clark Expedition
Pacific Exploration
Powell Expeditions
Russian Exploration
Space Exploration, Manned
Space Exploration, Unmanned
Wilkes Expedition

EXPLORERS AND SCIENTISTS

Amundsen, Roald
Andrews, Roy Chapman
Ballard, Robert
Banks, Joseph
Bates, Henry Walter
Bell, Gertrude
Bingham, Hiram
Bougainville, Louis-Antoine de
Bruce, James
Burton, Richard Francis
Byrd, Richard E.
Carter, Howard
Cheesman, Lucy Evelyn
Cook, James
Cope, Edward Drinker
Cousteau, Jacques-Yves
Darwin, Charles
Earle, Sylvia
Flinders, Matthew
Hanbury-Tenison, Robin, and Marika Hanbury-Tenison
Hedin, Sven
Henson, Matthew
Heyerdahl, Thor
Horner, John R.
Humboldt, Alexander von
Jones, Albert José
Kingdon-Ward, Frank
Kingsley, Mary
Leakey Family
Livingstone, David, and Henry Morton Stanley
Mackenzie, Alexander
Malinowski, Bronislaw
Marsh, Othniel Charles
Mexia, Ynes
Mouhot, Henri
Nansen, Fridtjof
Nordenskjöld, Adolf Erik
Ostrom, John H.
Park, Mungo
Peary, Robert E.
Schliemann, Heinrich
Schultes, Richard
Schweinfurth, Georg August
Scoresby, William
Scott, Robert Falcon
Shackleton, Ernest
Speke, John Hanning
Stark, Freya
Thomas, Elizabeth Marshall
Van der Post, Laurens
Wallace, Alfred Russel
Washburn, Bradford
Waterton, Charles
Watkins, Gino

FIELDS OF STUDY AND PRACTICE

Maps and Mapmaking
Oceanography, History of
Space Exploration, Manned
Space Exploration, Unmanned

GEOGRAPHIC REGIONS AND LOCATIONS

Amazon River and Basin
Antarctica
Arctic
Como Bluff, Wyoming
Everest Expeditions
Gobi Desert
Pacific Exploration
Russian Exploration

SOCIETIES, ORGANIZATIONS, INSTITUTIONS

African Association
Explorers Club
Hakluyt Society
International Geophysical Year
International Polar Year
National Geographic Society
Royal Geographical Society
Society of Woman Geographers

INTRODUCTION

At the start of his historic voyage west across the Atlantic Ocean, Christopher Columbus made the following entry in his journal:

> This present year of 1492, after Your Highnesses had brought to an end the war with the Moors who ruled in Europe and had concluded the war in the very great city of Granada . . . and later . . . because of the report that I have given to Your Highnesses about the lands of India . . . you thought of sending me, Christobal Colon, to the said regions of India to see the said princes and the peoples and the lands, and the characteristics of the lands and of everything and to see how their conversion to our Holy Faith might be undertaken. And you commanded that I should not go to the East by land, by which it was customary to go, but by the route to the West, by which route we do not know for certain that anyone has previously passed.

Looking back on the momentous decision by King Ferdinand and Queen Isabella of Spain to send him in search of the East Indies, Columbus recounts much about the state of the world and the reasons for his voyage. Not least among the motivations for Columbus and the Spanish Crown, aside from the possibility of economic and territorial gain, was to protect Catholicism against the Moors—who had a stronghold on the Iberian Peninsula dating back to the early eighth century—and against the spread of Islam. If Catholicism could be carried to the East Indies, it might establish a beachhead against Muslim expansion. And if Catholics in the East could unite with Catholics in Europe, the Muslims might be surrounded and defeated.

In this respect, Columbus was a historical figure firmly rooted in the prescientific era, motivated by the religiosity and sectarian interests that had predominated for centuries. Yet in setting out on his historic voyage, the forty-year-old navigator from Genoa—who had an abiding interest in maps and claimed to have made his first ocean voyage at age ten—also exhibited a modern scientific curiosity in his desire to explore uncharted waters and sail headlong into the unknown. In doing so, he relied, in part, on the experiences and records of the Portuguese, who, under Prince Henry the Navigator in the early fifteenth century, had begun to sail south toward the coast of Africa, as well as on centuries of cartographic, navigational, and mathematical development—unsophisticated and imprecise as it often was—in both the Christian West and the Muslim East.

Historians continue to debate the extent to which the efforts by Columbus, the Portuguese, and other early explorers represented a truly scientific approach. According to one view, the early overseas expeditions were "guided in part by the new spirit of empirical science . . . that impelled men if, for instance, they heard about the existence of unicorns, to go out and try to find some." According to the renowned historian of exploration, J.H. Parry, however, the answer remains elusive. As Parry wrote in *The Age of Reconnaissance, 1450–1650* (1963), "How far explorers and promoters of exploration were directly and consciously motivated by scientific curiosity, is impossible to say on the scanty evidence which remains."

At the very least, Columbus and his Portuguese predecessors represented enough of a break from—and challenge to—the superstitions of the Middle Ages that their explorations rightly can be categorized as part of the beginning of the scientific revolution. More important, their expeditions unleashed a flood of scientific endeavors—by researchers, navigators, mapmakers, instrument makers, engineers, and theoreticians—to discover new lands, new oceans, new societies, new flora and fauna, and new ideas.

It is with these explorers, then, that this encyclopedia begins—chronologically at least. The work is organized alphabetically, with each letter containing an assortment of articles on scientists and explorers, expeditions, geographic locations, fields of study, and notable institutions.

Every entry begins with a thumbnail chronology that summarizes the major events of an individual's life, a scientific expedition, an area of endeavor, or an organization. Many entries contain short sidebars that present interesting background information on scientific principles, vessels and instruments, procedures and technologies, the natural environment, society and culture, and unresolved questions. And every article concludes with a list of recommended sources for further research and background reading.

This book is about the people and technologies that have marched hand in hand into geographic and empirical frontiers. It is not intended to be comprehensive in its coverage of explorers and exploration in general. Rather, it is meant to provide an embarkation point for a wide-ranging investigation into the history of scientific exploration from the Age of Discovery to the twenty-first century.

Toward that end, the encyclopedia presents information on scientific explorers and expeditions from a variety of fields in all seven continents. Polar explorers include Roald Amundsen, Richard E. Byrd, Matthew Henson, Fridjtof Nansen, Robert E. Peary, Robert Falcon Scott, and Ernest Shackleton. Paleontologists are represented by Roy Chapman Andrews, Edward Drinker Cope, John R. Horner, Othniel Charles Marsh, and John H. Ostrom. African explorers include James Bruce, Richard Francis Burton, Mary Kingsley, David Livingstone, Mungo Park, John Hanning Speke, and Henry Morton Stanley. Among the archaeologists and anthropologists are Gertrude Bell, Howard Carter, the Leakey family, and Heinrich Schliemann.

The great natural scientists Charles Darwin and Alfred Russel Wallace are discussed in detail, as are the natural scientific expeditions in North America of Meriwether Lewis and William Clark, William Dunbar and George Hunter, and John Wesley Powell. So, too, are the eighteenth-century Pacific explorers James Cook and Matthew Flinders and the modern oceanographers Robert Ballard and Jacques-Yves Cousteau. Not to be excluded are explorers—both in the field and in the laboratory—in the areas of conservation, entomology and botany, geology, and photography, from the inestimable naturalists Alexander von Humboldt and Joseph Banks to the ethnobotanist Richard Schultes and the mountaineering photographer Bradford Washburn.

Subjects meriting longer survey entries include the Age of Discovery, maps and mapmaking, the history of oceanography, Russian exploration, and space exploration—the latter covered in separate articles on manned and unmanned missions.

Other entries are devoted to important geographic locations—such as the Amazon River and Basin, Antarctica, the Arctic, Mount Everest, and the Gobi Desert—and to influential institutions and organizations—such as the African Association, Hakluyt Society, National Geographic Society, and Royal Geographical Society.

On Sunday, November 4, 1492, a few short weeks after his arrival in what would come to be called the New World, Christopher Columbus made the following journal entry (referring to himself, as he sometimes did, in the third person):

> The Admiral showed cinnamon and pepper to a few of the Indians of that place . . . and he says that they recognized it; and they said by signs that nearby to the southeast there was a lot of it. He showed the gold and pearls, and certain old men answered that in a place that they called Bohio there was a vast amount. . . . Moreover, he understood that there were big ships and much trade and that all of this was to the southeast. . . . The Admiral decided to return to the ship to wait for the two men whom he had sent and to decide whether to leave and seek those lands.

The lands he sought, of course, were part of the West Indies rather than the East Indies—a miscalculation of thousands of miles. Yet in attempting his voyage—for whatever combination of religious, economic, and scientific reasons—Columbus had taken a major step in launching the great Age of Discovery, opening the way to far-flung expeditions of the Earth and outer space, and setting forth into the new world of scientific research and understanding.

Neil Alexander Hamilton

A–Z Entries

A

AFRICAN ASSOCIATION

1788: Naturalist Joseph Banks and several other prominent Englishmen form the African Association to explore West Africa
1790: The association issues its first report
1795: Scottish explorer Mungo Park navigates the Niger River for the association
1831: The association merges with the Royal Geographical Society

The African Association was a private British exploration group that sponsored expeditions into the African interior in the eighteenth and nineteenth centuries in the hope of advancing scientific and geographic knowledge, as well as Britain's economic and political interests.

In eighteenth-century London, dining clubs emerged at which the wealthy socialized and discussed a wide range of issues. One such group, the Saturday Club, included Joseph Banks, the famed British naturalist who had sailed with Captain James Cook on voyages to the Pacific Ocean in the late 1760s. On June 9, 1788, Banks and eleven other men in the club met at St. Alban's Tavern, where they founded the Association for Promoting the Discovery of the Interior Parts of Africa, more commonly called by its members the African Association.

The association was created at a time when Europeans were showing a greater interest in Africa, but the British government, which was financially strapped, had no plans to finance expeditions to that vast continent. Europeans already had some familiarity with the interior of Africa. The French had established trading posts 600 miles (960 kilometers) inland on the Senegal River in the early 1700s, English traders had sailed a good distance up the Gambia River, and the Portuguese had explored the lower reaches of the Congo River.

Maps of the African interior, however, displayed large blank spots where Europeans had yet to venture. Geographic obstacles were partly responsible for keeping Europeans from penetrating deep into the continent. The transatlantic slave trade required no inland travel by Europeans, as African tribes generally brought slaves to the coast to be loaded onto ships. In addition, for many years, there were no other known commodities sufficiently attractive to draw foreigners inland.

In time, however, Europeans sought to know more about the African interior so that they could expand their trade with the native peoples. By the mid-1700s, Britain and France were competing for greater influence in western Africa. Concurrently, the Enlightenment stimulated curiosity about distant lands, as did the far-flung expeditions of James Cook, James Bruce, and others. Added to these developments, Europeans who worked to end slavery wanted to learn more about the African societies that were involved in the practice.

From the outset, the African Association displayed a sense of European superiority toward Africa. Its first report, issued in 1790, declared that the association sought to bring the benefits of science and mechanics to "nations hitherto consigned to hopeless barbarism." The association was headed by a secretary; the first was Hugh Beaufoy, an antislavery Quaker. Second to the secretary in standing was the treasurer; Joseph Banks was the first to serve in that position.

The primary interests of the association were to find new items of trade; expand scientific knowledge, especially botanical; and map geographical features. Among the questions on the minds of members were where the Niger River began and ended, whether there existed any great empires in central Africa, and where there might be gold. The founders of the association stated,

> Resolved that as no species of information is more ardently desired, or more generally useful, than that which improves the science of Geography; and as the . . . continent of Africa . . . is still in great measure unexplored, the members of this Club do form themselves into an Association for promoting the discovery of the inland parts of that quarter of the world.

As the group wanted to do more than promote trade or satisfy the members' curiosity, it supported the British drive to acquire new colonies in Africa. For example, in 1793, the association pushed for Great Britain to control the trade between the Barbary states (the North African states of Tripolitania, now part of Libya, Tunisia, Algeria, and Morocco) and Central Africa. Six years later, Banks advocated the British sending an army into the land around the Gambia and crushing any African forces that might oppose it.

The association sponsored several expeditions into the African interior. Some of these expeditions failed and resulted in the deaths of their leaders, while others achieved their goals. In 1795, the Scotsman Mungo Park navigated the Niger River. In 1797, Friedrich Hornemann left Cairo in an attempt to find Timbuktu (a legendary, ancient city, now called Tombouctou, in Mali), but he disappeared and was never heard from again. Later explorers learned that he had contracted dysentery and died after reaching the Niger River.

As a result of the club's efforts, much more was known about African geography by the early 1800s. In addition, Park's book *Travels in the Interior Districts of Africa: Performed in the Years 1795, 1796, and 1797,* which was published in 1816, stimulated interest in the association.

The African Association existed for forty-three years. Over this time, it counted a total of 212 subscribing members, with its largest membership for any single year, 109, occurring in 1791. Among its members were the Duke of Grafton and the Earl of Bute, and at least one woman, the Countess of Aylesbury.

In the 1820s, the British government began sponsoring expeditions to Africa, which reduced the need for the association to do so. In 1831, the African Association merged with the Royal Geographical Society, which had been founded the previous year. The association had expanded the geographic and scientific knowledge of Africa, served as the forerunner to later private organizations dedicated to the study of geography, encouraged the British government to explore the continent, and paved the way for increased British trade and imperialist expansion.

Further Reading

Hallett, Robin, ed. *Records of the African Association, 1788–1831*. London: Thomas Nelson and Sons, 1964.

Sattin, Anthony. *The Gates of Africa: Death, Discovery, and the Search for Timbuktu*. New York: St. Martin's, 2003.

See also: Banks, Joseph; Park, Mungo; Royal Geographical Society.

AMAZON RIVER AND BASIN

1541: Francisco de Orellana of Spain is the first European to discover the Amazon River at its confluence with the Napo River

1637–1638: Pedro Teixeira of Portugal journeys along the Amazon River system and reaches Quito in Ecuador

1800: With Frenchman Aimé Bonpland, the Prussian naturalist Alexander Von Humboldt makes the first modern scientific exploration of the Amazon basin

1817–1820: German naturalist Johann Baptist von Spix and botanist Carl Friedrich Philipp von Martius explore the Amazon in Brazil

1914: Former U.S. President Theodore Roosevelt leads a scientific expedition into the Amazon basin

1971: American author-photographer Loren McIntyre locates the source of the Amazon River in the southern highlands of Peru

2000: Polish-American explorer Andrew Pietowski uses the Global Positioning System to more accurately pinpoint the source of the Amazon

The Amazon watershed in equatorial Brazil includes the largest tropical plain in the world. The river itself stretches for 4,000 miles (6,400 kilometers) from source to mouth, making it second only to the Nile River in length.

The Amazon River ranges from 1 mile wide to 30 miles wide (from 1.6 to 48 kilometers) during floods. The estuary of the Amazon (where it empties into the Atlantic Ocean) is so wide, measured at more than 150 miles (240 kilometers), that the first Europeans to explore the South American coast had no idea they had come across a river. In fact, the river's vastness caused the early Portuguese explorers to name it *O Rio Mar*, the River Sea. At times, ocean-sized, 16-foot-high (5-meter-high) waves pound against the banks of the river's lower reaches. The size of the river, dense tropical growth, and treacherous conditions combine to make the Amazon difficult to investigate yet enticing to generations of scientific explorers.

Scientific and mapping expeditions to the Amazon basin continued into the early twentieth century, but it took later technological innovations—aerial photography and the satellite-based Global Positioning System—to confirm the source of the river. *(Library of Congress)*

The first European to discover the Amazon River (the region had long been inhabited by indigenous peoples) was the Spanish conquistador Francisco de Orellana, who, in 1541, left Quito, Ecuador, in search of gold. Orellana and his party headed east and crossed the Andes Mountains. Decimated by illness, the party eventually descended to the Napo River, which rises in Ecuador and flows through northeastern Peru, where it empties into the Amazon River. Upon reaching the Napo, they built a boat, arriving at the river's junction with the Amazon River in February 1542. In August, they descended the Amazon and reached the Atlantic Ocean.

The first journey upriver by a European began in 1637, when the Portuguese Pedro Teixeira left Belém, Brazil, near the mouth of the Amazon. His massive party, which consisted of some 2,000 people in more than thirty canoes, reached Quito early the following year. Teixeira undertook a return trip from Quito to Belém through the Amazon basin in 1638–1639 with the Jesuit father Cristóbal de Acuña, who wrote extensive observations about the forests, fish, wildlife, and native people they encountered.

Much as they did in other parts of the Western Hemisphere, the indigenous people of the Amazon basin suffered grievously from diseases—such as smallpox—brought by the Europeans. Perhaps 90 percent of the native population died due to epidemics during the early years of European exploration. Many long-standing indigenous settlements in the Amazon basin (Amazonia) were decimated.

The first modern scientific expedition in the Amazon region was led by Alexander von Humboldt, a Prussian naturalist, in 1800. With French botanist Aimé Bonpland, Humboldt explored the Orinoco River in Venezuela and, later, the region in Peru where the Amazon River begins. Together, they proved that the Orinoco River system connects with the Amazon River system.

Johann Baptist von Spix, a German naturalist, and Carl Friedrich Philipp von Martius, a German botanist, traveled to the Brazilian Amazon in 1817–1820 at the behest of the king of Bavaria. They collected specimens of 6,500 plants, 2,700 insects, 350 birds, 150 amphibians, 116 fish, and eighty-five mammals. Englishman Henry Walter Bates spent eleven years, from 1848 to 1859, in the interior of Amazonia, where he compiled the single largest collection of insects ever made by one individual in the region.

Numerous other expeditions have conducted scientific research in the region, including one led by former U.S. President Theodore Roosevelt in 1914 and others; the trip was sponsored by the U.S. National Geographic Society and the Brazilian government. Accompanying the expedition was George Cherrie, an American naturalist who had spent thirty years exploring the region. Roosevelt was one of the few other American explorers to that time to venture into the Amazon basin.

Cândido Mariano da Silva Rondon, a renowned Brazilian explorer, joined Roosevelt in leading the expedition. Rondon recently had discovered what he called the Rio da Duvida, or River of Doubt (which begins in northwestern Brazil and flows 400 miles, or 640 kilometers, to the Aripuanã River), while planning for the building of a railroad, but he had no idea where the river went. The Roosevelt expedition aimed to explore and map the river.

The party experienced numerous hardships along a river punctuated by dangerous rapids. Illness and the loss of canoes and supplies hampered the explorers, and Roosevelt nearly died from malaria. He wrote in May 1914,

> We have had a hard and somewhat dangerous but very successful trip. No less than six weeks were spent . . . forcing our way down through what seemed a literally endless succession of rapids and cataracts. For forty-eight days we saw no human being. In passing these rapids we lost five of the seven canoes. . . . One of our best men lost his life in the rapids. Under the strain one of the men went completely mad . . . and when punished by the sergeant he . . . murdered the sergeant and fled into the wilderness.

Still, they traveled more than 1,000 miles (1,600 kilometers) on the river, collected more than 3,000 specimens, and mapped the entire

River of Doubt—being the first to do so. "Colonel Roosevelt is not a fool scientist," said Cyrus C. Adams, editor of the *Bulletin of the American Geographical Society*, in 1914. "No one can doubt that he is a careful student and cautious contributor to science, and especially that he is a most careful geographer."

In 1971, author-photographer Loren McIntyre, working in cooperation with the National Geographic Society, used aerial photos to locate the source of the Amazon River. He traversed Peru's Apurímac River, an Amazon tributary, and then hiked through the southern highlands of Peru to reach the Continental Divide. From a ridge on a mountain named Nevado Mismi, McIntyre sited a small pond, at 17,220 feet (5,250 meters) above sea level and identified it as the source.

Yet the finding came into dispute. As a result, in 2000, a National Geographic team led by Andrew Pietowski, a Polish immigrant living in Carmel, New York, used the Global Positioning System (GPS) to pinpoint the source. Pietowski's team consisted of twenty-two explorers from the United States, Peru, Canada, Spain, and Poland. They confirmed McIntyre's finding of Nevado Mismi as the source of the Amazon River.

See also: Humboldt, Alexander von.

Further Reading

Medina, Toribia José, ed. *The Discovery of the Amazon.* New York: Dover, 1988.

Palmatary, Helen Constance. *The River of the Amazons: Its Discovery and Early Exploration, 1500–1743.* New York: Carlton, 1965.

AMUNDSEN, ROALD (1872–1928)

1872: Born on July 16 in Borge, Norway
1897: Joins the Belgian Antarctica Expedition as second mate
1904: Fixes the position of the North Magnetic Pole
1905–1906: Becomes the first explorer to traverse the Northwest Passage in a single voyage in a single ship
1911: Becomes the first explorer to reach the South Pole
1918–1920: Journeys along the northern coasts of Europe and Asia to Nome, Alaska
1926: With Italian Umberto Nobile and three other explorers, flies over the North Pole in a dirigible
1928: Lost during a mission to search for Nobile in the Arctic

A Norwegian explorer who was the first to traverse the Northwest Passage (a sea route from the Atlantic to the Pacific through the Arctic Ocean) and the first to reach the South Pole, Roald Amundsen also found the location of the North Magnetic Pole and paved the way for further scientific discoveries in Antarctica.

Roald Engelbregt Grauning Amundsen was born on July 16, 1872, in Borge, Norway, to a family of ship owners and captains. His father was Jens Amundsen, and his mother was Gustava Sahlquist, and he was raised in Oslo.

Roald's mother wanted him to become a doctor, but he was not attracted to the profession. In fact, to hear Amundsen tell it, by age fifteen, he had determined to become an explorer as a result of having read the works of John Franklin. A Briton, Franklin had died while searching for the Northwest Passage in the 1840s. Amundsen said that he read Franklin's works with a "fervid fascination." Amundsen wrote in his autobiography, *My Life as an Explorer* (1927),

> Strangely enough, the thing in Sir John's narrative that appealed to me most strongly was the sufferings he and his men endured. A strange ambition burned within me to endure those same sufferings.

As a boy, Amundsen began to prepare himself for his chosen career, developing a strong physique from skiing and hiking in his mountainous homeland. He wrote,

> At every opportunity of freedom from school, I went out in the open, exploring the hills and mountains which rise in every direction around Oslo, increasing my skill in traversing ice and snow and hardening my muscles for the coming great adventure.

Yet another formative influence on Amundsen was the first crossing of Greenland by the Norwegian explorer Fridtjof Nansen in 1888. Nansen had shown that with the right technique and technology, polar exploration could be successful. Nansen's use of skis, moreover, fit perfectly with Amundsen's own talent. Dreaming of becoming a hero such as Nansen, Amundsen continued to hone his skiing abilities while also learning how to handle sled dogs, manage a crew, and properly supply an expedition.

Following the death of his father in 1886 and his mother in 1893, Amundsen abandoned all thoughts of becoming a doctor, entered the military, and took to the sea. In 1897, he joined the Belgian Antarctica Expedition as second mate. He and the other men aboard the *Belgica* were the first Europeans to winter in Antarctica, after their ship became locked in by sea ice near the Antarctica Peninsula. The experience strengthened Amundsen's already keen interest in Antarctica, but it also revealed to him the perils of such an environment, including illnesses such as scurvy and dementia caused by the long periods of feeling closed in.

Northwest Passage

Amundsen turned his attention northward and determined to become the first person to sail the Northwest Passage from beginning to end in one trip. He would do so, he said, in "the service of science." In 1901, he bought a small fishing vessel, the 47-ton *Gjoa,* in Norway. Then, he went about raising funds for the expedition and collecting supplies. Despite his efforts, money was a constant problem. When creditors threatened to repossess his ship, he quickly gathered his crew of seven men, and under the cover of darkness and heavy rain, they sailed from Norway on June 16, 1903.

The Northwest Passage had been the object of explorers since the first Europeans had arrived in the Americas hundreds of years earlier. Amundsen called it "that baffling mystery to all the navigators of the past." He would spend three years, from 1903 to 1906, on his arduous journey.

He had selected the *Gjoa* with the idea that a small ship could better navigate the dangerous icy waters than could a large one. The *Gjoa* was only 72 feet (22 meters) long and 11 feet (3.4 meters) wide, with a shallow

Roald Amundsen and his party planted the Norwegian flag at the geographic South Pole on December 14, 1911. They spent the next three days making observations and conducting studies. *(Bob Thomas/ Popperfoto/Getty Images)*

DOGSLEDS

Dogsleds allowed explorers in the Arctic and Antarctic to journey far from their ships. The sleds, of various designs, had runners to provide a gliding motion over the snow and ice.

Europeans did not turn substantially to dogsledding until the 1820s and 1830s, during the second Arctic voyage of the Englishman William Parry, and the second and third voyages of the Scottish explorer Sir John Ross. These sledding forays were limited to short distances, but with knowledge gleaned from the Eskimos, Europeans learned the techniques of sledding.

During the second search for Sir John Franklin and his team in 1848, the extensive use of dogsleds showed the explorers how valuable sledding could be to an expedition. Sir James Ross, who served with Parry and John Ross, brought his knowledge of dogsleds with him to the Franklin search. James Ross was familiar with the sleds used in northern Canada and in Greenland; he had previously been on a sledding trip of nearly thirty days.

The American explorer Robert E. Peary relied on dogsleds for his trek to the North Pole in 1909. His wooden sleds were each 12 feet long (3.5 meters) and 2 feet wide (.5 meters) and could carry loads of up to 500 pounds (225 kilograms). Peary's sleds were pulled by teams of eight dogs.

The most effective use of sled dogs was a matter of considerable debate. Some explorers argued that during a long journey it was more efficient to kill some of the dogs as the trip proceeded. This would mean less food would be needed for the dogs, and the dead dogs could serve as food for the expedition.

Whatever the case, one explorer remarked that with the dogsleds "the ice which arrests the progress of the ship forms the highway for the [sled]."

draught. It had one mast and one mainsail, along with an auxiliary motor. Amundsen crammed the ship with supplies; even the deck was loaded with crates.

At Greenland, Amundsen picked up huskies to pull his dogsleds. In August 1903, he and his men stopped at Beechy Island (at the western end of Devon Island between the Beaufort Sea and Baffin Bay in the Canadian Arctic). Then, they headed south into Peel Sound (also in the Canadian Arctic, between Prince of Wales Island and Somerset Island), where they battled a fire in the engine room, crashed into a rock, and endured a violent gale.

In September, they set anchor at a small harbor off King William Island (part of the Canadian Arctic Archipelago in what is today Nunavut). They called the harbor Gjoa Haven, and it became their refuge for the coming winter.

To fix the position of the North Magnetic Pole, Amundsen traveled from the harbor to Boothia Peninsula (northeast of King William Island, across James Ross Strait); the round trip took seven weeks and the challenging conditions required the use of dogsleds. In spring 1904, through an interpolative method involving four readings, he fixed the position of the magnetic pole on the peninsula at a site slightly farther north than the earlier fix in 1831, by James Clark Ross, a British explorer. (Shortly thereafter, scientists debated the accuracy of Amundsen's readings and concluded they were deficient. Today the North Magnetic Pole, which moves rather than remaining stationary, is located well north of the Boothia Peninsula, in the Arctic Ocean.)

Ultimately, Amundsen and his crew spent two years at Gjoa Haven, where they set up a magnetic observatory containing photographic recorders to conduct more studies of the magnetic pole. From 1903 to 1905, Amundsen interacted extensively with the local Inuit, the people called Netsilik. Amundsen claimed that he and his men "showed them the marvels of our equipment, and treated them with the greatest consideration." However, his writings of them reveal at least an initial condescending European attitude:

> This was truly a thrilling moment in the lives of these poor savages. No one of them had ever seen a white man before, yet white men were a part of the legendary tradition of their tribe. Seventy-two years earlier, their grandfathers had met Sir James Clark Ross on almost this very ground.

During the time that the *Gjoa* was anchored off King William Island, some 200 men, women, and children erected fifty "Eskimo huts" near the ship. In his contact with the Netsilik, Amundsen collected samples of clothing, cooking implements, and other items that he intended for a museum exhibit. He took a keen interest in Netsilik cultural practices and praised some of them, including the skill of the women at making clothes from caribou skins. In all, he made important ethnographic studies of the Netsilik, while learning from them how to build snow houses and treat frostbite—skills he later needed for an expedition to the South Pole.

Amundsen and his men departed Gjoa Haven in August 1905. For the next three weeks, the shallow channels hampered their progress and nearly forced them aground. Finally, on August 26, they sighted the *Charles Hansson,* a whaling ship from San Francisco. This sighting meant that they would soon enter deeper waters and had nearly completed their journey through the Northwest Passage. "We had succeeded!" Amundsen later wrote. "What a glorious sight that was—the distant outlines of a whaling vessel in the west!"

Still, ice forced the crew of the *Gjoa* to spend the winter at King Point (near Herschel Island off the coast of the Yukon Territory in Canada), and they did not conclude their trip until they reached Nome, Alaska, in August 1906. Earlier, Amundsen had traveled more than 500 miles (800 kilometers) overland by skis and snowshoes to Eagle City, Alaska, where he wired news of his accomplishment. The completion of the journey made him the first person to traverse the entire Northwest Passage in a single voyage in a single ship.

The South Pole

Amundsen also had wanted to be the first person to reach the North Pole, but when he learned that the Americans Frederick Cook and Robert Peary already had accomplished the feat (Cook in 1908, Peary in 1909, although Cook's feat largely has been discredited), he set his sights on the South Pole.

He made this decision in secret, for he feared he would be beaten by a competitor, perhaps the British explorer Robert Scott, in the race to Antarctica. In fact, when Amundsen's ship, *Fram*, sailed from Morocco, even his crew thought that Amundsen had set the North Pole as his destination. He did not tell them otherwise until the ship was well into the Atlantic Ocean that the South Pole would be their goal.

Amundsen recruited eighteen men for the mission to Antarctica. He appointed Thorvald Nilsen as captain of the *Fram* and made himself second-in-command. He also brought with him sled dogs from North Greenland, known for their hardiness. While he intended to engage in scientific research during the expedition, his most important objective was getting to the South Pole.

The *Fram* reached Antarctica in January 1911, and Amundsen established his base camp, which he called Franheim, on the eastern edge of the Ross Ice Shelf at an inlet named the Bay of Whales. He chose the location because, as he later recalled, from the Ross Ice Shelf, "We could . . . go farther south in the ship than at any other point—a whole degree farther south than Scott could hope to get in McMurdo Sound, where he was to have his station." The site also was abundant in seals and penguins that could be killed for food.

On October 19, 1911, Amundsen and his party, consisting of four other men (Olav Bjaaland, Helmer Hanssen, Sverre Hassel, and Oscar Wisting) and four sleds pulled by fifty-two dogs, began their trek to the South Pole, some 870 miles away (1,400 kilometers). This was their second attempt, as they had been forced to abort an earlier attempt in September.

The explorers had to dodge crevasses that, hidden beneath the ice, could swallow up men, sleds, and whole dog teams. At one point, Amundsen and his men had to fight hard to keep a sled from meeting such a fate. For nourishment, the men consumed food they earlier had placed in caches along the first stages of the route. As they journeyed farther, they shot and ate several of the dogs.

The party battled blizzards whipped by winds of 35 miles (56 kilometers) per hour and struggled to find their way through thick fog. Yet, in all, the weather favored them, and on December 8, Amundsen and his men passed the point where, in 1908, British explorer Ernest Shackleton had been forced

THE WANDERING NORTH MAGNETIC POLE

Prior to the current age of the Global Positioning System, the North Magnetic Pole was extremely important to navigation, since it makes possible the functioning of the magnetic compass; however, it was difficult to pinpoint.

Not long after Europeans began using the compass, in the twelfth century, they sought to explain its directional properties. In 1600, English physician and philosopher William Gilbert published his *Book de Magnete,* in which he accurately postulated that no single place on Earth is magnetic; rather, he stated, the Earth is a giant magnet, and this is the reason that compasses pointed north. In effect, currents within the Earth's core produce the magnetic pole by emitting an electrical current. The magnetic pole moves because the currents change.

By the early 1800s, research showed that the North Magnetic Pole was located not at the geographic North Pole but somewhere in Canada. British explorer Sir James Ross located the North Magnetic Pole in 1831 at Cape Adelaide on the Boothia Peninsula in northern Canada.

Since then, the North Magnetic Pole has drifted considerably to the northwest. In 2001, it was located near Canada's Ellesmere Island, which lies at 81° N 80' W. In 2005, it was estimated to be at 82.7° N and 114.4' W. Should the trend continue—and it is moving at about 6 to 25 miles (10 to 40 kilometers) a year—the North Magnetic Pole soon could wind up in Siberia.

Despite its movement and the development of new satellite technology, the North Magnetic Pole's location remains important to navigators who still rely on their compasses for direction.

to turn back. This put them 95 miles (150 kilometers) from the pole. By then, the men were suffering from frostbite; however, they were worried that Scott might yet beat them, so they pushed ahead at full speed.

At 3 P.M. on Friday, December 14, 1911, the sleds were halted. The men had reached the South Pole. With their battered hands, they planted the Norwegian flag at the spot. Amundsen named the surrounding plain King Haakon VII's Plateau. That evening, the men celebrated with a meal of seal meat. Amundsen wrote in his diary: "So we arrived and were able to plant our flag at the geographical South Pole. God be thanked!"

Over the next three days, the party completed observations to confirm that they had reached the South Pole. Before leaving, they erected a tent and left a message inside of it to inform Scott of their accomplishment.

Their return trip to the *Fram* took thirty-nine days; they reached the ship on January 25, 1912. There followed a journey of several weeks to Tasmania, Australia. On March 7, 1912, Amundsen cabled his brother from Hobart, Tasmania, with the news that he had reached the South Pole.

Amundsen's adept use of dogs and skis, his single-minded determination to reach the pole, and his ability to supply his party with food and other necessities, all contributed to his success. He said as much when he later wrote,

> I may say that this is the greatest factor—the way in which the expedition is equipped—the way in which every difficulty is foreseen, and precautions taken for meeting or avoiding it. Victory awaits him who has everything in order.

Northeast Passage and North Pole

In 1918, Amundsen began a trip through the Northeast Passage. (Also known as the Northern Route, it comprises the Arctic Ocean along the northern coast of Eurasia). He planned to have his ship, the *Maud*, drift along the currents that bear the ice floes of the Arctic Ocean and then cross the North Pole, but he failed to reach the pole. Instead he sailed along the northern coast of Europe and Asia and, in 1920, reached Nome, Alaska. He was the first person to sail along the entire northern coast of Europe and Asia since Adolf Erik Nordenskiöld, a Swedish explorer, had done so in the 1870s.

Despite Amundsen's failure to reach the North Pole, important scientific work was accomplished during the journey by his colleague, Harald Sverdrup, who studied ocean currents and posited that the effects of the Earth's rotation could best be observed in the currents of the polar regions. Sverdrup's work aboard the *Maud*, including work he did after the trip of 1918–1920, enabled him and other scientists to better understand the physical oceanography of currents. He also researched meteorology, magnetics, and tidal dynamics.

In May 1926, Amundsen joined with the Italian explorer and engineer Umberto Nobile and the explorers Lincoln Ellsworth (an American), Hjalmar Riiser-Larsen (a Norwegian), and Oscar Wisting (also a Norwegian), to fly across the North Pole in the dirigible *Norge* ("Norway"). Nobile had designed and built the airship, and the men flew it from the island of Spitsbergen, Norway, to Teller, Alaska, near Nome, in a little more than seventy hours. Their journey included passage over unexplored regions of the Arctic Ocean north of Alaska. (The American explorer Richard Byrd claimed to have flown over the North Pole forty-eight hours before Amundsen, in an airplane, but there still is some debate over whether he in fact did this.)

Amundsen and Nobile argued over which of them should get most of the credit for the flight. Despite this disagreement, when Nobile was lost during a polar flight in 1928, Amundsen volunteered to help find him. Searchers found Nobile, but, in the effort, Amundsen disappeared.

Amundsen was last heard from on June 28, 1928, after taking off in a plane from Norway. A pontoon from the plane was found on August 31, but Amundsen's body was never recovered. He had fulfilled his "service [to] science," and in the end, service to a friend.

Further Reading

Huntford, Roland, ed. *The Amundsen Photographs.* New York: Atlantic Monthly Press, 1987.

———. *The Last Place on Earth: Scott and Amundsen's Race to the South Pole.* New York: Modern Library, 1999.

Langley, Andrew, and Kevin Barnes. *The Great Polar Adventure: The Journeys of Roald Amundsen.* New York: Chelsea House, 1994.

Vaeth, J. Gordon. *To the Ends of the Earth: The Explorations of Roald Amundsen.* New York: Harper and Row, 1962.

See also: Antarctica; Scott, Robert Falcon.

ANDREWS, ROY CHAPMAN (1884–1960)

1884: Born on January 26 in Beloit, Wisconsin
1908: Writes scientific paper on right whales
1909–1912: Leads expeditions to study cetaceans in Japan, China, the Philippines, Borneo, Celebes Island, and Korea
1922: Organizes his first Central Asiatic Expedition
1923: With George Olsen, discovers dinosaur eggs in the Gobi Desert of China
1930: Leads his last Central Asiatic Expedition to eastern Inner Mongolia
1935: Becomes director of the American Museum of Natural History in New York City
1960: Dies in Carmel, California, on March 11

An American naturalist whose pursuit of whales in the Pacific Ocean and fossils in China rewrote the history of the Earth's development, Roy Chapman Andrews is, according to some accounts, the model for the fictional movie character Indiana Jones. Yet Andrews neither pursued the Holy Grail, nor did he advocate risky undertakings. To him, science and careful preparation came first.

Andrews was born on January 26, 1884, in Beloit, Wisconsin, to Charles Ezra Andrews, a wholesale druggist, and Cora May Chapman. He enjoyed bird watching and decided early on to become an explorer and work in a natural history museum. Self-taught in taxidermy (the preparing and stuffing of dead animal skins so that they appear lifelike), he studied physiology and anatomy at Beloit College while working as a taxidermist at the Logan Museum of Anthropology.

In 1905, when Andrews was in his junior year of college, he experienced a traumatic event. During an outing with a friend, the canoe in which they were riding capsized. Andrews's friend drowned, while Andrews nearly perished. As he struggled to come to terms with his friend's death and his own near death, Andrews concluded that, since life was so short and precarious, he must do everything reasonably possible to pursue his desire for museum work.

In 1906, Andrews received his bachelor's degree from Beloit. Then, with $30 in his pocket, he journeyed to New York City, where he sought a position at the American Museum of Natural History (AMNH). Anxious to be hired, he offered to do anything, even scrub floors. The museum's director, Hermon C. Bumpus, impressed by the young man, made him an assistant to James L. Clark in the Department of Taxidermy. Andrews later recalled his first day on the job:

> I shut my eyes and made a little prayer, then walked to the entrance on Seventy-Seventh Street, and, for the first time, went through the doors of the American Museum as an employee.

Cetaceans

Andrews helped build models of cetaceans (aquatic mammals such as whales, porpoises, and dolphins), including a model of a blue whale. In 1908, he wrote a scientific paper on the anatomy of a right whale based on his study of the skeleton of one from the North Atlantic.

Shortly thereafter, Andrews volunteered to travel for the museum, without pay, to British Columbia and study whales there. At shore-whaling stations, where whales were butchered by commercial hunters, Andrews measured the animals, took photographs, and studied their internal organs and skeletons. In all, he studied more than 100 whales.

Over the next few years, Andrews led several expeditions to continue his study of cetaceans: to Japan, China, the Philippines, Borneo, and Celebes Island in 1909 and 1910, and to Korea in 1911 and 1912. For his master's degree in mammalogy from Columbia University (which he received in 1913), he wrote a thesis based on a stunning discovery.

While in Korea, he had noticed that the flukes and markings of a species known as the Korean devilfish were the same as those of the California gray whale, a species that was believed to be extinct. Andrews discovered that the two mammals were one and the same, but had been misidentified as distinct species. His finding established his reputation as an authority on Pacific cetaceans.

Central Asiatic Expeditions

Accompanied by his wife, photographer Yvette Borup (whom he married in 1914 and with whom he had two children), Andrews led expeditions to Burma and to Yunnan province in China in 1916 and 1917. While traveling along the edge of the Gobi Desert in 1919, he noticed evidence of fossils.

Based on this observation, Andrews envisioned putting together an expedition to study Mongolia's geology, paleontology, archeology, zoology, and botany. He wanted to test a theory offered by the scientist Henry Fairfield Osborn, who was president of the AMNH, that central Asia was the origin of mammalian life, including human ancestors. Newspapers sensationalized Andrews's announcement of the upcoming expedition, calling it a search for the "missing link."

Andrews believed in thoroughly preparing for the expedition, as he abhorred taking chances or did not believe in engaging in adventure for the sake of adventure. Clearly, though, adventure was a part of the trip, whether it was in the excitement of finding fossils or the danger in capturing thieves who tried to rob the expedition's camps.

In his planning, Andrews put together an innovative strategy of using automobiles in the desert. The autos allowed for the transport of equipment and supplies on a scale that meant a tremendous amount of work could be accomplished in a short time. Although the cars and trucks did get stuck from time to time in deep sand and mud, he later said,

> The automobile was the answer to the transportation problem. With motors we could go into the desert as soon as the heavy snows had disappeared, penetrate the farthest reaches of Mongolia, and return before cold and snow set in.

Moreover, Andrews brought together an impressive team of geologists, archeologists, and paleontologists. All in all, it ended up being an expensive undertaking and required him to raise money. The financier J.P. Morgan donated $50,000 to the expedition, as did John D. Rockefeller, Jr.

Andrews's first Central Asiatic Expedition began in 1922 and departed from the Mongolian city of Kalgan in the spring. Seventy-five camels loaded with supplies were led by a Mongol named Merin. The scientists traveled in Dodge cars and Fulton trucks. During the initial foray, paleontologist Walter Granger uncovered dinosaur bones in the Gobi—the first such find there. Granger patiently excavated the site, carefully removing sand from the fossils and cleaning the teeth and bones. Andrews admitted he had little patience for such work. "I was inclined to employ [a] pickax," he commented.

The explorers also found dinosaur nests with eggs. The discovery of the eggs, uncovered at Flaming Cliffs (in the Gobi Desert), stunned even the scientists. Initially they could not believe what they had uncovered and thought that the reddish-brown items, 9 inches (23 centimeters) long, might be some kind of geological deposit. But Andrews later said, "it was evident that dinosaurs did lay eggs and that we had discovered the first specimens known to science."

Andrews speculated that the dinosaurs had found Flaming Hill to be an attractive breeding place because the sand was just the right consistency to allow heat and air to pass through the eggs after they had been covered and left to hatch. Paleontologist George Olsen, who was on the expedition, thought that the eggs might have been laid by the beaked herbivore *Protoceratops*, although he cautioned that he could be wrong. It is now believed that the eggs were laid by *Oviraptors*, dinosaurs belonging to the group called theropods and known for their birdlike skeletal features and feathers.

While Andrews was wrong about theirs being the "first specimens" (the first dinosaur eggs were found in France in 1859), it was a monumental find. Nevertheless, Andrews considered the most important discovery of the expedition to be seven tiny skulls of the shrewlike *Zalambdalestes*. They, too, were uncovered at Flaming Cliffs and showed that mammals had shared the Earth with dinosaurs.

Newspapers around the world gave extensive coverage to the expedition's finds, particularly the dinosaur eggs. In 1924, more than 4,000 people turned out to hear Andrews present his first lecture in New York City, at the AMNH. Crowds packed the hall of the museum to see the eggs. Andrews became famous as feature stories about him appeared in the *Saturday Evening Post*, *Harper's*, *Cosmopolitan*, and many other publications. To many, he seemed to be an adventurer, yet he also was an erudite scientist able to regale audiences with his tales of discovery.

American naturalist and adventurer Roy Chapman Andrews examines 10-million-year-old dinosaur eggs, which he discovered in the Gobi Desert of Central Asia in 1923. *(Topical Press Agency/Stringer/Hulton Archive/Getty Images)*

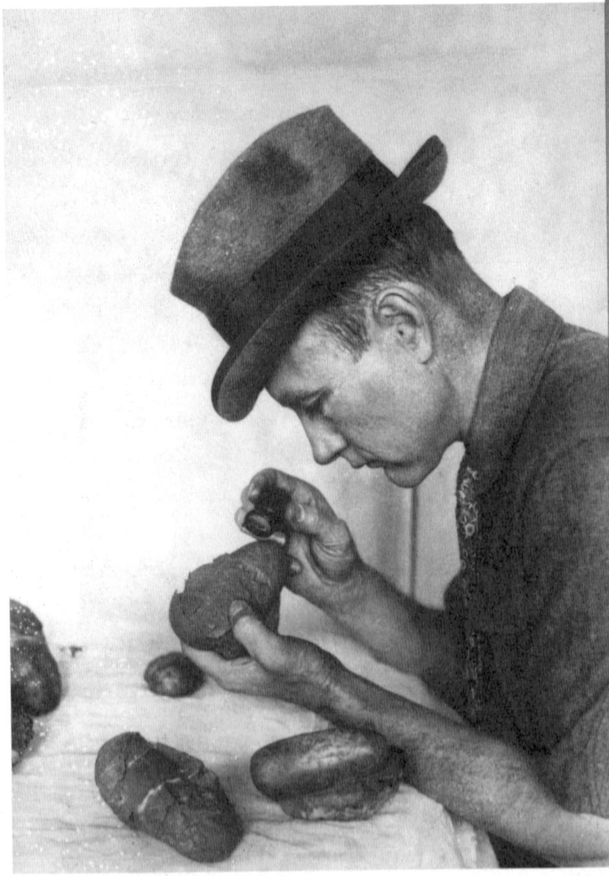

Andrews used the publicity surrounding him and his accomplishments to raise money for additional central Asian expeditions. He even staged a "Great Dinosaur Egg Auction." Unfortunately, the auction antagonized the Chinese and the Mongols, crucial supporters of his missions, because they thought he was making money by exploiting their lands.

The second Central Asiatic Expedition, in 1923, also traveled to Mongolia. In 1925, came the third and largest expedition, consisting of forty men, who explored Outer Mongolia. War in China in 1926 and 1927 precluded any expeditions in those years, but Andrews and his scientists returned in 1928; in 1930, the last of his expeditions explored eastern Inner Mongolia. The expeditions ended when revolutionary turmoil in China and financial constraints due to the Great

FOSSIL EXTRACTION

Fossils are the remains of plants and animals found in sedimentary rock or other parts of the Earth's crust and usually date back to the prehistoric period. They include organic remains and their impressions, as well as the trails, tracks, and habitats of organisms. Because all of these deteriorate over time, they cannot become fossilized unless they are embedded in a protective material such as sediment.

When Roy Chapman Andrews discovered fossils in the Gobi Desert, he left it to Walter Granger to excavate the site—he did not trust himself with such a delicate task. Removing fossils from the ground is delicate and painstaking work, because fossils can easily break during the process.

The usual tools for removing fossils from an outcrop (rock that protrudes above the surface of the ground) are hammers and chisels. On occasion, large fossils are removed using shovels and picks.

Often, it takes hours just to uncover and remove a single bone. The fossil then must be carefully packaged for transport in a box or bag, or wrapped in paper or burlap, and taken to a laboratory. Once the excess rock has been removed, the fossil can be analyzed.

Depression made them no longer feasible. By then, more than 10,000 specimens had been collected.

American Museum of Natural History

When Andrews returned home in 1931, he became vice director of the AMNH. Four years later, he became director, although he felt himself ill suited for the position and disliked administrative work. Also in 1935, Andrews, who had divorced in 1931, married Wilhelmina Anderson Christmas.

As museum director, Andrews despaired over the dwindling funds available to sponsor explorations. At the same time, critics accused him of being ineffective and more attuned to adventure than to the mundane policies necessary to running a museum. In 1941, he retired from the museum.

Over the years, Andrews had written several books, including *Whale Hunting with Gun and Camera* (1916), *Camps and Trails in China* (1918), and the best-selling *On the Trail of Ancient Man* (1926). In retirement, he wrote popular books about his life and explorations, including *Under a Lucky Star* (1943) and *An Explorer Comes Home* (1947). He also wrote books for young people, such as *Meet Your Ancestors* (1945) and the novel *Quest of the Snow Leopard* (1955).

Andrews retired to Carmel, California, in 1942. He died there on March 11, 1960, of a heart attack at Peninsula Community Hospital.

Although Andrews failed to find the bones of an early primitive human being or prove Osborn's theory about central Asia being the originating point for mammalian life, his central Asiatic expeditions proved extraordinarily valuable to paleontologists and paved the way for numerous other explorations of the Gobi. Since the 1940s, American, Canadian, Chinese, Mongolian, Polish, Russian, and Swedish scientists have explored the desert. Still to be definitively answered is the question of why the Gobi contains so many dinosaur skeletons in such a well-preserved state.

Further Reading

Archer, Jules. *Science Explorer: Roy Chapman Andrews.* New York: J. Messner, 1968.

Gallenkemp, Charles. *Dragon Hunter: Roy Chapman Andrews and the Central Asiatic Expeditions.* New York: Viking, 2001.

Pond, Alonzo W. *Andrews: Gobi Explorer.* New York: Grosset and Dunlap, 1972.

Roy Chapman Andrews Society. http://www.roychapmanandrewssociety.org.

See also:
Gobi Desert.

ANTARCTICA

1773: English explorer James Cook crosses the Antarctic Circle
1821: James Davis of the United States makes the first known landing on Antarctica
1895: Norwegian whaler Henryk John Bull makes the first recorded landing on Antarctica outside the Antarctic Peninsula
1911: Roald Amundsen of Norway becomes the first to reach the South Pole
1929: Richard E. Byrd of the United States flies from the Ross Ice Shelf to the South Pole
1957: The International Geophysical Year begins with substantial scientific work in Antarctica
2004: Observations indicate that global warming has contributed to the accelerated melting of Antarctica's glaciers

Windswept, frigid, and forbidding, with a mean temperature of 71 degrees below zero Fahrenheit (-57 degrees Celsius) and an ice sheet that averages nearly 7,100 feet (2,200 meters) in depth, Antarctica was the last continent to be explored by human beings. It has become important to scientific exploration, providing insights into the Earth's climate and geological history.

As late as 1819, no human being had ever set eyes on Antarctica. Yet stories about it abounded in the Western world. Medieval maps showed a continent called Terra Australis where Antarctica is. In the 1600s and 1700s, Europeans explored several islands near the continent, including the South Sandwich Islands, South Georgia, and the Kerguelen Islands.

In 1773, the British navigator James Cook, dodging icebergs while sailing on the *Resolution*, crossed the southern latitude 71° 10′, the farthest south anyone had traveled. He thus became the first to cross the Antarctic Circle, but he did not sight the continent.

Expeditions

Russian naval expeditions in 1819 and shortly thereafter, along with sealers from several different nations, continued to probe around the mysterious continent. In 1821, Captain John Davis of the United States made the first known landing on Antarctica, going ashore at Hughes Bay at the Antarctic Peninsula, which juts into the Atlantic Ocean near Argentina and Chile. Over the five years from 1838 to 1843, several other explorers arrived in the area, with James Wilkes of the United States skirting the coast and confirming that Antarctica was indeed a separate continent.

In 1895, the Norwegian whaler Henryk John Bull made the first recorded landing on the continent outside the Antarctic Peninsula, when he debarked at Cape Adare near the Ross Sea. That same year, the Sixth International Geographical Conference in London urged further exploration of the continent, and, in 1899, a British expedition led by Carsten Borchgrevnik became the first group of Europeans to spend a winter on the ice mass. (In 1897, the *Belgica*, a ship of the Belgian Antarctic Expedition, had become locked in sea ice near the Antarctic Peninsula, and thus was the first to spend a winter at Antarctica, but in the water and not on the ice mass itself.)

British naval officer Robert Falcon Scott and his party reached Antarctica on the ice ship *Terra Nova* in early 1911. Beaten to the South Pole by the Roald Amundsen expedition later that year, Scott and four others died on the journey back to base camp. (*Time & Life Pictures/Getty Images*)

Between 1901 and 1904, the British National Antarctic Expedition under Robert Falcon Scott spent two winters in McMurdo Sound in the Ross Sea. Members of the expedition tried but failed to reach the South Pole. There followed several more efforts aimed at reaching the pole. In 1908, Ernest Shackleton led a British expedition across the Queen Maud Mountains and came within about 110 miles (175 kilometers) of the pole. In doing so, he pioneered a route across the Ross Ice Shelf that other explorers would follow. He also brought back samples of coal that proved Antarctica was once semitropical.

The South Pole finally was reached in December 1911, when an expedition led by the Norwegian explorer Roald Amundsen pushed 700 miles (1,125 kilometers) across the Ross Ice Shelf, fighting fierce storms and the debilitating effects of thin air at the 10,500-foot (3,200-meter) elevation of the ice plateau. Amundsen beat out Scott, who returned to Antarctica and reached the South Pole in January 1912, five weeks after Amundsen. Scott and his men died before completing their return trip.

In describing Amundsen's feat, *National Geographic* magazine reported,

> [Amundsen] has defined the eastern and southern boundaries of the Great Ice Barrier. . . . This enormous glacial ice plain is one of the wonders of the world. It is a solid mass of ice . . . approximately 800 to 1,600 feet [240 to 490 meters] thick, and covering an area of about 100,000 square miles [160,000 square kilometers], or considerably larger than New York, Massachusetts, New Hampshire, and Vermont combined.

Explorers penetrated Antarctica by air, too. In 1928, George Hubert Wilkins of Australia flew along the Antarctic Peninsula. The following year, Richard E. Byrd of the United States flew from the Ross Ice Shelf to the South Pole. He made additional flights from 1933 to 1935 to conduct a photographic survey. In 1935, another American, Lincoln Ellsworth, became the first to cross Antarctica by air.

The International Geophysical Year

Beginning in 1939, expeditions to Antarctica focused more on scientific projects. Richard Byrd established stations staffed with scientists; so, too, did the Argentines, Australians, British, Chileans, and French. (Science had its military applications, too. With the advent of the cold war in the 1940s, the American military monitored human experience in frigid conditions as a way to prepare for possible battle with the Soviet Union.)

A pivotal moment in scientific research occurred when, in 1952, the International Council of Scientific Unions proposed a series of global geophysical activities for January 1957 through December 1958, dubbed International Geophysical Year (IGY). Sixty-seven countries were involved in studying global geophysical phenomena.

Although the activities included projects in the equatorial region and the Arctic, Antarctica was the center of attention. A series of stations was established there to make continuous measurements, leading to advances in the study of meteorology, and, for the first time, scientists measured the thickness of Antarctica's ice mass. In support of the IGY, the U.S. Navy

McMURDO STATION

Situated on bare volcanic rock on Ross Island is the largest of Antarctica's scientific research stations, McMurdo. It is named for Archibald McMurdo, a British naval officer aboard the HMS *Terror* on an expedition that first charted the area in 1841 under the command of McMurdo's fellow Briton, Sir James Clark Ross. The station was founded in 1956 by the United States government to support scientific research for the International Geophysical Year (1957–1958).

Over the years, McMurdo has grown from a few buildings overlooking McMurdo Sound, an inlet of the Ross Sea, to a complex of more than 100 structures capable of supporting some 1,300 residents. McMurdo includes an outlying airport and a helicopter pad. The site is served by water, sewer, telephone, and power lines.

Most of the residents at McMurdo are support personnel, but the station is dedicated to scientific work. McMurdo is part of the U.S. Antarctic Program, which has as its goal researching the continent's ecosystem and its effect on the global climate.

The program also uses the continent as a base from which to study the upper atmosphere and outer space. For example, scientists at the station research stratospheric chemistry and aerosols, particularly as they relate to the ozone hole. They also study the sun and cosmic rays through long-duration balloon flights launched from the station.

The Albert P. Crary Science and Engineering Center (named for the geophysicist and glaciologist Albert P. Crary) opened in 1991. The center supports the biological, Earth, and atmospheric sciences, and it houses an aquarium.

In 1999, a telescope was set up at McMurdo to study cosmic background radiation. Other science facilities at McMurdo investigate the magnetic field around the Earth.

Scientists lower a current meter into the frigid water of McMurdo Sound, Antarctica, to study ice movements. The McMurdo Station research center was established by the United States in 1956 to collect data on the continent's ecosystem. *(David Boyer/National Geographic/Getty Images)*

established five coastal stations and three interior stations on Antarctica, and explored vast regions of Wilkes Land. In March 1958, a team led by Dr. Vivian E. Fuchs completed the first land crossing of Antarctica, traveling about 2,150 miles (3,460 kilometers) in ninety-eight days.

To keep Antarctica from becoming militarized, twelve nations, including Britain, France, the Soviet Union, and the United States, signed a treaty in 1959 in which they recognized "that it is in the interest of all mankind that Antarctica shall continue forever to be used exclusively for peaceful purposes and shall not become the scene or object of international discord." The treaty prohibited military bases and fortifications, weapons testing, and the like. It encouraged scientific programs and the exchange of scientific personnel and observations, but it failed to resolve the territorial claims made by several nations. The treaty was renewed in 1991, with a protocol banning mineral and oil exploration for fifty years and providing for wildlife protection.

Today, numerous scientific stations operate in Antarctica under the sponsorship of more than fifteen countries. They range in size from fewer than twelve people to the hundreds accommodated in summer by McMurdo Station (operated by the United States). Many scientists work indoors, while others do fieldwork and labor in difficult outdoor conditions. They study the plates of the Earth's crust, fossils, and meteorites.

One important discovery occurred in 1985, when British scientists discovered the ozone hole. The ozone layer, a bed of ozone molecules in the Earth's stratosphere, greatly reduces the amount of certain ultraviolet rays (UVBs) that reaches the planet's surface. Without this protection, UVB rays can harm human beings by increasing the risk of skin cancer and cataracts and by damaging immune systems. UVB exposure also can harm terrestrial plant life, single-cell organisms, and aquatic ecosystems.

The ozone hole—actually a reduction in the concentrations of ozone—was caused in part by chlorofluorocarbons (CFCs), a family of man-made chemical compounds developed for use in aerosol propellents and refrigeration. In 1987, several nations signed the Montreal Protocol, in which they pledged to stop making and using CFCs. By 2008, the protocol had been signed by 193 nations, more than had signed an environmental treaty ever before. Since the original signing of the protocol, CFC production has dropped nearly 97 percent. Yet in 2006, the ozone hole expanded to a record 11,400,000 square miles (29,500,000 square kilometers).

In 2004 and later, observations indicated that global warming had contributed to the accelerated melting of Antarctica's glaciers. For example, American and Argentine scientists have discovered how rising temperatures have caused an increase in the speed at which glaciers are moving, meaning that these ice masses are being pushed into the ocean more quickly, where they will melt.

Further Reading

Martin, Stephen. *A History of Antarctica*. Sydney, Australia: State Library of New South Wales Press, 1996.

Reader's Digest. *Antarctica: The Extraordinary History of Man's Conquest of the Frozen Continent*. New York: Reader's Digest, 1990.

Roberts, Leslie Carol. *The Entire Earth and Sky: Views on Antarctica*. Lincoln: University of Nebraska Press, 2008.

See also: Amundsen, Roald; Byrd, Richard E.; Cook, James; International Geophysical Year.

ARCTIC

1610: English explorer Henry Hudson explores Hudson Bay and searches for the Northwest Passage
1733–1743: Danish explorer Vitus Jonassen Bering leads the Great Northern Expedition and maps Russia's Arctic coastline
1790–1791: A Russian expedition sailing on the *Slava Rossii* charts the coastline of Russian America
1909: Americans Robert E. Peary and Matthew Henson reach the North Pole
1937: A Soviet team led by Ivan Papanin winters at the North Pole on the world's first drifting ice station
1957: The U.S. nuclear submarine *Nautilus* travels beneath the North Pole

The Arctic comprises all of the lands and waters north of the Arctic Circle. Beginning in the fifteenth century, Europeans explored the region in what is today northern Canada in search of the Northwest Passage, a sea route between the Atlantic and Pacific oceans. The entire Arctic has been the scene of extensive scientific research—both that which coincided with the search for the passage and that which came later.

Although Arctic temperatures are variable, winters generally are long and cold and summers are short and cool. The lowest temperatures of -90 degrees Fahrenheit (-68 degrees Celsius) are reached in Greenland and northern Siberia. But maximum temperatures of about 23 to 36 degrees Fahrenheit (-5 to +2 degrees Celsius) are common on the ice sheet, such as in Greenland, and highs of 70 to 100 degrees Fahrenheit (21 to 37 degrees Celsius) are common on land areas. During the summers, there is continuous sunlight; during the winters, continuous darkness.

The region generally is defined as lying north of the Arctic Circle (66° 33' N), which places it north of the tree line (the point beyond which trees do not grow). North of 75° latitude, ice is permanent, and icebergs flow (or "calve") into the ocean from western Greenland and northeastern Canada.

Long before Europeans arrived in the Arctic, the Inuit explored the region. Evidence also indicates that in ancient times a Greek navigator reached Iceland. And long before the scientific revolution emerged in Europe in the fifteenth century, Norsemen came here.

Search for the Northwest Passage

Much of the Arctic exploration by Europeans after 1492 was in search of the Northwest Passage, the hoped-for course that would allow easier and quicker travel between the Atlantic and Pacific oceans. In the sixteenth and seventeenth centuries, a string of failed efforts characterized the search.

In 1576, the Englishman Martin Frobisher sailed to Frobisher Bay, an inlet of the Labrador Sea at the southeastern corner of Baffin Island (which is located between Canada and Greenland). He thought the bay would lead to the Pacific but was proved wrong. Ten years later, John Davis, a fellow Englishman, sailed even farther north and reached the Davis Strait, between Baffin Island and Greenland.

In 1610, Henry Hudson, sailing for the English, explored the massive Hudson Bay (in Canada's Arctic region), thinking it would provide an outlet to the Pacific. But his crew, tired of the search, mutinied and set Hudson, his son, and several other men adrift on a small boat in June 1611. They were never seen again.

In 1616, the English navigators William Baffin and Robert Bylot journeyed as far north as Ellesmere Island and nearby Greenland. In the 1700s, several British expeditions tried to find an entrance to the Northwest Passage from the Pacific. Most notably, from 1776 to 1779 Captain James Cook sailed along the west coasts of Canada and Alaska.

Amid the search for the Northwest Passage, naval parties from Russia traversed the Arctic. From 1733 to 1743, Vitus Jonassen Bering, a Dane who had joined the Russian navy, led the Great Northern Expedition, organized in accordance with Czar Peter I's order to bring "glory" to Russia "through the arts and sciences." Bering explored from Arkhangelsk, along the White Sea, to Bolshoy Baranov Cape, along the East Siberian Sea. In 1741, he and Aleksi Illich Chirikov reached America, where they discovered for Russia the Aleutian and Komandorski islands. The expedition mapped much of Russia's Arctic coastline. That same year, Semyon Chelyuskin reached Eurasia's northernmost point, Cape Chelyuskin, a portion of tundra extending north from the Taymyr Peninsula.

In 1790–1791, an expedition sailing on the *Slava Rossii* (*Glory for Russia*) charted the coastline of Russian America from Prince William Sound (just east of present-day Anchorage) to Cape Prince of Wales (directly east of Russian Siberia), including Diomede Island and St. Lawrence Island. Their findings were used to help compile the *Atlas of the Northern Part of the East Ocean*, which was published in 1826.

Several Russian expeditions from about 1820 to 1840 surveyed the Bering Sea and Bering Strait, among other areas, which led to the publication in 1852 of the *Atlas of America's Northwestern Coast from the Bering Strait to Corrientes Cape and the Aleutian Islands*, an important contribution to nineteenth-century geographic studies. Also in the 1820s, a Russian army lieutenant, Pyotr Anzhu, traveled by dogsled, horse, and kayak to map the New Siberian Islands, along with parts of the Siberian coast.

John Ross of Britain located the North Magnetic Pole in 1831, and he found Boothia Peninsula (a large peninsula in the northern Canadian Arctic) and King William Island (in Canada's Kitikmeot Region). In 1845, John Franklin and his team vanished while searching for the Northwest Passage.

In the early 1850s, an expedition led by the Irish naval officer Robert McClure traversed most of the Northwest Passage by entering from the Pacific, but the explorers were forced to abandon ship before they could complete their journey. They returned in 1854 to finish the transit on another ship. Not until 1905 did Roald Amundsen, a Norwegian, complete the first journey through the Northwest Passage on a single voyage aboard a single ship, the *Gjoa*.

In the meantime, Adolf Erik Nordenskiöld navigated the Northeast Passage in 1879, a feat duplicated by Amundsen in 1918–1920, when he sailed along the northern coasts of Europe, Asia, and Alaska.

In 1900, the American explorer Robert E. Peary reached the northern point of Greenland and named it Cape Morris Jesup. His expedition proved that Greenland was an island, not a continent, and added to ethnographic studies of the Inuit and scientific studies of glaciers.

Seeking the North Pole

Many explorers tried to reach the North Pole. One, the Norwegian Fridtjof Nansen, failed in his effort from 1893 to 1896, but added considerably to European knowledge about the Arctic Ocean. On April 6, 1909, the Americans Robert E. Peary and Matthew Henson became the first explorers to reach the North Pole. Their small party, consisting of Peary, Henson, and four Inuits, did so by dogsled. (Historians and scientists debate Peary's claim; some say he missed the pole by a short distance.)

Members of the Russian-sponsored Hydrographic Expedition of the Arctic Ocean sailed in icebreakers to traverse the Northeast Passage in 1914–1915 and found the archipelago Severnaya Zemlya. The Americans Richard E. Byrd and Floyd Bennett claimed to have reached the North Pole in an airplane in 1926 (historians debate whether the two men reached the precise point of the pole). This was followed days later by an expedition in a dirigible led by Amundsen and his Italian colleague, Umberto Nobile.

In 1937, a research group from the Soviet Union, led by Ivan Papanin, wintered for 274 days near the North Pole. As the explorers drifted on an ice floe—their North Pole-1 was the first scientific drifting ice station in the world—they conducted hydrological, meteorological, and magnetic observations. The expedition took water samples, measured water temperatures, gathered bottom soil samples, and measured ocean depth. Their findings revealed that neither large landmasses nor small islands abut the North Pole; that warm Atlantic water reaches it; and that cyclones, rain, and fog occur there. Beginning in the early 1950s, the United States also operated drifting ice stations.

In 1955, during the cold war, the United States and Canada began building a radar network, the Distant Early Warning Line, or DEW Line, from Alaska to Greenland. The DEW Line was to provide protection from a surprise attack by the Soviet Union. The network was updated and moved some over the years; in 1993, it was renamed the North Warning System.

"All the News That's Fit to Print."

The New York Times.

COOK NOT NEAR POLE, SAYS PEARY; PROOFS STILL HELD BACK BY COOK

Two Eskimos Cited by Cook Told Peary He Never Went Far from Land.

SAYS "I HAVE COOK NAILED"

Cables His Wife Not to Worry About the Doctor's Claim to the Pole.

COOK TO ASK FOR AN INQUIRY

Says He Will Submit His Observations to Competent Scientists.

DOUBT OF HIS STORY GROWS

COMMANDER PEARY'S PRELIMINARY ACCOUNT OF HIS SUCCESSFUL VOYAGE TO THE NORTH POLE

He Sends to The Times by Wireless a Summary, to be Followed by His Full Report—Record of His Swift Progress to the Utmost North.

FROM CAPE COLUMBIA UP IN 37 DAYS, BACK IN 16 DAYS

Prof. Ross G. Marvin, of Cornell, Drowned on April 10, Forty-five Miles North of Cape Columbia, While Leading the Supporting Party.

BATTLE HARBOR, Labrador, Via Wireless Cape Ray, N. F., Sept. 8.—As it may be impossible to get my full story through in time for to-morrow's TIMES, partly as a prelude which may stimulate interest and partly to forestall possible leaks, I am sending you a brief summary of my voyage to the North Pole, which is to be printed exactly as written.

SUMMARY OF NORTH POLAR EXPEDITION OF THE PEARY ARCTIC CLUB.

The steamer Roosevelt left New York on July 6, 1908; left Sydney on July 17; arrived at Cape York, Greenland, August 1; left Etah, Greenland, August [illegible]; arrived Cape Sheridan, [illegible], September 1; wintered at Cape Sheridan.

The sledge expedition left the Roosevelt February 15, 1909, and started for the North. Arrived at Cape Columbia March 1; passed British record March 2; delayed by open water March 2 and 3; held up by open water March 4 to 11; crossed the 84th parallel March 11; encountered open lead March 15; crossed 85th parallel March 18; crossed 86th parallel March 23d; encountered open lead March 23d; passed Norwegian record March 23d; passed Italian record March 24th; encountered open lead March 26th; crossed 87th parallel March 27th; passed American record March 28; encountered open lead March 28; held up by open water March 29; crossed 88th parallel April 2; crossed 89th parallel April 4; North Pole April 6.

All returning left North Pole April 7, reached Cape Columbia April 23, arriving on board Roosevelt April 27.

The Roosevelt left Cape Sheridan July 18, passed Cape Sabine August 8; left Cape York August 26; arrived at Indian Harbor with all members of expedition returning in good health except Prof. Ross G. Marvin, unfortunately drowned April 10, when forty-five miles north of Cape Columbia, returning from 86° North Latitude in command of the supporting party.

ROBERT E. PEARY.

MAP SHOWING PEARY'S ROUTE TO THE POLE.

The September 9, 1909, issue of *The New York Times* carried Robert E. Peary's firsthand narrative of his conquest of the North Pole the previous April, which disputed Frederick Cook's claim of having reached the pole a full year earlier. *(Hulton Archive/Stringer/Getty Images)*

In accordance with the International Geophysical Year, 1957–1958, several countries established 300 research stations in the Arctic. In 1958, the U.S. nuclear submarine *Nautilus*, with a crew of 116 and commanded by William R. Anderson, became the first sub to cross the North Pole, although it did not surface there. It traveled from Alaska to Greenland, a total of 1,839 nautical miles (3,405 kilometers), underneath an ice pack for four days. One crew member, Lieutenant William G. Lalor, Jr., later said: "As we watched in awe, our gyrocompasses swung, finally to point back where we had been. . . . I asked how close we had come to the exact Pole." He was told that they "pierced it."

A year later, in 1959, another nuclear sub, the USS *Skate*, surfaced at ten different locations in the Arctic Ocean, including the North Pole. In 1977, the Soviet nuclear icebreaker *Arktika* became the first surface ship to reach the North Pole.

In 1995, the Canadian Richard Weber and the Russian Mikhail Malakhov reached the North Pole by traveling entirely on skis. Their 940-mile trip (1,500 kilometers) took 121 days to complete and entailed traveling to and from Ward Hunt Island.

The Arctic in the Twenty-First Century

Recent scientific studies conducted in the Arctic region and photographs taken from space show the Arctic is changing, largely as a result of global warming. High summer temperatures from 1995 to 2005 have resulted in a substantial loss of the Greenland ice pack. In 2006, the average annual sur-

ARCTIC DRIFTING STATIONS

The drifting ice stations begun by the Soviet Union and the United States have been labeled by one writer as "Arctic outposts of superpower science." On them, scientists have conducted hydrological, meteorological, and magnetic observations.

When, in 1937, the Russian Admiral Ivan Papanin led his team in founding North Pole-1, the Soviet government hailed the men as "polar heroes." The work of those scientists, however, was preceded by the establishment of polar stations on more stable terrain, the islands in and shores along the Arctic Ocean.

Following Papanin's effort, the Soviet Union founded North Pole-2 on an ice floe in 1950. From 1954 until 1991, the Soviets operated one to three stations, all of which made discoveries in physical geography. Eighty-eight polar crews occupied the ice floes for a total of 29,276 drift days. In 2003, the Russians returned to the ice floes with North Pole-32.

In March 1952, the United States founded a polar station on T-3, a 7-mile-long (11 kilometer-long) drifting ice island. T-3 was abandoned several months later and then reoccupied in 1957 as part of the scientific efforts linked to the International Geophysical Year. Abandoned once again, this time in the fall of 1961, T-3 was reoccupied in February 1962 and remained in use until 1975.

From 1952 to 1975, T-3 traversed a looping path from near the North Pole, south to the north coast of Alaska (where it temporarily ran aground), and then north along the western coasts of the Queen Elizabeth Islands, until it returned to the waters near the North Pole. The Americans also founded other drifting ice stations, including one in 1961 that meandered north from Barrow, Alaska.

Scientists at the North Pole-32 meteorological research station—one in a long series of Russian scientific facilities located on Arctic ice floes—had to be evacuated in 2004 due to melting ice. *(AFP/Stringer/Getty Images)*

face temperature for land areas north of 60° latitude were higher than the mean average for the twentieth century; in 2007 the summer sea ice reached a new minimum in area. Other developments have sent mixed signals as to the extent of warming in the Arctic. Undoubtedly, scientific study of the region will continue to provide important clues about global warming and climate change in general.

In the meantime, the Arctic is serving as a scientific incubator of sorts. In Spitsbergen, near the town of Longyearbyen, the Global Seed Vault has been bored into the middle of a mountain as part of a project directed by the Norwegian government, the Global Crop Diversity Trust (an international organization), and the Nordic Genetic Research Center (a cooperative effort of the Nordic countries). Since 2006, scientists have placed inside the cavelike structure thousands of seeds from around the world. The vault, whose internal temperature is monitored by a digital system, has been made to withstand bomb blasts and earthquakes, and it is protected by tight security. The Global Seed Vault is part of a program to protect the seeds of plant species that face extinction.

Further Reading

Berton, Pierre. *The Arctic Grail: The Quest for the North West Passage and the North Pole, 1818–1909.* New York: Lyons, 2000.

Fleming, Fergus. *Ninety Degrees North: The Quest for the North Pole.* New York: Grove, 2001.

Williams, Glyndwr. *Voyages of Delusion: The Quest for the Northwest Passage.* New Haven, CT: Yale University Press, 2003.

See also: Henson, Matthew; Peary, Robert E.

B

BALLARD, ROBERT (1942–)

1942: Born on June 30 in Wichita, Kansas
1971: Begins collecting ocean rocks that support the theory of continental drift
1973: Using the submersible *Alvin,* studies lava floes in the Atlantic Ocean
1977: Discovers life near hydrothermal vents in the deep ocean
1984: Investigates the site of the downed U.S. nuclear submarine *Thresher*
1985: At a depth of more than 12,000 feet (3,650 meters) in the Atlantic, with Jean-Louis Michel discovers the wreckage of the RMS *Titanic*
2001: Identifies ancient shorelines, drowned river valleys, and buildings in the Black Sea

An oceanographer and marine archeologist whose discoveries shattered assumptions about life in the deep ocean and expanded historical knowledge, Robert Duane Ballard earned worldwide fame for his discovery of the wreckage of the passenger liner RMS *Titanic*.

Born on June 30, 1942, in Wichita, Kansas, to Chester Ballard and Harriet May, he grew up in California. His father worked in aerospace design, and his job caused the family to move several times. In 1953, the family settled in Downey, California, where Robert played sports and took up scuba diving. He also excelled academically and loved to read stories of exploration and adventure.

His favorite books included Walter Lord's *A Night to Remember* (1955), about the sinking of the passenger ship *Titanic*, and *Twenty Thousand Leagues Under the Sea* (1869), the Jules Verne classic. "Submarines fascinated me," Ballard later wrote. "After I read [Verne] I was gripped by the challenge of actually exploring the hidden ocean depths." It was then that he started thinking about how he could make a career in diving.

In 1960, Ballard entered the University of California at Santa Barbara, where he majored in chemistry and geology. After he received his B.A. degree in 1965, he was accepted into the oceanographic program at the University of Hawaii. While studying for his master's degree, he worked at the nearby Oceanic Institute, where he helped train dolphins who performed for the public.

Ballard received his M.A. in geophysics in 1966. That year he also married Marjorie Hargas. He then decided to study for his doctoral degree at the University of Southern California. This was the time of the Vietnam War, however, and Ballard, who was in the military reserves (first the army and later the navy reserve) was called to duty. The U.S. Navy then assigned him to serve as a liaison between the Office of Naval Research and the Woods Hole Oceanographic Institution, on Cape Cod in Massachusetts.

Continental Drift and Deepwater Life

Ballard left the U.S. Navy in 1970. While continuing to work at Woods Hole, he enrolled in the doctoral program at the University of Rhode Island. For his Ph.D., Ballard researched plate tectonics—the drift of the continents. He focused his studies on the Appalachian Mountains and, in 1971 and 1972, used the submersible *Alvin* to collect rocks from the floor of the Gulf of Maine. He wanted to see if the rocks were identical to those on land, for this would indicate that the theory of continental drift as postulated by others was indeed correct. His samples contributed to the evidence backing the theory.

To further the study, Ballard and a team of American scientists joined with a team of French scientists in 1973 and 1974 to investigate the rift valley of the Mid-Atlantic Ridge, which is located several hundred miles southwest of the Azores. *Alvin* was again employed in what was called

Project FAMOUS. Ballard and the other scientists studied lava flows rising from the ocean floor. They concluded that the lava being squeezed from the Earth's interior moved the continents. They also confirmed that the African plate was pulling back at the rate of 1 inch (2.5 centimeters) per year.

During this expedition, Ballard experienced the first of several close calls under the ocean that nearly cost him his life. While he was aboard the French bathyscaphe *Archimedes* (used in addition to *Alvin* for the project), an electrical fire erupted. Ballard struggled to breathe emergency oxygen in order to survive, while the *Archimedes* made a rapid ascent.

In 1974, Ballard earned his doctorate from the University of Rhode Island in geological oceanography. Three years later, he joined a study of the Galápagos Rift off the Pacific Coast of South America. For him, and for marine science, it turned out to be a monumental expedition. Using the ANGUS underwater camera, which took still photograghs, Ballard and his colleagues searched for hot springs, or hydrothermal deep-sea vents, in the darkness of the deep ocean.

At these deep-sea vents, where the water temperature was much warmer than that only a few yards away, they discovered clams and mussels lying on lava; they saw orange puffballs, anemones, and starfish. It was a beautiful and amazing sight. "We realized we had stumbled onto a major scientific discovery," Ballard later said. And when asked what was the greatest find in his career, he said, "Well, it wasn't the *Titanic*. . . . My greatest discovery was . . . of exotic creatures living underwater in hot springs." On this expedition,

DEEP-SEA VENTS

Deep-sea vents appear where the sea floor is torn apart by the spreading of the Earth's tectonic plates. They usually are found along the spines of rifts and ridges.

When the tectonic plates separate, magma from beneath the Earth's crust surges upward and cools to form a new crust. The cracks and fissures in the new crust fill with seawater, which contains minerals from the surrounding rocks. Pressure then causes the mineralized water to erupt through vents. In this way, the oceans circulate through the rift system over millions of years.

The life-forms found around these deep-sea vents vary. According to *National Geographic* magazine, sometimes one species dominates a particular vent, as do giant white clams in the Pacific Ocean near 21° N. In the Lau Basin, near Fiji, snails dominate.

Scientists believe that most vents last only a few decades. When a vent collapses, the animals around it die.

The existence of the vents has led to questions about the appearance of life on Earth. Most scientists still believe that life first evolved in a sun-enriched environment, but others believe that the deep-sea vents might have enabled the first primitive organisms to evolve.

At the Woods Hole Oceanographic Institution in Massachusetts, Dr. Robert Ballard announces the discovery of the wreckage of the RMS *Titanic* off the coast of Newfoundland in September 1985. *(Cynthia Johnson/Time & Life Pictures/Getty Images)*

the scientists shattered the assumption that little life existed in the deep ocean.

But how could the animals survive, let alone thrive? They were far from the sunlight necessary to produce food through photosynthesis, which was thought necessary to support life. Instead, these creatures used chemosynthesis—they relied on a food chain consisting of bacteria living on the lava. The bacteria was eaten by microbes, which were, in turn, eaten by larger creatures.

Ballard continued to study hydrothermal vent sites. In 1982, he founded the Deep Submergence Laboratory at Woods Hole to develop underwater robots. Bringing together computer scientists and robotics specialists, Ballard developed *Argo,* an unmanned video camera sled that was equipped with sonar and tethered to a surface ship.

Search for the *Titanic*

Ballard used *Argo* in 1984, when he investigated the site of the *Thresher,* a U.S. nuclear submarine that had gone down in 1963 in 8,500 feet (2,600 meters) of water about 240 miles (390 kilometers) east of Cape Cod. While Ballard prepared to find the downed submarine, he already had in mind an expedition to locate the *Titanic,* the supposedly unsinkable passenger ship that had sunk during its maiden voyage in 1912 after a collision with an iceberg, about 95 miles (150 kilometers) south of the Grand Banks of Newfoundland. Ballard's interest in searching for the *Titanic* had been piqued by Bill Tatum, president of the Titanic Historical Society. Ballard later wrote, "Bill virtually made the tragic ship, its passengers, and crew come alive in my imagination."

An earlier attempt by Ballard to find the *Titanic,* in 1977, had ended in failure. This time, he undertook his mission in cooperation with a team of scientists from France. The French ship *Le Suroit,* which carried powerful sonar equipment, tried to find the *Titanic* but was unable to do so before being called away on another mission.

To continue his search, Ballard transferred to the *Knorr,* a ship from Woods Hole. The *Knorr* had just finished searching for the wreckage of a U.S. nuclear submarine, the *Scorpion,* in a mission financed by the U.S. Navy. Ballard and fellow scientist Jean-Louis Michel, from the French team, mapped out an area of 150 square miles (390 square kilometers) in which they believed they would find the *Titanic.*

When Ballard had searched for the *Thresher*, he had learned about the type of debris trail left by a sinking vessel. He planned to use this knowledge in finding the *Titanic*, starting at the point where passengers from the ship had been recovered in their lifeboats. His skeptical French colleagues agreed to go along after he explained that he expected the debris field to be half of a mile to 1 mile in length (approximately 1 to 1.5 kilometers), a much bigger target than the hull.

On September 1, 1985, with *Argo* tethered to the *Knorr*, Ballard and Michel found one of the *Titanic*'s boilers at 12,230 feet (3,730 meters). From there, they followed the debris trail until they reached what they suspected was the location of the hull. The next day, *Argo* was towed over the *Titanic*, as Ballard worried that the submersible's cables would become entangled in the wreckage below. Then, the hull appeared. Ballard remarked to his colleagues: "It's the side of the ship. She's upright." The *Titanic* had been found.

Ballard later wrote,

> It was one thing to . . . have found the ship. It was another thing to be there. . . . I could see the *Titanic* as she slipped nose first into the glassy water. . . . At the center of the circle of people whooping, hugging, and dancing wildly around us, Jean-Louis and I stood silently, overcome by the significance of the moment.

Ballard predicted that all of his previous scientific achievements "would be viewed by the public as arcane precursors to this spectacular success." And indeed they were.

Before leaving the site, Ballard used ANGUS to take still photos of the debris field. There appeared China teacups, silver serving platters, headboards, bedsprings, bottles of wine, and shoes—the detritus of the *Titanic*'s historic moment.

Ballard returned to the *Titanic* site in 1986. This time, he brought *Jason Junior* (*JJ*), a small remote-controlled underwater vehicle connected by cable to *Alvin*. *JJ* roamed inside the *Titanic*, moving along the staircase landing and deep into the interior, even discovering a nearly intact chandelier as a revealing reminder of the *Titanic*'s opulence.

JASON Projects and More Discoveries

In 1987, Ballard's book *The Discovery of the Titanic* reached the best-seller lists. At this time, he began the JASON Project. This series of expeditions has included exploring the undersea volcano Marsili Seamount in the Mediterranean and ship remains in the area from ancient Rome. As a part of the JASON Project, schoolchildren are able to view Ballard's explorations as they occur.

In 1989, Ballard looked for the German destroyer *Bismarck,* which had been sunk by the British Royal Navy on May 27, 1941, in the Denmark Strait. An earlier search had failed, but this time he found the ship.

Following his divorce from Marjorie Hargas in 1990, Ballard married Barbara Earle, a producer of the *National Geographic Explorer* television show, which he hosted. (They would have two children.) With Earle, he founded the Odyssey Corporation to produce TV specials for the television division of the National Geographic Society. In 1992, in a project funded partially by the U.S. Navy, Ballard explored Guadalcanal Island in the Pacific Ocean and identified eleven ships that had gone down there during World War II. Among the ships, he found the wreckage of the *Kirishima,* a Japanese battleship larger than the *Bismarck.* It had been sunk by the U.S. battleship *Washington* in November 1942.

Ballard led several other expeditions in the 1990s. In one, he explored the British ocean liner *Lusitania,* sunk by a German submarine during World War I. In another, he conducted chemical experiments on lava flows and volcanic gases near the island of Hawaii.

In 1995, Ballard used the *NR-1,* the U.S. Navy's smallest nuclear sub, to dive to the wreck of the *Andrea Doria,* which had gone down in a collision with a ship near Nantucket Island, Massachusetts, in 1956. Also in 1995 he used the *NR-1* to compile a map of ancient trade routes between Africa and Rome, once again merging his oceanographic and historical interests. He later said,

> I've always had a passion for history. . . . Where did we come from? . . . It's all about the opportunity to keep learning. History is a moving target. We don't know where it's going to be next.

Ballard retired from Woods Hole in 1997 and founded the Institute for Exploration at Mystic Aquarium in Connecticut. He dedicated the institute to deepwater archaeology. He intended to make the findings of his explorations available to the public by showing artifacts, through camera and computer hookups, as they existed on the sea bottom. Ballard was angered by salvagers who took artifacts from the *Titanic* graveyard for display in museums; he believed his approach avoided the type of degradation then occurring at such original sites.

In 1998, Ballard led three expeditions in four months as part of JASON Project IX. In May, following an eighteen-day search, he found the *Yorktown,* an American aircraft carrier sunk in World War II during the Battle of Midway.

In 2001, Ballard's Black Sea expeditions resulted in marine archaeologists identifying ancient shorelines, drowned river valleys, and buildings in about 300 feet (90 meters) of water off the coast of Turkey. This research

ALVIN

The first deep-sea submersible capable of carrying passengers, and thus known by scientists as a Human Occupied Vehicle (HOV), *Alvin* has been refitted and rebuilt over the years to the point that it now can dive untethered nearly 15,000 feet (almost 4,600 meters) into the ocean.

Alvin first went into operation in 1964. It is owned and operated by the Woods Hole Oceanographic Institute and is named for Allyn Vine, an engineer important to the vehicle's development.

With a weight of 16 tons (14 metric tons), *Alvin* contains a variety of equipment used in scientific explorations. Two hydraulic arms can lift up to 200 pounds (90 kilograms) each. Water samplers collect biological and geological evidence, and sensors take chemical readings. *Alvin* also has a computer, a recording system, navigation and sonar systems, and three view ports. Film and video cameras are mounted on its exterior, and its powerful lights are capable of penetrating the ocean darkness. The submersible can hold three people: the pilot and two scientists.

In 1966, *Alvin* was used to find a hydrogen bomb lost in the Mediterranean Sea. Two years later, *Alvin* itself was almost lost when, near Cape Cod, it broke away from the cables to which it was tethered and sank 5,000 feet (1,500 meters). It took eleven months to recover the sub. *Alvin* has been used to discover twenty-four hydrothermal vents in the Pacific and Atlantic oceans, as well as to discover new species of animals—about thirty in all.

Alvin usually is transported on the ship *Atlantis* and lowered into the water with a crane. It makes about 150 to 200 dives a year.

In 2008, the National Science Foundation (NSF) announced that *Alvin* will be replaced with a new HOV. Arden Bement, director of the NSF, said, "This new submersible will be the flagship for the next phase of deep-sea exploration, and the many exciting discoveries that are anticipated in coming decades."

While *Alvin* can only dive 2.8 miles (4.5 kilometers) down, its successor will be able to plunge 4 miles (6.4 kilometers) into the depths, which will open up 99 percent of the ocean floor to exploration. Development and construction of the new HOV originally were estimated to cost about $20 million, but, as construction has slowed, costs have mushroomed. The new HOV is expected to be operational in 2015.

Alvin, the first human-occupied deep-sea research submersible, has helped scientists discover new life-forms, confirm plate-tectonic theory, and explore hydrothermal vents on the ocean floor since it went into operation in 1964. *(Henry Groskinsky/Time & Life Pictures/Getty Images)*

has since stimulated debate over the history of the Black Sea and how it evolved through the centuries.

The following year, Ballard, in cooperation with the National Geographic Society, found *PT-109*, the patrol torpedo boat on which John F. Kennedy had served during World War II. The Japanese had rammed the boat in the Pacific, forcing Kennedy and the other crew members to cling to the bow of the ship to survive until they were able to swim to an island. From there, they were rescued.

In 2004, Ballard was appointed professor of oceanography and director of the Institute for Archaeological Oceanography at the University of Rhode Island. Looking back on his earlier expeditions, he described his descent in the submersibles as "risky." He observed,

> It's . . . like going into the lion's lair. . . . You can't buy a ticket to the deep sea. It's as alien and hostile as Mars. You need people who aren't terrified to go to Mars and who have the technology to do it. And those are oceanographers. They work with the social scientists, the marine geologists. And together we read the chapters.

Further Reading

Ballard, Robert D., ed. *Archeological Oceanography.* Princeton, NJ: Princeton University Press, 2008.

———. *The Discovery of the Titanic.* New York: Warner, 1987.

———. *Explorations: My Quest for Adventure and Discovery Under the Sea.* New York: Hyperion, 1995.

Hill, Christine M. *Robert Ballard: The Oceanographer Who Discovered the Titanic.* Berkeley Heights, NJ: Enslow, 1999.

BANKS, JOSEPH (1743–1820)

1743:	Born on February 13 in London
1760:	Enters Oxford University
1766:	Makes his first voyage, on the *Niger*, to Newfoundland and Labrador
1768:	Sets sail with Captain James Cook on the *Endeavour* for the South Pacific
1770:	With Swedish-born botanist Daniel Carl Solander, collects a massive number of plants at Botany Bay, Australia
1778:	Elected president of Britain's prestigious Royal Society
1795:	Receives investiture as Knight of the Bath
1820:	Dies on June 19 in London

English botanist Joseph Banks (depicted in a 1773 portrait by Sir Joshua Reynolds) amassed a vast collection of plant and animal specimens on several voyages. He also served as president of the Royal Society, Britain's national academy of science. *(Granger Collection, New York)*

An influential British botanist, Joseph Banks brought back from his voyages to the North Atlantic and South Pacific a vast quantity of species. He served for years as president of the Royal Society, sponsoring a number of scientific expeditions, and he was the leading founder of the African Association.

Banks was born on February 13, 1743, into a prominent London family. His father, William Banks, served in the House of Commons and owned a considerable estate. His mother, Sarah Bate, was a wealthy heiress. As a boy, Joseph attended Harrow School and then, between the ages of thirteen and eighteen, he went to Eton. But more than going to school, he liked to fish and, most notably, developed an interest in botany.

As the story has it, one day while at Eton, Joseph, having finished bathing in a river, noticed the beauty of some nearby flowers and concluded that he could learn more from nature than from studying Greek or Latin. So he began collecting plants. At about the same time, he discovered in his mother's possession a book, complete with engravings, that described specimens he had encountered. This intensified his botanical searches.

Banks enrolled at Oxford University in 1760 and studied botany under a tutor. He was attracted to the teachings of Carl Linnaeus, the Swedish naturalist who developed a system for classifying plants and was popular in Banks's time.

In 1761, Banks's father died, and, in 1764, at age twenty-one, Banks inherited his father's estate, Revesby Abbey in Lincolnshire. Later that year, he left Oxford without obtaining a degree and settled in London. There, he expanded his circle of friends, among them the Swedish-born botanist Daniel Carl Solander, who had studied under Linnaeus. By attending meetings of the British Museum, Banks made contacts with scientists in England and began writing to Linnaeus.

Banks made his first sea voyage in 1766, when he sailed on the *Niger* with a friend from Eton, Constantine John Phipps, to Newfoundland and Labrador. He returned to England in January 1767 with specimens or records of at least 340 plants and ninety-one birds, along with many fish and some mammals. The plants constituted the beginnings of a herbarium (a place where dried and pressed plant specimens are stored in special cabinets) that would become renowned for its scope.

Voyage with Cook

At this time, the Royal Society, to which Banks had been elected as a fellow, was encouraging the British government to send an expedition to Tahiti to participate in observing the transit of Venus over the surface of the Sun.

CARL LINNAEUS AND MODERN TAXONOMY

Sometimes called the "father of taxonomy" (the science of classifying organisms), the Swedish naturalist Carl Linnaeus (1707–1778) influenced Joseph Banks and other scientists of his day and provided a classification system that remains the standard in modern biology.

Linnaeus published his *System Naturae* in 1735, while enrolled at the University of Leiden in the Netherlands. In it, he presented his innovational taxonomic system, which he would modify over time. As Linnaeus stated in his most influential work, *Philosophia Botanica* (1751), he considered it the naturalist's duty to construct a system of classification dedicated to revealing the divine order created by God.

Linnaeus believed that all species of organisms could be grouped into higher categories called "genera," and that genera could be grouped based on shared features, and so on. This system created a taxonomy of genera grouped into orders, orders into classes, and classes into kingdoms. Thus, the following is an example of his classification for human beings:

Kingdom: Animalia

Class: Verterbrata

Order: Primates

Genus: Homo

Species: Sapiens

Linnaeus also developed a plant taxonomy (which has undergone numerous changes over the years). It was based on the number and arrangement of plants' reproductive organs, with the stamen determining the class and the pistil the order.

Linnaeus simplified the naming of species by assigning one Latin name to indicate the genus and another the species. The second name usually is an adjective describing the organism or its geographic location, or it may be based on the name of the person who discovered it. For example, the domestic dog is *Canis familiaris,* with *Canis* being the genus that includes dogs, wolves, and coyotes, and *familiaris* a descriptor assigned specifically to the domestic dog.

This system, called binomial nomenclature, became standard. Although scientists today classify species based on characteristics different from those used by Linnaeus, they still rely on his system of taxonomy.

The transit is the movement of Venus over the Sun's disk as seen from Earth, an event that has occurred only five times since the telescope was invented in 1609, and last occurred in 2004. By observing from widely spaced locations on Earth when the transit began and when it ended, astronomers could calculate the distance to Venus. From this, the scale of the rest of the solar system would follow.

King George III agreed to fund the mission, which set sail with James Cook as captain of the *Endeavour* in 1768. Banks convinced the Royal Society to back him in becoming part of Cook's voyage of science and discovery.

Banks kept an extensive, 250,000-word journal of the three-year journey. In it, he wrote about the beginning of the expedition on August 25, 1786:

> After having waited in [Plymouth] ten days, the ship, and everything belonging to me, being all that time in perfect readiness to sail at a moments warning, we at last got fair wind, and this day at 3 O'Clock in the even weig[he]d anchor, and set sail, all in excellent health and spirits perfectly prepared (in Mind at least) to undergo with Cheerfullness any fatigues or dangers that may occur in our intended Voyage.

At Tahiti, Cook observed the transit of Venus, although his measurements were imprecise. But clearly, the expedition was intended to accomplish more. Cook was under secret orders from the British government to discover new lands in the South Pacific, to "search between Tahiti and New Zealand for a Continent or Land of great extent," and to explore New Zealand. In addition, Banks sought to gather a wide range of information about plants, birds, and other animals, along with knowledge of the indigenous peoples.

Working with Solander and the Finnish botanist Herman Spöring, Jr., Banks collected about 800 specimens of Australian flora, pictures of which were drawn by Sydney Parkinson. In his journal, Banks effused about the plentiful birds and the bountiful plants he found in 1770 at Botany Bay and elsewhere along the Australian coast. One quote in particular reveals something about the methods he used:

> Our collection of Plants was now grown so immensely large that it was necessary that some extraordinary care should be taken of them least they spoil in the books. I therefore devoted this day to that business and carried all the drying paper . . . ashore and spreading them upon a sail in the sun kept them in manner exposed all day, often turning them. . . . By this means they came on board at night in very good condition.

Cook's first expedition ended after he sailed across the Indian Ocean to the Cape of Good Hope (the southern tip of Africa). The *Endeavour* arrived back in England in July 1771.

Banks wanted to sail with Cook on the captain's second expedition, intended to depart in 1772 in search of a land south of New Zealand. But a dispute over accommodations—Banks wanted most everything on the ship to be arranged to his liking—and his claim that the ship, *Resolution*, was unsafe, caused him to cancel his plans. Instead, the same year Cook set sail, Banks voyaged to the western islands of Scotland and to Iceland.

The Royal Society and a Vast Collection

In 1778, Banks was elected president of the Royal Society, a position he held until 1820. In this capacity, and in his role as an advisor to the British government on scientific issues, he sent botanists to gather specimens in New South Wales in Australia.

Banks's interest in Australia and in the development of the British Empire led him to advocate the settlement of New South Wales. In 1779, he argued before a committee of the House of Commons that convicts should be sent to Botany Bay to help relieve the crowded conditions in British prisons and to develop the new land as a British colony. But he also wanted free settlers to come to New South Wales, and he became intimately involved in the plans made to carry out this policy. Indeed, much correspondence passed between him and the territory's first four governors.

Banks organized the voyage of the *Investigator* to Australia in 1801–1803, during which Matthew Flinders mapped much of the continent's coast. He sent botanists to many lands to amass great collections, including expeditions to the Cape of Good Hope, West Africa, the East Indies, South America, and India.

When Cook set sail, in 1776, on his third expedition to find the Northwest Passage and again journey through the Pacific, Banks provided advice. Banks suggested that Cook take with him David Nelson, a gardener from London's Kew Gardens, to help in bringing back newfound species of plants. In fact, Banks played an instrumental role in the development of the gardens. The expeditions sponsored by the Royal Society while Banks was its president led to the Kew Gardens becoming the world's leading botanical gardens and resulted in a host of plant species being introduced into Europe.

Banks began compiling his massive *Florilegium* in the 1770s. This book contains the illustrations of his discoveries from the *Endeavour* mission—hundreds of previously unknown plants, insects, fish, reptiles, birds, and mammals. His London home, on Soho Square, which he bought in 1776, became a gathering center for scientific discussions and housed his many collections. One observer pictured Banks's collection shortly before he moved to Soho:

> His house is a perfect museum; every room contains an inestimable treasure. . . . The Armoury contains all the warlike instruments, mechanical instruments and utensils of every kind, made use of by the Indians in the South Seas. . . . The second room contains the different habits and ornaments of the several Indian nations they discovered. . . . The number of plants is about 3000, 110 of which are new genera, and 1300 new species which were never seen or heard of before in Europe. . . . [A third room] contains an almost numberless collection of animals, quadrupeds, birds, fish, amphibians, reptiles, insects and vermes [worms], preserved in spirits, most of them new and nondescript. Here I was most in amazement and cannot attempt any particular description.

For his scientific accomplishments, Banks was knighted by the British crown in 1795. In his later years, he remained deeply involved in scientific and community projects. In 1804, Banks and a group of friends founded the Royal Horticultural Society. He continued as president of the Royal Society and served on several government committees. He also was a trustee of the British Museum and presided over the Club of the Royal Philosophers.

During this time, Banks labored through great pain as he suffered from gout. After 1805, he was mainly confined to a wheelchair. Banks died on June 19, 1820.

Banks expanded scientific knowledge of plants and animals through his collections and those of the many other explorers whom he backed. He was, moreover, an intriguing combination of internationalist and nationalist. He believed in the advancement of science based on international cooperation, as evident in his substantial correspondence with scientists overseas, yet he also helped expand and advance the power of the British Empire, a main reason why, with Banks as president, the Royal Society worked so closely with the British government.

Further Reading

Chambers, Neil. *Joseph Banks and the British Museum: The World of Collecting, 1770–1830.* London: Pickering and Chatto, 2007.

Gascoigne, John. *Joseph Banks and the English Enlightenment: Useful Knowledge and Polite Culture.* New York: Cambridge University Press, 1994.

———. *Science in the Service of Empire: Joseph Banks, the British State and the Uses of Science in the Age of Revolution.* New York: Cambridge University Press, 1998.

O'Brian, Patrick. *Joseph Banks: A Life.* Chicago: University of Chicago Press, 1987.

See also: Cook, James; Flinders, Matthew.

BATES, HENRY WALTER (1825–1892)

1825: Born on February 8 in Leicester, England
1843: Publishes his first scientific paper, on insects
1848: Begins exploration of the Amazon region
1862: Presents paper describing his theory of mimicry
1864: Begins serving as assistant secretary of the Royal Society
1892: Dies on February 16 in London

A British explorer, naturalist, and entomologist (one who studies insects), Henry Walter Bates journeyed into the far reaches of the Amazon region in Brazil to collect insect specimens. He was an early supporter of the Darwinian concept of natural selection. And he proposed the theory of mimicry, the condition in which two or more species are similar in appearance or some other form but only one of the species carries the specific features that makes it repulsive to a predator.

Born on February 8, 1825, to a hosiery maker in Leicester, England, Henry Bates came from humble origins. He attended boarding school until age thirteen, at which point, he apprenticed to a hosiery manufacturer. While working long days, he also attended the local Mechanics Institute, where he studied Greek, Latin, and drawing, often staying up past midnight to complete his schoolwork.

During this time, Bates developed an interest in natural history, especially entomology, and he began collecting butterflies. Bereft of proper equipment, he stored them in the drawers of his furniture. Bates wrote about and drew descriptions of the butterflies and also began collecting beetles. In 1843, at age eighteen, he published a paper titled "Note on Coleopterous Insects Frequenting Damp Places."

Shortly thereafter, Bates met Alfred Russel Wallace, a teacher at the Collegiate School in Leicester, who shared his interest in entomology. The two men collected specimens together and began talking about journeying to far-off places to expand their pursuit.

Then, in 1847, W.H. Edwards published *Voyage Up the River Amazon, Including a Residence at Para*. Bates and Wallace read the book and became excited by Edwards's description of the beauty of the region and the kindness of its people. As a result, Bates decided to sail with Wallace across the Atlantic to Brazil.

Bates and Wallace arrived in Brazil in 1848, and settled at Para (today Belém), which they used as a base for short expeditions to collect birds and insects. For reasons now unclear, they went their separate ways in exploring Amazonia.

In 1851, Bates journeyed to Santarém, a Brazilian town located along the Amazon River where it joins with the Tapajós River. From there, he explored the remote reaches of the Tapajós, including one of its branches. He made contact with the Mundurucú Indians and gathered considerable ethnological information, along with biological and geographical facts.

The hardships were considerable, and, at one point, some 1,400 miles (2,250 kilometers) inland along the Amazon, Bates complained of not having received any supply packages from England in a long time. His clothes were tattered, his feet bare, and his spirit sapped. He had no books to read and claimed he had been robbed. At another point he suffered from yellow fever, which caused him to take a "decoction of elder blossoms as a sudorific" that led to his falling "insensible into my hammock."

Bates's procedure for collecting specimens is described in a letter he wrote from the Amazon:

> Between 9 and 10 A.M., I prepare for the woods: a coloured shirt, pair of trousers, pair of common boots, and an old hat, are all my clothing; over my left shoulder slings my double-barrelled gun, loaded. . . . In my right hand I take my net; on my left side is suspended a leathern bag with two pockets, one for my insect box, the other for powder . . . on my right side hangs my "game bag," . . . with . . . thongs to hang lizards, snakes, frogs, or large birds; one small pocket in this bag contains my caps, another papers for wrapping up delicate birds.

Bates collected a total of 14,712 species, at least 8,000 of which were new to science. Among his collection were 14,000 insects, 360 birds, 140 reptiles, 120 fish, and 52 mammals.

Perhaps his most lasting achievement came when he applied his scientific eye to some beautiful, two-toned butterflies. He found that one type of butterfly—heliconians—emitted an odor to repel birds and to keep the birds from eating them. Another type—Dismorphia—looked like the heliconians but emitted no repelling odor. The birds, however, thought the Dismorphia were the malodorous ones, and so refrained from eating them as well. In short, butterflies of one kind mimicked the appearance of another in order to protect themselves. Bates attributed this mimicry to natural selection, saying the characteristics had been adopted to survive in an environment filled with predators.

Bates did not return to Para until 1859, when declining health forced him to leave Brazil for England. Upon reaching England, he read Charles Darwin's recently published *On the Origin of Species* (1859) and embraced it. For his part, Darwin admired Bates's theory of mimicry and praised a paper that Bates wrote in 1862. Darwin called it "one of the most remarkable and admirable papers I ever read in my life," and said, "I am rejoiced that I

MIMICRY

In the time since Henry Bates first proposed his theory of mimicry, scientists have discovered many more instances of this evolutionary adaptation. Batesian mimicry is when two or more species are similar in appearance, or in some other way, but only one carries the features that make it repulsive to a predator. While visual mimics are most obvious to human beings, there are other forms of mimicry, such as smell.

One complex example of Batesian mimicry is evident in the appearance of the Papilio memnon butterfly of Indonesia. The female of this butterfly can produce one or more different female forms, including color and wing shape, that mimic any of five species of bitter-tasting butterflies. In another case, Batesian mimicry occurs between the coral snake and the king snake. Both snakes have alternating yellow, red, and black bands, but the coral snake is venomous, while the king snake is harmless.

In the 1870s, the German naturalist Fritz Muller postulated another form of mimicry to explain a phenomenon Bates had found puzzling: two or more species sharing similar features but also sharing the same mechanisms through which they protect themselves from predators, such as being unpalatable. Bates could not figure out why, if both species were harmful, they mimicked each other.

Muller explained that once a predator had learned to avoid a warning, such as a coloration in butterflies, it would then avoid all other similarly patterned species, edible or inedible. Thus, the number of individuals sacrificed in educating the predators would be spread over all of the species that share the same warning, allowing more individuals within each species to survive.

passed over the whole subject [of mimicry] in the 'Origin,' for I should have made a precious mess of it."

In 1863, Bates published his book *The Naturalist on the River Amazon*, an enthralling account of his expedition. In it, he reveals his eclectic interest in the people, terrain, birds, insects, fish, and mammals of the Amazon, to all of which he applied an explorer's curiosity. Also during this time, Bates developed a classification system for butterflies tied to the Darwinian theory of evolution, categorizing them from simple to more complex types. In 1861, Bates married Sarah Ann Mason; the couple had a daughter and three sons.

From 1864 until his death, Bates served as assistant secretary of the Royal Society and became editor of its journal, *Philosophical Transactions*. He also served as president of the Entomological Society of London (now the Royal Entomological Society) from 1868 to 1869 and again in 1878. He was elected a fellow of the Linnean Society in 1871 and of the Royal Society in 1881. In his later years, he sold his butterfly collection and concentrated on studying beetles.

His health weakened by exposure to disease in the Amazon, Bates died on February 16, 1892, in London from complications associated with influenza and bronchitis. To the present day, "Batesian mimicry" is regarded as important evidence of the theory of natural selection.

Further Reading

Bates, Henry Walter. *The Naturalist on the River Amazon.* 1863. New York: Routledge, 2004.
Woodcock, George. *Henry Walter Bates, Naturalist of the Amazon.* London: Faber, 1969.

See also:
Amazon River and Basin; Wallace, Alfred Russel.

BEAGLE, VOYAGE OF THE

1831: Charles Darwin begins his voyage on the *Beagle*
1835: Darwin explores the Galápagos Islands
1836: The *Beagle* returns home to England

The HMS *Beagle* was a small ship, only 90 feet (27 meters) long and 24 feet (7 meters) wide, but it left a large imprint on science. It was on this vessel, which flew the British flag, that Charles Darwin made the five-year voyage that led to his formulating the theory of evolution through natural selection.

When Darwin began his voyage in 1831, the *Beagle* was an eleven-year-old ship. Launched in May 1820, as a ten-gun brig in the British navy, the vessel saw no combat duty and had been moored for five years. In 1825, it was converted to a three-masted sailing ship and used on a mission by the British Admiralty to help in a hydrographic survey (charting waters, including their flow) of Patagonia and Tierra del Fuego, in South America.

For the *Beagle*'s second voyage, also under the direction of the Admiralty, the ship was refitted under the direction of Captain Robert FitzRoy. In fact, it had rotted so much it practically had to be rebuilt. FitzRoy had a new deck constructed, strengthened the hull, and added twenty-two chronometers and five modernized barometers, known for their accuracy.

In seeking someone to accompany him, FitzRoy turned to Darwin, a twenty-two-year-old naturalist whose observations, it was believed, would add to the knowledge gained on the voyage. The *Beagle* was to circumnavigate the globe, and FitzRoy believed Darwin would find evidence to confirm a literal interpretation of the Bible, especially the story of the great flood. Although Darwin had begun to read scientific accounts questioning such an explanation, at this stage he, too, took much of the Bible literally.

The start of the voyage was delayed, as problems arose with refitting the ship and with inclement weather. Finally, the *Beagle* got under way. On December 27, 1831, it departed Plymouth Sound (located in southwestern England on the English Channel).

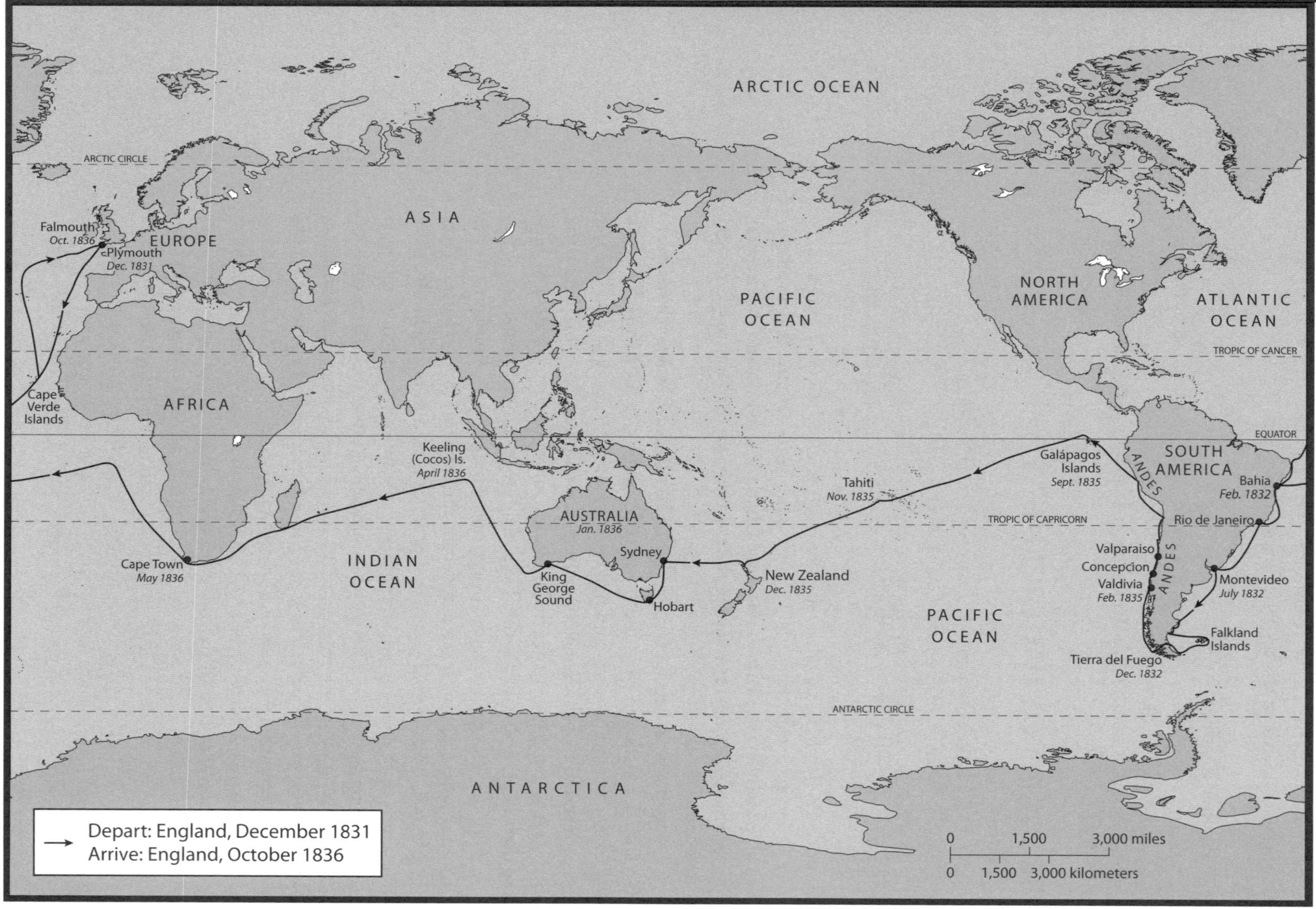
ARCTIC OCEAN
ARCTIC CIRCLE
Falmouth
Oct. 1836
Plymouth
Dec. 1831
EUROPE
ASIA
PACIFIC OCEAN
NORTH AMERICA
ATLANTIC OCEAN
TROPIC OF CANCER
Cape Verde Islands
AFRICA
EQUATOR
Keeling (Cocos) Is.
April 1836
Galápagos Islands
Sept. 1835
SOUTH AMERICA
ANDES
Bahia
Feb. 1832
Tahiti
Nov. 1835
AUSTRALIA
Jan. 1836
TROPIC OF CAPRICORN
Rio de Janeiro
Valparaiso
Concepcion
Valdivia
Feb. 1835
Sydney
Cape Town
May 1836
INDIAN OCEAN
King George Sound
Hobart
New Zealand
Dec. 1835
Montevideo
July 1832
PACIFIC OCEAN
Falkland Islands
Tierra del Fuego
Dec. 1832
ANTARCTIC CIRCLE
ANTARCTICA
Depart: England, December 1831
Arrive: England, October 1836
0 1,500 3,000 miles
0 1,500 3,000 kilometers

After major renovation and refitting—including the addition of extensive scientific equipment—the HMS *Beagle* carried young Charles Darwin on a five-year ocean voyage that would be a turning point in his life and the history of biological science. *(Hulton Archive/Stringer/Getty Images)*

The ship stopped first at St. Jago in the Cape Verde Islands, where the volcanic terrain made Darwin contemplate the mysterious workings of nature. In the rocks, he sighted a white band of shells and corals some 30 feet (9 meters) above sea level, and he wondered how it was that the shells and corals were no longer under water. He concluded that a sudden drop in the sea's level was not the cause of this exposure. Instead, he agreed more and more with the English geologist Charles Lyell, who argued that the Earth was changing constantly and slowly. This view conflicted with the widely accepted "catastrophic theory," which held that periodic catastrophes changed the Earth, the last great one having been the flood during Noah's time.

When the *Beagle* reached South America at Bahia in Brazil, on February 28, 1832, Darwin studied the life peculiar to the region and the different environments in which the animals there lived. He was stunned by the natural beauty he found in Brazil, particularly in the rain forests. He later wrote about "the luxuriance of the vegetation . . . the elegance of the grasses, the novelty of the parasitical plants, the beauty of the flowers." During the trip, he collected many biological specimens.

Arriving at Montevideo, Uruguay, on the River Plate (Río de la Plata) in July 1832, Darwin found a rebellion under way against the government. At Bahía Blanca, Argentina, he met with gauchos (South American cowboys) who told him of their warfare against the Pampas Indians. At Tierra del Fuego, which he reached in December, he saw "uncivilized" humans, and he observed that the "difference between savage & civilized man . . . is greater than between a wild & domesticated animal."

But it was in the Galápagos Islands, located in the Pacific Ocean about 650 miles (1,050 kilometers) off the coast of South America (today part of Ecuador), where Darwin made discoveries that would raise more questions in his mind about animals and their habitats. In the Galápagos, Darwin found tortoises so abundant, he said, "that a single ship's company here caught from 500–800 in a short time," and he found black lava rocks on the beach "frequented by large (2–3 ft) most disgusting, clumsy Lizards."

From October 8 to October 17, 1835, Darwin explored one of the Galápagos Islands, called James Island but also known as San Salvador or Santiago Island, which consisted of two volcanoes. He ventured into its little-traversed interior, all the while collecting specimens important to his scientific research.

Nicholas Lawson, a British official on the Galápagos, called to Darwin's attention that each island supported its own form of tortoises. Consequently, an observer could determine which island a tortoise came from just by looking at it. Darwin also observed that mockingbirds he collected from the Charles and Chatham islands (also in the Galápagos) were different from each other, and he noticed that finches displayed wide variations in the sizes and shapes of their beaks. Several years later, these discoveries would cause him to study the links between distinct but similar species and to contemplate the effects of the environment on them. That is, he considered the changeability of species. This later would lead to his theory of evolution through natural selection.

From the Galápagos, the *Beagle* proceeded to Tahiti, which had been visited by Europeans several times previously. There, Darwin hiked among the volcanic peaks, collected ferns, and canoed out to a reef. He was amazed to find that the reef had been formed by corals, which he called the "tiny architects" of the ocean.

In late November, the *Beagle* headed for New Zealand. On its arrival, Darwin observed the Maori people and concluded that they were shifty, cunning, and barbaric.

In January 1836, the expedition reached Australia. Darwin journeyed into the interior and hunted kangaroos. He also collected shells and fish and caught a native Australian bush rat. But he generally found the land to be uninteresting and was relieved when the *Beagle* departed westward across the Indian Ocean.

The ship rounded Africa and arrived at Falmouth, England, on October 2, 1836, thus completing its voyage.

Further Reading

Brown, Janet. *Charles Darwin: Voyaging.* New York: Alfred A. Knopf, 1995.

Desmond, Adrian, and James Moore. *Darwin.* New York: Warner, 1991.

BELL, GERTRUDE (1868–1926)

1868: Born on July 14 in Durham, England
1888: Graduates from Oxford University with a degree in history
1900: Makes contact with the Druze, a secret sect
1907: Publishes *Syria: The Desert and the Sown*
1913: Journeys to the oasis settlement of Ha'il in Saudi Arabia
1921: Becomes advisor to King Faisal I and begins the Iraqi Archaeological Museum
1926: Dies by suicide on July 12 in Baghdad

A British archaeologist known for her research and writings on the Middle East, Gertrude Bell also was a political strategist and intelligence officer who helped shape the modern nation of Iraq.

Gertrude Margaret Lowthian Bell was born into a wealthy family in Durham, England, on July 14, 1868. Her father, Hugh Bell, owned a coal-mining company. Precocious, intelligent, and curious, Gertrude excelled at school and in 1886 arrived at Oxford University. In just two years, she became the first woman to graduate from Oxford with a degree in history.

"To those bred under an elaborate social order," she once wrote, "few such moments of exhilaration can come as that which stands at the threshold of wild travel." Bell was, in fact, a prodigious traveler, and a mountaineer in Switzerland before she discovered her attraction to the Middle East.

Her travels were extraordinary for either a man or a woman given the arduous nature of transportation at the time, and more so because it was considered improper for a woman to journey great distances without a male companion, let alone into dangerous territory. Quite likely, travel for Bell provided more than excitement. No doubt it provided a sense of independence and accomplishment in a world where men held so much power.

The Druze and Archaeological Research

Bell studied archaeology and languages, and she became fluent in Arabic, Persian, French, and German. In 1892, she traveled to Persia and was enthralled by its culture. Seven years later, she traveled to Palestine and Syria, which were then under the rule of the Ottoman Turks. In 1900, she undertook a dangerous trip to Jebel Mountain to make contact with the Druze, a secret sect that had been fighting the Turks for some 200 years. There, she met with the Druze king.

British writer and archaeologist Gertrude Bell, an inveterate traveler of the Middle East during the early twentieth century, was also an intelligence officer, government advisor, translator of literature, and founder of the Baghdad Museum in Iraq. *(Harlingue/Roger Viollet/Getty Images)*

At the urging of the archaeologist Saloman Reinach, Bell returned to the Middle East in 1905 to study ancient ruins. She again met with the Druze, as well as with the Bedouin. Often, she camped alone on the desert sand, her tent an isolated outpost; many a time, she won the support of a sheik or chieftain with gifts and political stories and joined him in reciting Arab poetry. The contacts she made with desert rulers proved invaluable to her later political activities.

In 1907, she published her book *Syria: The Desert and the Sown*, a vivid description of the villages and cities she visited. Her prose made Middle Eastern culture accessible to Westerners. Her study of Turkish ruins, also in 1907, led her to write *A Thousand and One Churches* (1909) with the archaeologist and New Testament scholar William Ramsey.

Two years later, she began research at the ancient Hittite city of Carchemish in Mesopotamia, photographing and mapping the fortress ruin of Ukhaidir. There, she met the British scholar and soldier T.E. Lawrence, who later became famous as Lawrence of Arabia.

In 1913, Bell undertook what one historian has called her "most important achievement in the field of exploration," a dangerous journey to the oasis settlement of Ha'il (in Saudi Arabia). This trek, from Damascus across the northern third of the Arabian peninsula, was laden with geographical and political challenges, as Bell faced extreme desolation and encountered hostile tribal leaders. In fact, previous explorers had turned back from the arduous trip.

Bell successfully completed this journey, and she returned with more than 300 photographs of life in the desert, including images of the landscape and local architecture. (All told, she took more than 7,000 photographs during her extensive travels.) She had undertaken an unprecedented exploration of tribal life and a mapping of central Arabia and came away with a rich knowledge of tribal relations. The trip led to her appointment two years later to the British Military Intelligence Department at Basra, in Iraq.

Iraq and Its Archaeological Museum

With the outbreak of World War I, Bell became less a scientist and more a politician. In 1917, the British captured Baghdad, a feat heavily dependent on the intelligence and maps that she provided to the army. Bell also was instrumental in fostering cooperation between British and Arab leaders in their fight against the Turks.

In 1919, she was appointed Oriental secretary in Iraq. When the Paris Peace Conference was held at the end of World War I, Bell attended as one of Britain's delegates and helped draw up the modern boundaries for the country.

Bell supported T.E. Lawrence when he advocated to British authorities the consolidation of Iraq's three districts—Basra, Baghdad, and Mosul—into one kingdom. As a liberal imperialist, she wanted the British to rule Iraq for the benefit of British interests and as a way to educate and train Arabs in Western governance. She advised that Iraq be run by the Sunni religious sect rather than the majority Shiites, because she feared that the Shiites would establish a harsh, theocratic state. And she opposed a Kurdish state in the north, because she felt that balance should be maintained among the Sunnis, Shiites, and Kurds through British oversight, which, in turn, would give Britain access to Iraq's oil reserves.

In 1921, Bell and Lawrence successfully promoted Faisal bin Hussein to become king of Iraq, while the country remained under British control. Faisal had been born into a royal family in Saudi Arabia but had never before been to Iraq and thus was distrusted by some Iraqis. He had, however, sided with Great Britain in World War I and, with the help of Lawrence, had organized a revolt against the Ottoman Empire, thus forming a close relationship with the British.

Bell became a close advisor to Faisal, who was crowned King Faisal I in 1921. She was nicknamed "the Uncrowned Queen of Iraq," and many Iraqis called her "Khatun," meaning "great lady." A contemporary, British author Virginia Woolf, said, "Miss Bell has a very long nose like an Aberdeen terrier; she is a masterful woman, has everyone under her thumb, and makes one feel a little inefficient."

With King Faisal's help, Bell founded the Iraqi Archaeological Museum (today the National Museum of Iraq) and became its first director. (The

ARCHAEOLOGICAL DIGS

Archaeologists engage in the scientific study of the human past by investigating a variety of remains, such as fossils, the ruins of buildings, tools, and pottery. These often are uncovered through digs, or excavations.

Sites for digs can be determined by carefully analyzing the ground surface for potsherds (shards of pottery) and other such clues. Today, archaeologists also use radar and other technology to determine what might exist underground before they start digging.

Digs tend to be small in size and usually involve only a few researchers and their helpers. Once the digging has begun, archaeologists use computer-based mapping systems to survey the site and the designs of any buildings or other major finds within it.

Some archaeologists focus on the evolution of primates up until human beings evolved. Others focus on the ancient and classical civilizations of Europe and the Middle East. Still others focus on more recent societies and combine physical with written evidence.

Marine archaeologists study submerged settlements and sunken ships to better understand the interaction between human beings and the sea. For example, in 2007, archaeologists George Robb and Adrian Anastasi, along with dive master Howard Phoenix, working for the RPM Nautical Foundation, began compiling an underwater map intended to plot the position of sunken fleets from ancient and medieval times along Albania's Adriatic coast. In doing so, they uncovered 2,400-year-old artifacts.

museum officially opened in its permanent home shortly after her death in 1926.) In her work with the museum, she supervised numerous digs and identified and cataloged artifacts crucial to understanding ancient Iraq.

By 1926, Bell had become ill and depressed. She was afflicted with bronchitis, and her family had suffered financial setbacks, forcing the sale of her home in London. She ended her life on July 12, 1926, in Baghdad with an overdose of sleeping pills.

In her explorations and archaeological work, Bell had combined the old Iraq with the new, literally unearthing in her digs the story of the past, while forging in her politics the boundaries of a new nation. She once said,

> I like Baghdad and I like Iraq. It's the real East, and it's stirring; things are happening here, and the romance of it all touches me and absorbs me.

Further Reading

Bell, Gertrude. *The Desert and the Sown.* Boston: Beacon, 1985.

Howell, Georgina. *Gertrude Bell: Queen of the Desert, Shaper of Nations.* New York: Farrar, Straus and Giroux, 2007.

Wallach, Janet. *Desert Queen: The Extraordinary Life of Gertrude Bell, Adventurer, Adviser to Kings, Ally of Lawrence of Arabia.* New York: Anchor, 2005.

BINGHAM, HIRAM (1875–1956)

1875: Born on November 19 in Honolulu, Hawaii
1906: Retraces the steps of Simón Bolívar in South America
1911: Encounters the Incan settlement of Machu Picchu
1912: Begins excavating Machu Picchu
1922: Wins election as lieutenant governor of Connecticut
1926: Wins election to the U.S. Senate
1956: Dies on June 6 in Washington, D.C.

An American archaeologist, academic, and politician, Hiram Bingham III is best known as the "scientific discoverer" of the ancient Inca ruins at Machu Picchu in Peru.

Hiram Bingham III was born on November 19, 1875, in Honolulu, Hawaii, to Hiram Bingham and Clarissa Minerva Brewster, both of whom were Protestant missionaries, as was his grandfather, who had done much to Christianize the islands. As a boy, Hiram learned mountaineering from his father and climbed the mountains in Hawaii.

After graduating from Punahou School in Hawaii in 1892, Bingham attended Phillips Academy in Andover, Massachusetts, for two years and then Yale University from 1894 to 1898. He enrolled at the University of California at Berkeley for graduate work in history in 1899. He then studied at Harvard from 1900 to 1905, when he earned his doctorate in Latin American history. In 1900, he married Alfreda Mitchell, an heiress whose money provided him the independence to engage in scientific expeditions.

Bingham taught history and political science at Harvard and Princeton. In 1909, he was appointed as an assistant professor in Latin American history at Yale. During these years, he showed no interest in following his family's missionary calling, a decision that caused friction between him and his parents.

Early Explorations

Bingham was attracted to the study of South American history because so little research had been done there by anyone in the United States. As he considered writing a biography of the South American liberator Simón Bolívar, he became attracted to exploration and decided to retrace the route taken by Bolívar across the continent in 1819. He later wrote,

> I came to the conclusion that if I wished to understand this period in South American history, it would be necessary for me to undertake an expedition

> that should have for its object not only a study of the country where Bolívar lived and fought, and a visit to the scenes of his most important battles . . . but also an exploration of the route of his most celebrated campaign.

Bingham undertook this journey in November 1906; he subsequently published *The Journal of an Expedition Across Venezuela and Colombia, 1906–1907* (1909). In 1908 and 1909, he traversed southern South America and served as a delegate to the First Pan American Scientific Congress, in Santiago, Chile.

It was during his southern excursion, as he traveled from Buenos Aires, Argentina, to Lima, Peru, that Bingham was drawn to the Incas. While he was in Peru, the authorities there persuaded him to join an expedition to the Inca village of Choqquequirau. He was intrigued by the ancient culture and stories about an unknown region around the high mountains. He was further influenced by Clements Markham's book, *The Incas of Peru* (1910), which told of the Incas' flight, circa 1536, from Cuzco to Vilcabamba, a nearby land of canyons and mountains, to escape the Spaniards.

In 1911, Bingham returned to Peru, this time, on an expedition sponsored by Yale to explore the region northwest of Cuzco, in the Andes. His party included Isaiah Bowman, a geologist; Kai Hendrickson, a topographer; and H. Z. Tucker, an archaeologist.

Finding Machu Picchu

In late July of that year, a local farmer told Bingham of some ancient ruins, and the American decided to find out if they might be related to the Incas. He had heard other stories about the ruins at least several days earlier and had been told about their existence by Albert Giesecke, the rector of the University of Cuzco. Still, when Bingham began his climb up the mountains on July 24 to search for the ruins, he doubted they would be significant.

That afternoon, he came upon Machu Picchu. Although he took the dimensions of some of the buildings in this first visit, he spent only a few hours there. Nevertheless, he realized he had made an important find.

He told *The New York Times* that he had found the ancient city when he was led by some Peruvian Indians up an old goat path to a precipitous plateau at an elevation of approximately 2,000 feet (600 meters). There, they discovered an Incan temple, along whose ruins the Indians recently had planted corn. "The white granite stones used in the foundation of the temple," Bingham told the *Times*, "measured 8 by 12 by 6 feet, and were well chiseled and beautifully joined without mortar in Egyptian style."

Machu Picchu has been called "the lost city of the Incas." Built around 1460, it was abandoned 100 years later, when the Spanish conquered the

Incas. Its importance to the Incas is widely debated by archeologists and historians. Some think that it was a holy center. Others believe it was an estate of an Incan emperor, a center from which to control the local economies, or even a prison. It was one of the few Incan sites not plundered by the Spanish, who failed to find it, thus adding to the value of Bingham's find.

Hiram Bingham III, a Yale University historian, rediscovered the "lost" Inca city of Machu Picchu in the Peruvian Andes in July 1911. Yale, which had cosponsored the expedition, agreed in 2007 to return thousands of relics he had removed from the site. *(Granger Collection, New York)*

Bingham believed that his team were the first white men to gaze on the city of Machu Picchu since the time of the Spanish invasion. On that point, however, he was wrong. In 1902, Agustin Lizarraga, who lived nearby in the town of San Miguel, had reached the ruins, and two local missionaries, Thomas Paine and Stuart McNairn, may well have reached the site in 1906. Still, Bingham was the first to publicize the importance of the ruins to the understanding of ancient Incan society and to methodically explore them. This is why he is often called their "scientific discoverer."

On leaving Machu Picchu, Bingham and his party mapped the Urubamba River and then climbed Mount Coropuna, at 21,763 feet (6,633 meters) the second-tallest peak in South America (after Mount Aconcagua in Argentina). The icy conditions forced them to use crampons (climbing irons) in their ascent. At the summit, they planted the Yale flag and left a canister containing a record of their feat.

Bingham returned to Machu Picchu in 1912 to excavate the site. The following year, he wrote about his findings for *National Geographic* magazine. (The National Geographic Society had supported his expedition.) At one point during his excavation trip, both his mules and his native guides deserted him, leaving him wandering on a mountain for two days with little food. He was saved when he met an Indian, who led him down a path to his base camp.

At Machu Picchu, Bingham found the skulls and skeletons of prehistoric human beings, along with bronze tables. He returned to the United States with some of the human remains, several of the tables, and some pottery. The Peruvian government questioned his removal of these items and, in general, distrusted his work at Machu Picchu, thinking he would disfigure or remove valuable items. In 2007, Yale agreed to return thousands of artifacts unearthed by Bingham and his colleagues, including mummies and ceramics.

Life after Machu Picchu

During World War I, Bingham served in the U.S. Army Air Service. In 1918, he commanded the flying school at Issoudun, France.

Entering politics after the war, he served as lieutenant governor of Connecticut from 1922 to 1924. In the latter year, he was elected governor of the state but served only two days before being elected to the U.S. Senate, as a Republican, to fill a vacant seat. Reelected in 1926, he faced an uphill battle for a third term in 1932.

By then, the Senate had censured Bingham for placing a lobbyist on his payroll. At the same time, the Republican president, Herbert Hoover, and the Republican-controlled Congress were largely reviled for their ineptitude in handling the economic crisis of the Great Depression. Bingham thus went down to defeat.

He subsequently engaged in banking and, during World War II, lectured at naval training schools. A zealous "communist hunter" during the cold war, he chaired the Civil Service Commission's Loyalty Review Board from 1951 to 1953. He died in Washington, D.C., on June 6, 1956.

Over the years, Bingham wrote three books based on his expedition to Machu Picchu: *Inca Land* (1922), *Machu Picchu, Citadel of the Incas* (1930), and *Lost City of the Incas* (1948). As a result of these works and his expedition, his name remains indelibly linked to the ancient Inca ruins at Machu Picchu.

Further Reading

Miller, Char. *Fathers and Sons: The Bingham Family and the American Mission.* Philadelphia: Temple University Press, 1982.

———, ed. *Selected Writings of Hiram Bingham, 1814–1869: To Raise the Lord's Banner.* Lewiston, NY: E. Mellen, 1988.

BOUGAINVILLE, LOUIS-ANTOINE DE (1729–1811)

1729: Born on November 12 in Paris

1753: Writes a paper on integral calculus that earns him membership in Britain's prestigious Royal Society

1766–1769: Circumnavigates the globe and writes detailed descriptions of the plants and animals he finds

1771: Publishes a book that portrays the island of Tahiti as a paradise and influences utopian philosophers

1811: Dies on August 20 in Paris

Louis-Antoine de Bougainville, the first Frenchman to circumnavigate the world, is greeted by natives in Tahiti—which he later described as an earthly paradise—in 1767. His account made Tahiti famous in Europe and reinforced the concept of the "noble savage." *(Granger Collection, New York)*

A French explorer, Louis-Antoine de Bougainville contributed to the scientific findings of the Enlightenment by circumnavigating the globe to discover new lands for his country and record the geography, plants, and animals that he found.

Bougainville was born on November 12, 1729, in Paris to Pierre-Yves de Bougainville, a wealthy notary in the city's courts of law, and Marie-Françoise d'Arboulin. As a young man, he showed a talent for mathematics. Bougainville studied under Alexis Clairaut, a prominent mathematician and astronomer, and, in 1753, he wrote a paper on integral calculus that was so impressive it earned him membership in Britain's prestigious Royal Society.

Bougainville initially prepared to become a lawyer, but he lost interest in an endeavor he considered dry and boring. Instead, he entered the French army in 1753. Three years later, he traveled to Canada, where he fought in the French and Indian War, sometimes called the Seven Years' War, against the British. There, he served as an aide-de-camp to Louis-Joseph de Montcalm-Grozon, the major general in command of French troops.

The war had begun in North America but escalated into a nearly worldwide fight for empire. When it ended in 1763, the French suffered a tremendous defeat and lost control of New France to the British. Following the war, Bougainville spent money from his personal fortune to settle displaced Acadians (French people from Canada) on the Falkland Islands, but the colony proved short-lived.

In 1766, the French government, under King Louis XV, gave Bougainville command of two ships, *La Boudeuse*, a frigate, and *L'Etoile*, a transport, for a voyage of discovery around the globe. On November 15, Bougainville left Nantes, on the western coast of France. Among those accompanying him was the botanist Philibert Commerçon.

Bougainville clearly wanted to add to the world's scientific knowledge at a time when more and more educated Europeans were embracing rational thought as part of the Enlightenment. He was a nationalist who wanted to advance the power of France, but he also was an internationalist, who worked with scientists from other countries.

The expedition sailed westward through the Strait of Magellan, at the southern tip of South America. In the spring of 1767, Bougainville arrived at Tahiti. He then journeyed to Samoa and New Hebrides (today Vanuatu), both located in the central South Pacific, and sailed through the Solomon Islands, located just to the east of New Guinea, where he named Bougainville Island, to the northeast of Australia, for himself.

Following an attack by islanders against his crew, Bougainville continued on to the Moluccas (in Indonesia). He completed his circumnavigation of the globe on March 16, 1769, when he arrived at Saint-Malo, on the northwestern coast of France, making him the first Frenchman to sail around the world.

Throughout his voyage, Bougainville kept journals that he filled with keen observations about plants and geography, including his identification of natural harbors at which ships could anchor. A South American climbing plant, the *Bougainvillea*, was later named for him.

In 1772, he published his *Description from a Voyage Around the World*, in which he portrayed Tahiti as a paradise. Utopian philosophers, who bemoaned the corruption of Western society while insisting that people were good when living within a state of nature, embraced this vision. In one of his journal entries, Bougainville wrote about Tahiti and its people:

> Our white skin delights them, they express admiration in this regard in the most expressive manner. Furthermore, the race is superb, with men 5 feet 10 inches tall, many reaching six feet, a few exceeding this. Their features are handsome. They have a head of hair they wear in various ways. Several also have a long beard which they rub as they do their hair with cocoanut oil. The women are pretty and, something [that] is due to their food and water, men and women and even old men have the finest teeth in the world. There people breathe only rest and sensual pleasures. Venus is the god they worship. The mildness of the climate, the beauty of the scenery, the fertility of the soil everywhere watered by rivers and cascades, the pure air unspoiled

by even those legions of insects that are the curse of hot climates, everything inspires sensual pleasure.

From 1779 to 1782, Bougainville again commanded a naval ship. He participated in the French blockade of Yorktown, Virginia, which helped the American colonies defeat Great Britain in the Revolutionary War. During this time, he married Flore-Josephe Longchamp de Montendre, with whom he would have three sons.

In 1787, Bougainville was made a member of the French Academy of Sciences. He obtained the rank of vice admiral in 1791, but shortly thereafter retired to his estate in Normandy, having escaped the indignity of imprisonment and the fate of execution that befell many of the elite in the bloody French Revolution. Bougainville died in Paris on August 20, 1811.

Further Reading

Hamilton, Edward P., trans. and ed. *Adventure in the Wilderness: The American Journals of Louis Antoine de Bougainville, 1756–1760.* Norman: University of Oklahoma Press, 1964.

Kimbrough, Mary. *Louis-Antoine de Bougainville, 1729–1811: A Study in French Naval History and Politics.* Lewiston, NY: E. Mellen, 1990.

Suthren, Victor J.H. *The Sea Has No End: The Life of Louis Antoine de Bougainville.* Toronto, Canada: Dundurn, 2004.

BRUCE, JAMES (1730–1794)

1730: Born on December 14 in Stirling County, Scotland
1763: Appointed consul to Algiers
1765: Explores the Roman ruins at Barbary
1770: Reaches the source of the Blue Nile River
1790: Publishes a five-volume account of his journey to the Nile
1794: Dies in Scotland on April 27

A Scottish explorer, James Bruce attempted to solve for Europeans the mystery of where the Nile River begins when, in 1769–1770, he ventured into the highlands of eastern Africa and mapped one of the river's tributaries, the Blue Nile.

Bruce was born on December 14, 1730, in Stirling County, Scotland. He was educated at Harrow School and Edinburgh University and later studied for the bar. His pursuit of a law career ended, however, when he married the daughter of a wine merchant and entered that business. After his wife died in 1754, he traveled to Portugal and Spain.

Energetic, skilled as a horseman and a marksman, and possessing a forceful personality along with an explosive temper, Bruce impressed almost everyone he met. He certainly impressed several British leaders, with whom he worked during Great Britain's fight against Spain in 1762 (as part of the Seven Years' War), for they appointed him consul to Algiers. He assumed the post in 1763.

But Bruce had more than political duties in mind. He wanted to explore, not only as an adventurer, but also as an archaeologist and a cartographer. He learned Arabic (along with several other languages) and became a competent linguist, astronomer, historian, and botanist. He also drew well.

In 1765, he resigned as consul and journeyed into the interior of the kingdoms of Algiers and Tunis in northern Africa. Thereafter, he sailed to Crete, nearly losing his life when a storm drove his boat onto a large rock. He explored ruins in Lebanon, at Baalbek, where he found a temple dating from ancient Rome, and in Syria, at Palmyra, an oasis location that had served as a Roman colony.

His greatest desire, though, was to find the source of the Nile River, the cradle of ancient Egyptian civilization and one of the most dominant natural features in the world. Bruce was convinced he would find the river's wellspring in Abyssinia (today, Ethiopia). The source of the Nile had long played on the human imagination: Ptolemy, the ancient Greek astronomer and mathematician, said the river's waters originated in a group of massive mountains in Africa, known by natives as the "Mountains of the Moon."

Bruce believed that of the Nile's two main tributaries, the White Nile and the Blue Nile, the Blue Nile was the most important, because it was the Nile of the ancients. Despite Bruce's claim, both the Blue Nile and the White Nile were important to the Nile itself, for while the Blue Nile contributed most of the Nile's water volume, the White Nile was much longer.

Bruce began his journey at Alexandria, then traveled to Thebes (the current location of the towns of Karnak and Luxor) and crossed the desert to Kosseir. Donning the outfit of a Turkish sailor to traverse what was then part of the Ottoman Empire, he sailed along the coast of the Red Sea and debarked at Jidda, on the coast of Saudi Arabia, in May 1769. He then departed from Loheia (today a part of Yemen) and sailed directly across the Red Sea, which he had mapped, reaching Massawa, then a Turkish possession, in September.

He arrived at Gondar, the capital of Abyssinia, in February 1770, which placed him near the source of the Nile. He carried with him the scientific instruments crucial to his mapping and goal of pinpointing the source of the Blue Nile. To reach Gondar, his men had to carry a heavy quadrant over steep mountains.

Bruce lived in Abyssinia for two years, caught amid the internecine conflict and bloody war then gripping the land. Abyssinians distrusted white Europeans, but Bruce's courage, athleticism, and confidence won over King Ras Michael, as did his treating the queen mother's grandchildren for smallpox. The king even made Bruce a cavalry commander.

In November 1770, Bruce traveled overland from Gondar in his continuing effort to find the source of the Blue Nile. He reached the southern shore of Lake Tana, its waters studded with islands. Bruce said eleven of the islands were likely inhabited, although the local people claimed many more of them to be so.

Today, most geographers believe there are thirty-seven islands in Lake Tana. They also consider the lake to be the source of the Blue Nile, and that, by reaching Lake Tana, Bruce had accomplished his goal. The Abyssinians, however, considered the source to be a spring at Gishe Abbay, about 70 miles (110 kilometers) from the lake. ("Gishe" means "source" and "Abbay" means "Nile"; Ethiopians still call Gishe Abbey the sacred source.) With guidance from the Abyssinians, Bruce, who also believed Gishe Abbay to be the source, pushed on and reached the more distant site.

As it turned out, Bruce was not the first European to find the source of the Blue Nile at Lake Tana. That feat had been accomplished by Father Pedro Paez, a Spanish Jesuit missionary, in 1615. Although few Europeans were aware of Paez's discovery, Bruce knew about it, yet he claimed the Spaniard's memoirs had been fabricated.

In 1771–1772, Bruce descended the Blue Nile, all the way to its confluence with the White Nile at present-day Khartoum. He thus became the first European to follow the full course of the river.

Following a harrowing return to northern Africa across the desert of Sudan—a trip on which he was beset by thirst and hunger—Bruce arrived in France in 1773. There, he was praised for his accomplishment by French naturalist Georges Louis-Leclerc, Comte de Buffon.

But when Bruce arrived in London in 1774, his reports were met with widespread skepticism. In 1790, he published his five-volume *Travels to Discover the Source of the Nile in the Years 1768–1773*, but many ridiculed his stories as fake. His tales of warfare, cavorting with women, and engaging in barbarous feasts with the Abyssinians, along with his graphic descriptions of bloodthirsty encounters, seemed too sensational to believe.

It was all true, though, as was the seemingly incredible combination of adventure and science in which Bruce had engaged. To his study of ruins and landscape Bruce applied critical observation and careful measurement. In doing so he represented both the spirit and practicality of the modern scientific method.

Bruce died in Scotland on April 27, 1794. His autobiography was published posthumously in 1805.

Further Reading

Bredin, Miles. *The Pale Abyssinian: A Life of James Bruce.* London: HarperCollins, 2000.

Bruce, James. *Travels to Discover the Source of the Nile in the Years 1768–1773.* 1790. New York: Horizon, 1964.

Reid, J.M. *Traveller Extraordinary: The Life of James Bruce of Kinnaird.* London: Eyre and Spottiswoode, 1968.

BURTON, RICHARD FRANCIS (1821–1890)

1821: Born on March 19 in Herefordshire, England
1840: Enters Trinity College at Oxford University
1842: Joins the army of the British East India Company
1853: Makes a pilgrimage to the Islamic holy cities of Mecca and Medina
1854: Travels to the Somalian city of Harar, a site usually closed to Christians
1858: Discovers Lake Tanganyika in eastern Africa
1890: Dies of a heart attack in Trieste, Austria-Hungary, on October 20

An English explorer who discovered Lake Tanganyika in eastern Africa, Richard Francis Burton was a modern Renaissance man—an archaeologist, linguist, ethnographer, diplomat, soldier, author, and translator—all wrapped in a flamboyant, irascible, explosive personality.

Richard Francis Burton was born on March 19, 1821, in Herefordshire, England, to Joseph Netterville Burton, a captain in the British army, and Martha Baker. A few months after he was born, the family moved to Tours, France. They would move several more times during Burton's youth, living in towns in France and Italy.

He had the reputation for being a wild child and caused problems for his parents as he rebelled against authority. On one occasion, he stole his father's rifle and shot out a church's stained-glass windows. As a teen, he frequented taverns and brothels, gambled, and experimented with opium. Partly in an effort to "tame" the young man, his father sent him to Trinity College at Oxford University in 1840. Although Burton was bright, he had little preparation for college and frustrated his tutors by rejecting his schoolbooks in favor of Italian novels.

India, the Middle East, and Africa

Burton hated Oxford from the start and thought it boring and pretentious. He earned the nickname "Ruffian Dick" for challenging students to duels.

In 1842, he was expelled and joined the army of the British East India Company, whereupon he was sent to India.

Ever the individualist, Burton did what most Britons in India refused to do: He immersed himself in Hindu culture. While his fellow soldiers criticized him for embracing the local customs, Burton learned to speak Hindustani, Gujarati, and Marathi. (Later in his life, he added Persian, Arabic, and some twenty-seven other languages.) He went undercover to investigate male brothels and, in a report colonial authorities later suppressed, alleged that the customers included British officers.

In 1847, Burton journeyed to the Portuguese possession of Goa on the Indian coast. Two years later, he returned to Europe. In 1850, he published a guide to the region, *Goa and the Blue Mountains.*

In 1853, the Royal Geographical Society sponsored Burton in an expedition to Arabia. He undertook a hajj, or pilgrimage, to the Islamic holy cities of Mecca and Medina. It was a dangerous trip. If he had been discovered, he likely would have been arrested or even killed. To prepare for the journey Burton studied Islamic culture. (He learned so much about it that he later praised Muslim beliefs and practices.) In 1855, he published *A Personal Narrative of a Pilgrimage to Al-Medinah and Meccah.*

Flamboyant and multitalented, Richard Francis Burton discovered the great lakes of Central Africa in the late 1850s. He wrote dozens of books on his travels and other subjects, including swordsmanship and falconry, and mastered more than thirty languages. *(Granger Collection, New York)*

Burton returned to his regiment in India in 1854 and volunteered to undertake an assignment recently proposed by the Royal Geographical Society: to journey into the interior of Somalia to investigate its natural resources. In October, he arrived in Aden, then a British colony, on the Arabian Peninsula. There, he met John Hanning Speke, a Briton who had served in the Indian army and had explored the Himalayas and Tibet.

Burton next traveled on his own to Harar in Somalia, a city that was closed to Christians, because they were considered a threat to Islam. Along the way, he studied the customs and language of Somali clans. He stayed at Harar for ten days and, while there, met the emir.

Back in Aden, Burton prepared to return to East Africa, this time with Speke, with the intention of again entering Harar and then finding and following the Nile River. In April 1855, Burton led a party that included forty-two men, camels, horses, and mules. They made camp near the Somali settlement of Berbera.

For reasons unclear but perhaps in search of plunder, tribesmen attacked the expedition. Burton was struck by a tribesman's javelin that entered one of his cheeks and came out the other, taking four of his teeth (it would leave a permanent scar). He was forced to elude his attackers with the javelin still stuck in him. One of his colleagues was killed, and Speke was wounded and captured. He escaped and, dripping blood, staggered into Berbera, then walked another three miles before he was found by a rescue party. The expedition was ruined.

The Sea of Ujiji

Despite this failure, the Royal Geographical Society decided to fund a search by Burton to find the Sea of Ujiji and the source of the Nile. (Today, the Sea of Ujiji is called Lake Tanganyika. It is situated between the Democratic Republic of the Congo and Tanzania.) Again working with Speke, Burton prepared for the expedition while in Bombay, India.

In 1856, the team arrived in Zanzibar, off the coast of present-day Tanzania, where Burton studied the island's geography, language, history, flora, and fauna, and made ethnological observations; he spent six months exploring the Zanzibar and neighboring coasts. On June 17, 1857, Burton and Speke departed Zanzibar for the African mainland. Ten days later, they began their journey inland, traveling westward across Tanzania.

Depending heavily on a local guide, Sidi Mubarak, the two men traversed a caravan path used by Arab slave traders. Their expedition included two gun-bearers, thirteen soldiers provided by the sultan of Zanzibar, ten slaves, and forty-one helpers. Burton took with him numerous scientific devices, including two chronometers, two prismatic compasses, a pocket thermometer, a sundial, a rain gauge, an evaporating dish, two sextants, a mountain barometer, measuring tape, two boiling thermometers, a telescope, a pocket pedometer, and what was described as a box of "mathematical instruments."

Problems beset Burton and Speke almost from the start. Malaria decimated the party. Burton grew weak and depressed, as his body felt as if it were on fire, and Speke could hardly walk. Quarrels broke out among the members of the expedition, men and animals ran away, food supplies dwindled, and most of the scientific instruments broke. Nevertheless, Burton and Speke pushed on.

On February 13, 1858, they arrived at the "sea" they had been searching for, actually the vast Lake Tanganyika. By this time, however, Speke's eyesight was so badly damaged that he could make out nothing more than a smeared image. (He later recovered from his blindness.) Unlike on his pre-

CHRONOMETERS

When Richard Burton journeyed inland into East Africa, he took with him a device that many explorers considered essential: a chronometer. A chronometer is an extremely accurate clock or watch. From the mid-1700s until the 1920s, these tools were important to navigators on land and sea in determining longitude.

The principle of determining longitude by chronometer is based on the movement of the sun across the sky each day. The sun's apparent daily orbit around the Earth takes twenty-four hours to pass through the 360 degrees of the Earth's circumference, or 15 degrees each hour, or 1 degree every four minutes. A navigator could determine his ship's longitude by determining the difference between the time of his local noon with that of local noon at a known reference longitude and then multiplying the result by the speed of the sun's movement across the sky. Importantly, an accurate measurement required that the sun's position be calculated precisely at noon—even a one-second error could adversely affect the result.

Until 1735, however, no timepiece approached the accuracy required for such a measurement. That year, John Harrison, an English carpenter, finished designing a marine chronometer that would be affected only minimally by a ship's motion. But the device was cumbersome. So, over the next thirty years, Harrison worked on building smaller and more accurate chronometers. His fourth model, also meant for use aboard ships, was completed in 1762 and proved to be accurate to within five seconds at the end of an eighty-one-day voyage.

A year later, French clockmaker Pierre Le Roy created a chronometer more resistant to errors caused by fluctuations in temperature. This required adding adjustments to the spring so that temperature changes would not affect it.

Chronometers began to lose much of their importance in the 1920s, when accurate times were broadcast by radio. The later emergence of Global Positioning Systems operating via satellites relegated chronometers to a backup role.

John Harrison's marine chronometer of 1759—his fourth attempt at such a device—accurately measured east-west position, or longitude, over long distances. It was a major breakthrough for exploration at sea as well as on land. *(Granger Collection, New York)*

vious journeys, which were more adventure than science, this time Burton had made an important geographical discovery.

Lake Victoria and Dispute with Speke

The following day, the expedition entered the settlement of Ujiji on the shores of the lake. Shortly thereafter, Burton heard of another lake to the north. At that point, he made what some historians consider to be a "great mistake." He decided to stay at Ujiji while Speke headed north.

Speke said it was his idea to search out what was later called Lake Victoria. Burton said he was the one who told Speke to undertake the mission. Whatever the case was, Burton failed to add another discovery to his accomplishments, one that would have ranked him among the most renowned explorers of Africa.

Why did Burton make this mistake? Four reasons were at play: he doubted Speke would find much; he wanted to continue to gather information from the people in the place where he was camped; he wanted to regain his health; and he believed that he already had accomplished what he had set out to do. As it was, Speke found Lake Victoria, among the greatest of the European discoveries in Africa.

In 1860, Burton published *Lake Regions of Central Africa,* a detailed account of the geography of the region and a description of the cultural practices of the people who lived there. He also traveled to the United States, met with the Mormon leader Brigham Young in Salt Lake City, and published a report on polygamy.

The following year, he married Isabel Arundell. She was from a prominent English family, and he had first met her at Boulogne in France.

In 1863, Burton cofounded, with James Hunt, the Anthropological Society of London. By this time, Speke and Burton had had a falling out. Tension had long existed between the two men because of their differing personalities; now, they quarreled over who owed the outstanding debts from their last expedition. Burton also disputed Speke's claim—an accurate one, as it turned out—that Lake Victoria was the source for the White Nile. He called Speke's evidence inconclusive and asserted that Speke's survey had been inadequate.

The two men were scheduled to debate the importance of Lake Victoria on September 15, 1864, before the British Association for the Advancement of Science (now the British Science Association). The day before the debate, Speke died from a gunshot wound while hunting. It still is uncertain whether he shot himself accidentally or committed suicide. Burton was greatly shaken by Speke's death.

In the early 1860s, Burton served as British consul to Fernando Póo (today the island of Bioko in Equatorial Guinea) and while there explored the west coast of Africa. In 1865, he was transferred by the British foreign service to Brazil. He explored the country's central highlands and canoed down the São Francisco River. But he disliked the country and considered his time there to be "banishment."

In 1869, he was appointed consul to Damascus, and, in 1877, he became consul to Trieste in Austria-Hungary. He was knighted by Queen Victoria in 1886. Burton died of a heart attack in Trieste on October 20, 1890.

Burton wrote several travel books that were poorly received, in part because of his accounts of foreign sexual practices that were at odds with Victorian standards. He also published several English-language translations of Asian classics, including the erotic *Kama Sutra*. His most celebrated translation, however, was *The Book of the Thousand Nights and a Night* (1885), more commonly called *The Arabian Nights*, which originally was written in Arabic.

Burton's conclusions and theories, while often wrong, challenged accepted thinking. His expedition to central Africa resulted in a mixed record: On the one hand, he had found Lake Tanganyika and, through Speke, Lake Victoria. On the other hand, he had explored the region only haphazardly and failed to traverse the Nile River.

Further Reading

Brodie, Fawn. *The Devil Drives: A Life of Sir Richard Burton*. New York: W.W. Norton, 1984.

Farwell, Byron. *Burton: A Biography of Sir Richard Francis Burton*. New York: Viking, 1963.

Kennedy, Dane Keith. *The Highly Civilized Man: Richard Burton and the Victorian World*. Cambridge, MA: Harvard University Press, 2005.

See also: Speke, John Hanning.

BYRD, RICHARD E. (1888–1957)

1888: Born on October 25 in Winchester, Virginia
1912: Graduates from the U.S. Naval Academy
1925: Commands naval air unit in an expedition to Greenland
1929: Becomes the first person to fly over the South Pole and maps Antarctica
1933: Lives alone at Advance Base in Antarctica
1955: Becomes head of Operation Deep Freeze
1957: Dies in Boston on March 11

An American explorer long believed to have been the first to fly over the South Pole, Richard Evelyn Byrd charted substantial portions of Antarctica and researched the continent's meteorological and geographical features.

Byrd was born on October 25, 1888, in Winchester, Virginia, to Richard E. Byrd, a wealthy lawyer, and Eleanor Flood, both of whom came from prominent families in the state. When Richard was twelve years old, he visited the Philippines. Although he stayed there for only a year, he developed a sense of adventure and expressed his desire someday to journey to the North Pole.

In 1908, Byrd entered the U.S. Naval Academy; he was commissioned in 1912. Four years later, he broke his ankle in an accident, which ended

Polar explorer and aviator Admiral Richard E. Byrd led five expeditions to Antarctica. He was said to be the first man to fly over both the North Pole (1926) and the South Pole (1929). His claims regarding the former were later called into question. *(Imagno/Hulton Archive/Getty Images)*

his assignment as a midshipman on a battleship. During World War I, he learned to fly and, in 1918, became a naval aviator. (He never flew in combat during the war.)

In 1925, Byrd commanded a U.S. Navy air unit as part of an expedition to Greenland led by a civilian, Donald Baxter MacMillan. The mission had as its goal studying the region's natural phenomena and surveying large expanses of the uncharted ice. The following year, Byrd and his colleague Floyd Bennett made what they claimed to be the first flight over the North Pole.

A recent analysis of Byrd's diary, however, indicates he may not have made it to his destination. The diary, discovered in the mid-1900s and published for the first time by Ohio State University in 1998, includes messages from Byrd to his pilot, Bennett (the noise in the plane required the two men to pass written messages to each other), which indicate that Byrd believed he had reached the North Pole. In one of them, he states,

> We should be at the Pole now. Make a circle. I will take a picture. Then I want the sun. Radio that we have reached the pole and are now returning with one motor with bad oil leak but expect to make Spitzbergen.

But the diary also contains still-legible erasures of navigational calculations. Some analysts insist that these calculations show that Byrd had not reached the exact location of the North Pole.

Base in Antarctica

In 1927, Byrd and the Norwegian American Bernt Balchen, along with Bertrand B. Acosta and George O. Noville, were the first to fly a transatlantic mail route from New York to France.

Over the next several months, Byrd finalized his plans to lead an expedition to Antarctica with the goal of flying over the South Pole. He bought three airplanes for the trip: a Ford trimotor monoplane, which was the main aircraft, and two other monoplanes to serve as backups and help transport scientists. These planes, along with much other equipment, were hauled aboard two ships to Antarctica.

In late December 1928, Byrd and his expedition selected the site for a base camp on the Ross Ice Shelf, on the east side of the Bay of Whales. They called their camp Little America and erected two main buildings, several smaller ones, and rooms carved out of the snow and covered with tarpaulin roofs. The buildings contained a library, hospital, and radio lab.

Radio transmitters and receivers were crucial to the expedition. Byrd was not the first to use such communications in Antarctica, but his expedition, he claimed, provided "the most elaborate system of communication ever proposed in a Continent where radio conditions are notoriously bad."

Byrd made his first Antarctic flight in mid-January 1929. On a second flight two weeks later, he discovered and named the Rockefeller Mountains. In March, three members of the expedition flew in one of the backup planes to the mountain range. They surveyed the terrain and collected geological samples. Then, a tremendous windstorm tore their airplane from its moorings and destroyed it. The men had to be rescued by Byrd.

When winter set in, Byrd and his men hunkered down at Little America. They endured blizzards and subzero temperatures as commonplace, along with weeks of complete darkness.

Flyover

In November 1929, a team from the expedition, led by Laurence Gould, began a geological investigation of the Queen Maud Mountains. The journey took several weeks and involved maneuvering around dangerous crevasses. At Mount Fridtjof, they found sandstone and coal, proof that the Queen Maud Mountains were not volcanic.

While this expedition continued its work, on November 28, 1929, Byrd readied his plane, the *Floyd Bennett,* for the flight over the South Pole. The plane had been transported in sections to Antarctica and had sat through an entire frigid winter. Before takeoff, the engines were warmed by torches. The pilot, Balchen, revved up the engines, let them die down, and then revved them up again to test them.

It was a beautiful day, with bright sunshine glistening on the snow and ice—a beauty that belied some of the dangers involved in the trip. High winds could make flying impossible; for miles, the terrain blended into an indistinguishable sameness; a magnetic compass was useless so close to the pole; and a fuel dump had to be set up in the Queen Maud Mountains to provide enough gas for the party's return to Little America.

Along with Byrd, who served as navigator, and Balchen, the crew consisted of Harold June, the copilot and radio operator, and Ashley C. McKinley, the aerial photographer. They faced a journey of 1,600 miles (2,600 kilometers) to and from the South Pole. *The New York Times* later described the beginning of the flight:

> A huge gray plane slipped over the dappled Barrier at 3:29 o'clock this afternoon, the sun gleaming on its sides, reflected in bright flashes from its metal wing and whirling propellers. With a smooth lifting movement, it rose above the snow in a long, steady glide.

At Liv Glacier, the plane proved too heavy to make it over an 11,000-foot (3,350-meter) pass, so the explorers had to jettison empty gasoline cans and packages of food. Finally, the plane cleared the pass by a few hundred yards.

Byrd and his colleagues reached the South Pole at 1:14 A.M. on November 29, 1929, whereupon Byrd dropped a small American flag at the site. After they flew around the area for eleven minutes, they returned to Little America as the first explorers to have flown over the South Pole.

In addition to the geological findings and the historic flight, Byrd's expedition mapped 150,000 square miles (390,000 square kilometers) of Antarctica and discovered the Edsel Ford Range, Marie Byrd Land (named by Byrd for his wife), Sulzberger Bay, and Paul Block Bay. His discovery of the entire eastern boundary of the Ross Sea was considered by many to be the most important accomplishment of the expedition.

On his return to the United States from Antarctica, Byrd was feted at celebrations in New York, Virginia, and Washington, D.C. At a ceremony held at the Washington Auditorium in June 1930, the demand for seats far exceeded the building's capacity. President Herbert Hoover presented Byrd with a special gold medal from the National Geographic Society; the event was broadcast over national radio.

Alone at Advance Base

In March 1933, during a second Antarctic expedition that lasted until 1935, Byrd began a five-month stay in a shack called Advance Base. He wanted to investigate the weather from an inland location and study the aurora.

Byrd originally planned to locate Advance Base at the foot of the Queen Maud Mountains and live in it with two other men. But his plans changed, because the prebuilt shack was too difficult to transport such a distance and because Byrd feared that three men living in such close

THE TIN GOOSE

Richard E. Byrd advanced the use of aircraft in cold-climate expeditions, beginning in 1925 when he became involved in the investigation of the Arctic conducted by Donald Baxter Macmillan. For that mission, Byrd piloted a biplane, designated by the U.S. Navy as an OL-2. It had a maximum speed of 122 miles per hour (196 kilometers per hour). Byrd saw the mission as a way to test out planes in an Arctic environment. From it, he learned much about the challenges posed to aircraft operating in extreme cold conditions.

While Byrd's two backup planes for his Antarctic expedition were a Fokker Universal with a 425-horsepower engine and a Fairchild folding-wing monoplane, his main airplane was the *Floyd Bennett,* a trimotor transport known as the 4-AT. Manufactured by Henry Ford, the 4-AT was adapted from a German design. Unusual for the time, the 4-AT was made completely of metal—no fabric covered its wings—thus, it was nicknamed the Tin Goose.

The *Floyd Bennett* had a length of 50 feet (15 meters) and a wingspan of 78 feet (24 meters). It featured three air-cooled radial engines designed by Charles L. Lawrence, president of the Wright Company: a 525-horsepower Cyclone engine was mounted in the nose, and there were two 220-horsepower Whirlwind outboard engines. Together, the engines gave the plane substantial hauling capacity; the airplane could carry a total load of about 15,000 pounds (6,800 kilograms).

Flown by a crew of three, the 4-AT was known for its reliability and effective design. The model was in production from 1925 until 1933. About that time, Henry Ford decided to leave the building of airplanes to other companies.

The all-metal Tin Goose (a nickname for the Ford tri-motor monoplane) was produced for civil transport beginning in 1925 and later used by the military. Richard E. Byrd flew one called the *Floyd Bennett* over the South Pole in 1929. *(Underwood and Underwood/ Time & Life Pictures/Getty Images)*

confines would get on one another's nerves. So Advance Base was set up about 120 miles (200 kilometers) from Little America and occupied only by Byrd.

In this incredibly harsh environment, Byrd dealt with the isolation and extreme cold. He was nearly killed when the ventilation system malfunctioned. He later wrote,

> This much should be understood from the beginning: that above everything else, and beyond the solid worth of weather and auroral observations in the hitherto unoccupied interior of Antarctica . . . I really wanted to go for the experience's sake. So the motive was in part personal. . . . The novocaine in my medical kit froze and shattered the glass tubes. So did the chemicals in the fire bombs. Two cases of tomato juice shattered their bottles. Whenever I brought canned food inside the shack I had to let it stand all day near the stove to thaw.

Byrd led another expedition to Antarctica from 1939 to 1940, during which he discovered more than 100,000 square miles of area (259,000 square kilometers), and a third one from 1946 to 1947, which was an official U.S. Navy expedition involving thirteen ships and several planes. During the expedition, about 845,000 square miles (2.2 million square kilometers) were mapped, roughly one-third of which were newly discovered lands, and Byrd again flew over the South Pole.

In 1955, Byrd was appointed head of Operation Deep Freeze, which was part of the International Geophysical Year and included the exploration of Antarctica. In 1956, he made his last flight over the South Pole. Over the years, he had written several books, including *Skyward* (1928), *Little America* (1930), *Discovery* (1935), *Exploring with Byrd* (1937), and *Alone* (1938).

After suffering from poor health for several months, Byrd died in Boston on March 11, 1957, from a heart ailment.

Further Reading

Goerler, Raimund, ed. *To the Pole: The Diary and Notebook of Richard E. Byrd, 1925–1927*. Columbus: Ohio State University Press, 1998.

Rodgers, Eugene. *Beyond the Barrier: The Story of Byrd's First Expedition to Antarctica*. Annapolis, MD: Naval Institute Press, 1990.

Rose, Lisle A. *Explorer: The Life of Richard E. Byrd*. Columbia: University of Missouri Press, 2008.

See also:
Antarctica.

C

CARTER, HOWARD (1874–1939)

1874: Born on May 9 near London
1891: Egypt Exploration Fund hires him as a draftsman
1893: Serves as main artist for excavation of the temple of Queen Hatshepsut
1899: Egyptian government appoints him as First Chief Inspector General of Monuments
1922: With Lord Carnarvon, enters the tomb of King Tutankhamen
1923: With Lord Carnarvon, enters the burial chamber of King Tutankhamen
1939: Dies from cancer in Kensington on March 2

A British Egyptologist who labored for years in general obscurity, although with considerable renown among archaeologists, Howard Carter gained worldwide fame when he discovered the tomb of King Tutankhamen, an Egyptian pharaoh of the eighteenth dynasty, in 1922.

Howard Carter was born on May 9, 1874, in the village of Kensington, near London. His father, Samuel Carter, was an artist who painted portraits of family pets for the local residents. When Howard was a child, his father taught him how to draw.

Attracted to stories of ancient Egypt, Carter longed to explore the desert land at a time when archaeologists were becoming interested in the artistic wonders and scientific secrets held in Egypt's ancient tombs. In addition, the potential monetary value of such discoveries meant that expeditions were being financed in hopes of returning a profit.

Carter got his chance when, at age seventeen, he was hired by the Egypt Exploration Fund as a draftsman to copy drawings and inscriptions. At Alexandria, he copied scenes from the walls of the tomb of Bani Hassan, a sovereign prince who lived sometime around 2000 B.C.E.

In 1892, Carter worked for Flinders Petrie, the noted British archaeologist and Egyptologist who had earlier excavated the Great Pyramid of Giza. The two men undertook excavations at El-Amarna, an ancient Egyptian capital. Petrie trained Carter in archaeological excavation and was impressed when the young man made several finds.

In 1893, Carter served as the main artist for the Egypt Exploration Fund's excavation of the temple of Queen Hatshepsut at Deir el Bahbri. After six years of this work, the Egyptian government appointed Carter to be the First Chief Inspector General of Monuments as part of the Egyptian Antiquities Service. In this position, he supervised archaeological digs in the Nile Valley, first in the Upper Nile and later in the Lower Nile.

Carter resigned his post in 1905, after the Egyptian government demoted him because of his involvement in a dispute involving some French tourists. The tourists had engaged in a brawl with several Egyptian guards at a historic site, and Carter got into trouble for siding with the guards and refusing to apologize to the tourists.

For Carter, there followed three years of struggling to make ends meet, until he was introduced by Gaston Maspero, his former supervisor at the Antiquities Service, to George Edward Stanhope Herbert, the fifth Earl of Carnarvon. Educated at Eton College and the University of Cambridge, the wealthy Lord Carnarvon had developed an interest in Egyptian antiquities, and he hired Carter to excavate several sites.

By this time, Carter longed to unearth the tomb of King Tutankhamen, who had reigned from 1333 to 1324 B.C.E. Carnarvon agreed to back Carter in his quest. The two men worked in the field, digging first in the western part of the Valley of the Kings in 1915 and then, from 1917 to 1922, in the main valley. Carnarvon, however, grew frustrated with their lack of success. He agreed to continue with the search only after Carter pleaded for just one more season to excavate.

In October 1922, Carter focused on the site of Ramses VI's tomb near Luxor. His team removed some 70,000 tons (63,000 metric tons) of sand and gravel over several months, still apparently without reward, until

THE CURSE OF KING TUT

Was there a curse surrounding the tomb of King Tut? The popular press thought so. It spread word of one when one of the discoverers of the burial site, Lord Carnarvon, died in 1923, just two months after the opening of the tomb. By 1929, supposedly eleven people connected with the discovery of the tomb had died, and, by 1935, the press had upped the count to twenty-one.

Yet one researcher later concluded that of the twenty-two people present when the tomb was opened in 1922, only six had died by 1934, and of the twenty-two people present at the opening of the sarcophagus in 1924, only two had died by 1934. Also, of the ten people who were present when the mummy was unwrapped in 1925, all survived until at least 1934. Still, could any of the eight deaths that occurred by 1934 be attributed to a curse?

Rather than a curse, there may be a scientific explanation. Later research revealed that the archaeologists and their workers might have been exposed to toxins that come from the mold within mummies. Such toxins can be harmful to those with weakened immune systems. (For this reason, archaeologists now wear protective masks and gloves when unwrapping a mummy.) Moreover, some tomb walls are covered by bacteria that is dangerous to human respiratory systems.

As for Lord Carnarvon, he was chronically ill long before he came upon King Tut. In fact, Howard Carter observed that given the overall unsanitary conditions in Egypt at the time, Lord Carnarvon might have been better off inside the tomb than outside of it.

Archaeologist Howard Carter examines the sarcophagus of King Tutankhamen, discovered during the excavation of his tomb in Egypt's Valley of the Kings in 1923. The tomb and its treasure had lain largely undisturbed for more than 3,000 years. *(Granger Collection, New York)*

a worker discovered what appeared to be a carved stone step. Carter described it in his diary as "the beginning of a steep excavation cut in the bed rock" and wrote that "it was of the nature of a sunken staircase entrance to a tomb of the type of the XVIIIth Dyn., but further than that nothing could be told until the heavy rubbish above was cleared away." This was done, revealing more steps leading downward to a royal seal.

Carter later wrote, "Here before us was sufficient evidence to show that it really was an entrance to a tomb, and by the seals, to all outward appearances that it was intact." Breaking the seal, he found a doorway and a passage behind it. On November 26, 1922, Carter and Carnarvon entered the tomb of King Tutankhamen.

Startling items, many with gold inlay, came into view—a treasure trove of couches, chairs, alabaster vases, chariots, a throne, stools, chests. They discovered four chambers, all enclosed by golden doors. Carter wrote, "We were astonished by the beauty and refinement of the art displayed by the objects surpassing all we could have imagined—the impression was overwhelming."

On February 16, 1923, Carter and Carnarvon entered the burial chamber. There lay King Tutankhamen's sarcophagus, which had on it four goddesses carved in high relief. Inside the sarcophagus were three coffins, one inside the other; the innermost one contained the pharaoh's body. It was wrapped in linen bandages, and the king's face was covered with a mask of gold.

King Tutankhamen's reign had been limited and of little political consequence. He became pharaoh at about the age of nine and ruled until his death at about the age of eighteen. Despite the brevity of the young king's reign, the plethora of objects discovered by Carter and Carnarvon revealed the life of ancient Egyptians in great detail.

It took ten years for the contents of the tomb to be moved to the Cairo Museum. Carter retired from his active participation in excavating the site later in 1923; in 1924, he went on a lecture tour of the United States. He spent the rest of his life as a collector of Egyptian antiquities. Carter died at Kensington on March 2, 1939, from cancer.

As for King Tutankhamen, in 2007 the remains of his mummified body were removed from the original sarcophagus and placed in a climate-controlled glass case to keep it from further deterioration. Visitors to the underground tomb in the Valley of the Kings can see his face—black, leathery, and displaying the king's buck teeth—and his feet. The rest of the body remains covered by linen.

Since the discovery of King Tutankhamen, Carter has been criticized for what today would be considered shoddy archaeological methods. For example, the mummy was exposed to sunlight for hours, which risked its deterioration, and the body was damaged in the removal of the golden mask from its face. Carter also may have violated his archaeological permit by taking some items from the tomb to be placed in his home.

Nevertheless, his discovery was nothing short of monumental in archaeological circles and contributed mightily to historical knowledge. "The news of the discovery spread fast all over the country," wrote Carter, "and inquisitive enquiries mingled with congratulations from this moment became the daily programme." To this can be added that, through Carter's discovery, today the shortened version of King Tutankhamen's name, King Tut, is recognized around the world.

Further Reading

James, T.G.H. *Howard Carter: The Path to Tutankhamun.* London: Kegan Paul International, 1992.

Vandenberg, Philipp. *The Golden Pharaoh.* New York: Macmillan, 1980.

Winstone, H.V.F. *Howard Carter and the Discovery of the Tomb of Tutankhamun.* Manchester, UK: Barzun, 2006.

CHEESMAN, LUCY EVELYN (1881–1969)

1881: Born in Westwell, England
1923: Becomes record keeper for an expedition to the South Pacific
1928: Receives a grant to collect insects in New Hebrides
1933: Explores Papua New Guinea
1969: Dies on April 15 in London

A British entomologist, Lucy Evelyn Cheesman explored dangerous regions of the South Pacific to collect insects and study the connection between those on New Guinea and those found elsewhere in the South Pacific.

Cheesman was born in 1881 in Westwell, an English country village in Kent. Her father, Robert Cheesman, was a man of inherited wealth, and so Evelyn (the name she preferred to use) grew up in comfort. Although she was frail, she liked to collect snails, plants, and flowers, and she examined glowworms to see what made them glow. She wanted to become a veterinarian, but no colleges were willing to admit women to study the subject at that time.

During World War I, Cheesman worked as a clerk for the Admiralty, the British government department in charge of naval affairs. Later, she worked as a secretary at the Imperial College of Science in London.

Around 1919, she was given the opportunity to take charge of the long-neglected Insect House at the Zoological Society of London. She delved into entomology and, in 1923, accepted an appointment as the record keeper for a government-sponsored research expedition to the South Pacific. Among its many stops, the expedition visited the Galápagos Islands, Marquesas Islands, and Tuamotu Archipelago.

Cheesman often broke away from the main group to collect insects on her own. At Tahiti, she quit her government job to engage in her own research. She explored the island, as well as Bora Bora and other islands in French Polynesia. During this time, she traveled light and relied on the local people for support. On her return to England in about 1926, she donated 500 insect specimens to the British Museum of Natural History.

In 1928, Cheesman received a grant from the museum to collect insects in the Pacific islands of New Hebrides (today Vanuatu). There, on mountainous Malekula, she lived among the Big Nambas, a Melanesian people known at that time for their cannibalism, but she became friends with King Ringapat, who protected her.

For Cheesman, the greatest danger came from the wildlife. She had to dodge crocodiles and, at one point, to escape Nephila spiderwebs—large, strong webs that momentarily entrapped her. She collected hundreds of insects, along with specimens of orchids, ferns, and mosses. But as she prepared to leave for England in 1930, her entire collection was ruined when a British official left it out in the rain.

In 1933, Cheesman explored Papua New Guinea, where, at one point, she set up a cloth screen at night to collect insects attracted to a light. She had in mind studying the connection between insects on New Guinea and those elsewhere in the South Pacific. She later wrote,

> My collection of insects made in the Territory of Papua in 1933–34 suggested to me that there must have been formerly [an] older land connected

> with New Guinea, which possibly had not been entirely submerged during the Late Cretaceous [period].

She also explored the Cyclops Mountains in the remote western part of New Guinea and spent a year in nearby Waigeo and the Japen Islands. She left New Guinea in 1942 when the Japanese invaded the island. In England during World War II, she helped her country by sharing her knowledge of the South Pacific with the British government.

After the war, Cheesman climbed the mountains of New Caledonia to collect more insects. In 1953, following the replacement of one of her hips, which had been damaged in a railroad accident, she journeyed to Aneityum, the southernmost inhabited island in the Vanuatu archipelago.

Cheesman died in London on April 15, 1969. The London *Times* said in her obituary that she was "single-minded in her devotion to natural history."

Further Reading

Cheesman, Lucy Evelyn. *The Two Roads of Papua*. London: Jarrolds, 1935.
Tinting, Marion. *Women Into the Unknown: A Sourcebook on Women Explorers and Travelers*. Westport, CT: Greenwood, 1989.

COMO BLUFF, WYOMING

1877: Teams working for paleontologist O.C. Marsh begin excavating large numbers of dinosaur bones
1897: Walter Granger discovers Bone Cabin Quarry, the site of several tons of dinosaur bones

A geological formation in Wyoming, Como Bluff is the site of the discovery, in the late nineteenth century, of a large number of dinosaur bones that contributed to the emergence of modern American paleontology.

The finds included the bones of Stegosaurus (a plated dinosaur with a spiked tail), Camptosaurus (large herbivorous dinosaurs), Camarasaurus (a short-necked dinosaur known for its large teeth), Allosaurus (which grew to 35 feet, or 10.5 meters), Diplodocus (a huge dinosaur known for its long tail and powerful hind legs), and Brontosaurus. (Later renamed Apatosaurus, the Brontosaurus was one of the largest of all land animals and measured 70 feet, or 21 meters, in length.)

Como Bluff, a ridge produced millions of years ago by geological folding (which results from two layers of rock pressing together), runs in an east-west direction between Rock River to the south and Medicine Bow River to the north, amid the Medicine Bow Mountains in the southeastern part of Wyoming. In 1877, railroad workers discovered large bones near Como Bluff and notified the paleontologist Othniel Charles Marsh about their find.

Between 1877 and 1889, teams working for Marsh excavated large numbers of bones. Soon after Marsh's men began their work, another team, under paleontologist Edward Drinker Cope, also began digging at the site. Marsh and Cope had been engaged in fierce competition for prominence in the field of paleontology, and their efforts at Como Bluff continued and intensified the contest.

In 1897, the Bone Cabin Quarry was discovered near Como Bluff. It was named for a cabin made of dinosaur bones that had been built there by a local trapper. From 1898 until 1905, several tons of dinosaur bones were removed from the quarry as the result of full-scale excavations.

Later excavations at Como Bluff occurred under the direction of the American Museum of Natural History. One such effort, in 1968–1970, produced only small numbers of dinosaur bones. A few more have been collected since.

Three geological formations have been exposed at Como Bluff: the Sundance, the Morrison, and the Cloverly, each containing fossils from the Late Jurassic period (between 199 and 145 million years ago) of the Mesozoic era (known as the "age of reptiles"). The dinosaur remains found in these formations generally were well preserved, and the Morrison Formation additionally revealed fossilized remains of turtles, crocodiles, and fish.

Como Bluff produced the only known specimen of Coelurus (a small carnivorous dinosaur with elongated legs). It was found at Reed's Quarry 13. In all, the bluff produced significant finds from twenty-two sites.

The findings at Como Bluff had a tremendous impact on the study of paleontology by encouraging further explorations and kindling popular interest in dinosaurs. The bluff ranks as perhaps the greatest collection of dinosaur remains in North America, and it is listed on the National Register of Historic Places.

Further Reading

Jaffe, Mark. *The Gilded Dinosaur: The Fossil War Between E.D. Cope and O.C. Marsh and the Rise of American Science.* New York: Crown, 2000.

Ostrom, John H., and John S. McIntosh. *Marsh's Dinosaurs: The Collections from Como Bluff.* New Haven, CT: Yale University Press, 2000.

See also: Marsh, Othniel Charles.

COOK, JAMES (1728–1779)

1728: Born on October 27 in Marton, England
1758–1759: Charts the St. Lawrence River to aid England in its war with France
1763: Admiralty appoints him to survey the coasts of Newfoundland
1768–1771: Makes his first voyage to the South Pacific, on the *Endeavour*
1769: Measures the transit of Venus and begins exploring the coasts of New Zealand
1772–1775: Undertakes his second voyage to the Pacific and becomes the first person to circumnavigate Antarctica
1776–1780: Aboard the *Resolution*, searches for the Northwest Passage
1779: Killed on February 14 by natives at Kealakekua Bay on Hawaii

A British sea captain, navigator, and cartographer, James Cook made three voyages in the Pacific Ocean. He extensively surveyed the ocean and its lands, proved Antarctica was a frozen mass of ice, showed that New Zealand consisted of two islands, and collected flora and fauna previously unknown to Europeans.

James Cook was born on October 27, 1728, in Marton, North Yorkshire, England, to James Cook, a Scottish farmer, and Grace Pace. Young James worked with his father before apprenticing to William Sanderson, a shopkeeper in nearby Staithes, in 1745.

At the shop, James stocked shelves and sliced cheese and bacon. Staithes was a small fishing village, and James spent hours listening to fishermen tell stories about the sea. Wanting to go to sea himself, he studied math, geography, and astronomy—subjects he would need to know if he ever were to command a ship.

Cook became a seaman in 1746, when he was apprenticed to a ship owner in Whitby and began learning navigation. By 1752, he was a first mate, and second in command to the captain. Three years later, he joined the Royal Navy and, with his background and penchant for hard work, soon moved up the ranks to become a ship's master, meaning that he could navigate a ship.

In the ensuing Seven Years' War between Great Britain and France, Cook served as master of the *Pembroke*. In the winter of 1758, he plied the waters of the St. Lawrence River in a small rowboat and discovered a route that General James Wolfe would use in July 1759 in his historic landing to fight the French at Quebec. Cook's feat earned him the respect of the navy's commanders but, when the war ended in 1762 and the *Pembroke* returned to England, he was discharged. That same year, he married Elizabeth Batts; the couple would have five children.

Cook's reputation as a navigator continued to impress his colleagues and commanders in the navy. In 1763, the British Admiralty hired Cook as the "main surveyor of the coasts of Newfoundland and Labrador." As captain of the *Grenville*, a schooner that he converted to a brig, he surveyed the northwest coast of Newfoundland in 1763 and 1764, the south coast in 1765 and 1766, and the west coast in 1767.

Captain James Cook, known as the greatest ocean explorer of the eighteenth century, conducted three major Pacific voyages, spanning nearly nine years in all. Cook is known for applying scientific methods and new technology to exploration and mapping. *(Granger Collection, New York)*

The work was of considerable importance, for Newfoundland was, militarily, critical to Britain's new role as possessor of Canada and, economically, invaluable for its cod fisheries. Cook used land-based trigonometry (in which he used a reference object and two observation points and then measured the angles of the sight lines and the distances between the observation points to calculate lengths) and made soundings in a small boat to chart the coasts. From these efforts, he produced detailed, highly accurate maps. Moreover, in 1766, he made observations of the Sun's eclipse that earned him a reputation as an able mathematician and astronomer.

Voyage of the *Endeavour*

Two years later, in 1768, Cook was commissioned as a first lieutenant and appointed to command the *Endeavour*, a refitted coal-hauling ship, on a scientific mission for the British government, which had been encouraged to act by the Royal Society. His announced assignment was to sail to Tahiti, where he was to observe the transit of Venus across the face of the Sun, but he also was given secret orders to thoroughly explore the geography of the South Pacific. This was to include a search for a continent between Tahiti and New Zealand, a terra incognita, or unknown land, that was thought to exist.

Reaching Tahiti would be no easy task. Unknown to Europeans until the year before, it was a tiny speck of an island in the vast Pacific, an ocean the Western world knew little about. And Cook had no reliable way of determining longitude, since the chronometer (a precision timepiece) had not yet been widely disseminated.

On August 25, 1768, Cook and his party, ninety-four men in all—among them the naturalist Joseph Banks—departed Plymouth. "We took our leave of Europe for heaven knows how long," Cook wrote in his journal, "Perhaps for Ever."

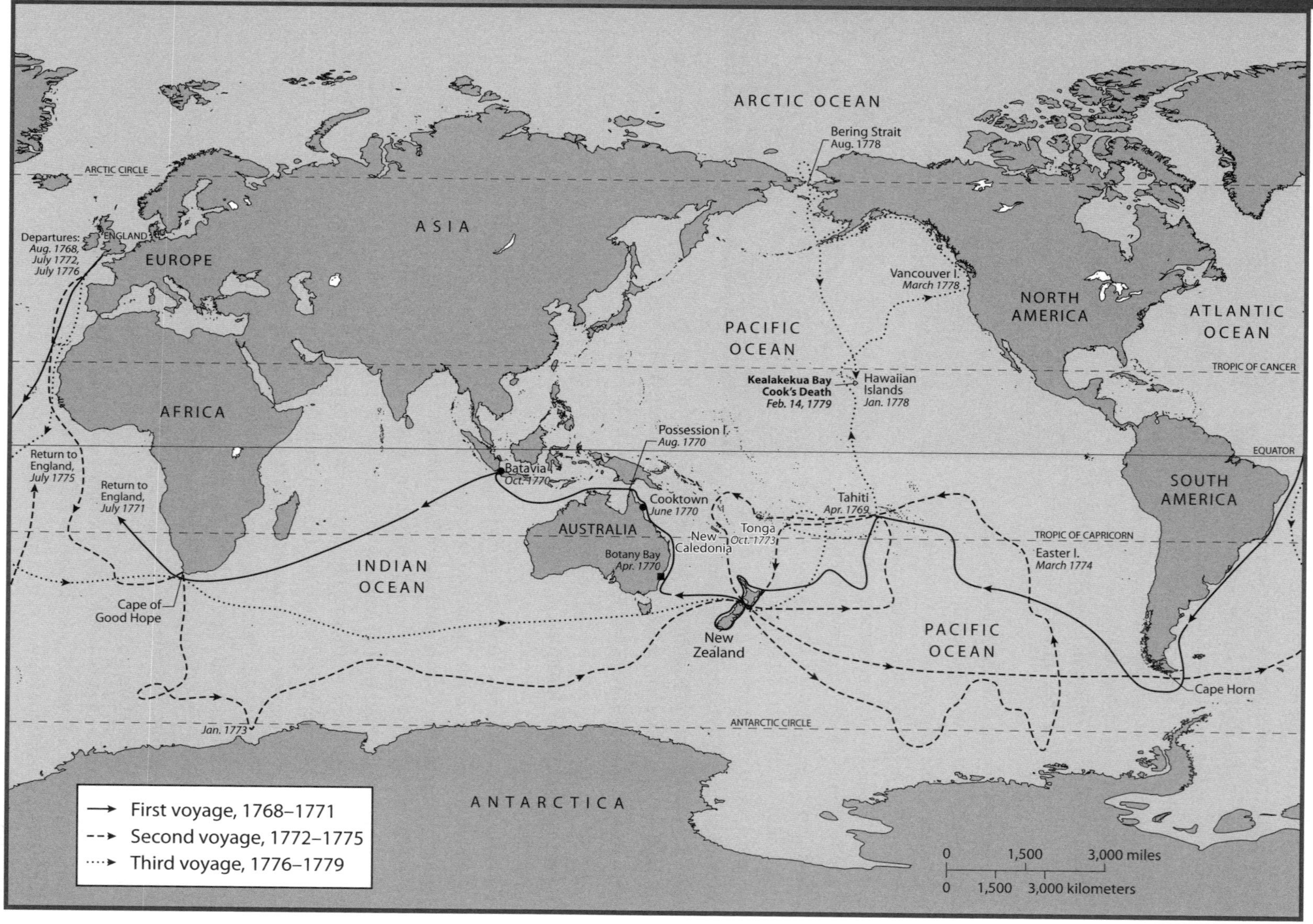
ARCTIC OCEAN
ARCTIC CIRCLE
Bering Strait
Aug. 1778
ASIA
EUROPE
ENGLAND
Departures:
Aug. 1768,
July 1772,
July 1776
AFRICA
PACIFIC OCEAN
Vancouver I.
March 1778
NORTH AMERICA
ATLANTIC OCEAN
TROPIC OF CANCER
Kealakekua Bay
Cook's Death
Feb. 14, 1779
Hawaiian Islands
Jan. 1778
Possession I.
Aug. 1770
EQUATOR
Return to England,
July 1775
Return to England,
July 1771
Batavia
Oct. 1770
Cooktown
June 1770
Tahiti
Apr. 1769
SOUTH AMERICA
AUSTRALIA
New Caledonia
Tonga
Oct. 1773
TROPIC OF CAPRICORN
Easter I.
March 1774
INDIAN OCEAN
Botany Bay
Apr. 1770
Cape of Good Hope
New Zealand
PACIFIC OCEAN
Cape Horn
Jan. 1773
ANTARCTIC CIRCLE
ANTARCTICA
First voyage, 1768–1771
Second voyage, 1772–1775
Third voyage, 1776–1779
0 1,500 3,000 miles
0 1,500 3,000 kilometers

For this voyage, the *Endeavour* became a scientific laboratory. On it, Cook measured the transit. He experimented with his crew's diet to see if scurvy, caused by a shortage of vitamin C, could be avoided. He became an ethnographer, observing and recording foreign cultural practices. And through the actions of Banks, he collected flora and fauna unknown to Westerners.

Setting off, Cook pointed the *Endeavour* south to the Madeira Islands, off the west coast of Africa, before directing it westward across the Atlantic. When he left Madeira on September 18, 1768, he journeyed into regions Europeans knew little, if anything, about.

Cook reached Brazil and then rounded South America en route to Tahiti, where he was to observe the transit. But on the way, he headed south toward Antarctica, which he hoped to sight.

On January 30, 1769, after a fruitless five-day search for Antarctica, Cook resumed his voyage to Tahiti, and reached the island in April. His crew arrived there largely unblemished by the dreaded scurvy, having been fed fruits and a considerable quantity of sauerkraut. "At this time we had but very few men upon the Sick list," Cook wrote. The Tahitians greeted Cook in friendship, and he called the island an idyllic paradise.

At Tahiti, he observed the transit of Venus across the Sun, which lasted six hours. Measuring the transit was considered important to determining the distance between the Earth and the Sun. Cook wrote in his journal,

> This day proved as favorable to our purpose as we could wish. Not a cloud was to be seen the whole day and the air was perfectly clear, so that we had every advantage we could desire in observing the whole of the planet Venus over the sun's disk. We very distinctly saw an atmosphere or dusky shade around the body of the planet.

Despite the good viewing conditions, Cook found it difficult to pinpoint when Venus began crossing the Sun. So his observations were inconclusive.

From Tahiti, he proceeded south, although not directly so. As he frequently did during his expeditions, he followed circuitous routes, in the hope that he might discover new lands, in this case even crossing his own path.

In October 1769, he arrived at New Zealand and spent the next six months exploring its coasts. He was prevented from traveling inland because of opposition from the indigenous Maoris, whose cannibalism terrified Cook's men. With this expedition, Cook established that New Zealand consisted of two islands and was not a part of Antarctica.

On April 19, 1770, Cook sighted the coast of Australia (then called New Holland) and explored and named Botany Bay (along which the town of Sydney later was founded). In June, he ran aground on the Great Barrier Reef. It took seven weeks for his men to repair the *Endeavour.*

THE *ENDEAVOUR*

For all of its glory as Captain James Cook's expedition ship, the *Endeavour* was intended for a more mundane mission. Built at Whitby, North Yorkshire, England, and launched in 1764 as the *Earl of Pembroke,* it originally was a "merchant collier," used to haul coal. Consequently, the vessel, which measured 106 feet (32 meters) long and about 29 feet (9 meters) wide, had a large hold and a flat-bottomed hull to enable it to sail in shallow waters.

When, at the urging of the Royal Society, the British government decided to finance a scientific expedition to the Pacific Ocean, the *Earl of Pembroke* was purchased in 1768 and renamed the *Endeavour.* It then underwent a refitting that included adding a third deck and equipping it with ten guns.

In 1988, a replica of the *Endeavour* was built in Fremantle, Australia, based on plans preserved at the National Maritime Museum in Greenwich, England. In the new vessel, however, some changes were made in the materials used for construction.

For example, British ships in the eighteenth century were traditionally built from elm, oak, and spruce, which for the modern project were too expensive to buy. These woods were replaced by the West Australian hardwood jarrah, along with old Douglas fir imported from the United States for the masts and spars. The sails were made of synthetic material rather than flax sailcloth, as had been used in the original. And modern navigation and communications equipment was added, although it was hidden away.

The replica *Endeavour* ultimately sailed to numerous locations around the world on several voyages from 1994 to 2005. Today, it is docked in Melbourne, Australia, as a museum ship.

But what became of the original *Endeavour*? There is no clear answer. The British Admiralty used it as a store ship and then sold it in 1775. Bought by a merchant company, it was renamed the *Lord Sandwich* in 1777. According to some reports, the vessel later became a French ship; other reports claimed it was moored on the Thames River. Quite likely, though, the *Endeavour* was sunk by the British in August 1778 to create a blockade against the French navy near the town of Newport, Rhode Island.

His Majesty's Bark *Endeavour,* commanded by Captain James Cook on his first Pacific voyage (1768–1771), underwent a major overhaul before setting out on this extended scientific mission. *(Robert W. Nicholson/ National Geographic/Getty Images)*

From Australia, Cook traveled to New Guinea and to Batavia (today part of Indonesia), and then west to the Cape of Good Hope, and finally north to England. On their arrival home, Joseph Banks portrayed himself as the essential person on the voyage; however, the publication of Cook's journal earned the captain considerable fame for his navigational abilities, his documentation of his discoveries, and his mapping of the Pacific.

Return to the South Pacific

Cook began a second expedition to the South Pacific in 1772, this time, with two ships. While he captained the *Resolution,* which was a mere 110 feet long (34 meters) and 35 feet wide (11 meters), Tobias Furneaux, a navigator, commanded the *Adventure,* which measured just 98 feet long (30 meters) and 30 feet wide (9 meters).

Cook's experience on his return to Tahiti in 1773 showed how Europeans were changing the local society. This time, the Tahitians, enticed by Western goods, tried to steal almost everything from Cook's ships.

In December, Cook traveled farther south than any previous European explorer when he crossed the Antarctic Circle. His trip dispelled lingering reports about Antarctica being a fertile land. In January 1774, as ice hung from the *Resolution*'s sails and blocked the ship's path, Cook turned away from the region. He reported in his journal for January 30,

> The outer or northern edge of [an] immense ice field was composed of loose or broken ice so close packed together that nothing could enter it. About a mile in began the firm ice, in one compact solid body and [it] seemed to increase in height as you travel it to the south. In this field we counted ninety-seven ice hills or mountains, many of them vastly large.

He later amended his journal to say he believed that "the ice extends all the way to the pole or perhaps joins to some land." Cook never did lay eyes on the Antarctic landmass, but his expedition was the first to circumnavigate Antarctica.

The journal entry of January 30 reveals Cook's drive and the confidence he had in his abilities. "I, whose ambition leads me not only farther than any man has gone before me, but as far as I think it possible for man to go," he said in reference to his search for Antarctica. Cook clearly knew he was the best navigator, the best explorer.

During this second expedition, Cook traveled a distance roughly equal to triple the equatorial circumference of the Earth, some 70,000 miles (110,000 kilometers). He plotted the exact position of Easter Island (2,237 miles, or 3,600 kilometers, west of continental Chile, of whose territory the island is today a part) and sent an exploratory party inland, where they

THE TRANSIT OF VENUS

Cook arrived at Tahiti in 1769 with the goal of measuring the transit of Venus. A rare event, it occurs when Venus passes between the Earth and the Sun and thus appears as a small, black disk moving across the Sun's surface.

By measuring the transit, astronomers can determine the distance between the Earth and the Sun and thus calculate a scale for the solar system. They make their measurement by observing the difference in time of either the start or the end of the transit from several points on the Earth's surface. The distance between the points then can be used as a baseline to calculate the distance to Venus and the Sun through the process of triangulation.

The only person previously known to have scientifically observed the transit was Jeremiah Horrocks. A British clergyman and astronomer, he made his sighting in November 1639. Writing in 1716, British astronomer Edmund Halley proposed that observations of the transit from different parts of the world would provide the most accurate measurement. In 1761, expeditions sponsored by Britain and France observed a transit, but with limited results.

Two obstacles hindered Cook from making an accurate observation. For one, the intense sunlight filtering through Venus's atmosphere blurred the edge of the planetary disk and made it difficult to discern exactly when Venus began its motion across the Sun. For another, when Venus approached the Sun, the black of space behind the Sun's edge produced a shadowy effect that, again, made it difficult to discern when the planet began crossing the Sun.

These were problems not only for Cook but also for scientific observers around the globe—some seventy-six in all. Consequently, their observations failed to produce an accurate measurement.

came across the ruins of "three platforms of stone work." At their top had been four large statues, since fallen. One of the statues, lying on the ground but still intact, was 15 feet long (4.6 meters). "Each statue had on its head," wrote Cook in his journal, "a large cylindrical stone of red color, wrought perfectly round."

Among Cook's other discoveries were New Caledonia and Norfolk Island, along with the Isle of Pines. When he finished exploring the South Pacific, he sailed east to Tierra del Fuego and across the Atlantic to the Cape of Good Hope before returning once again to England.

Seeking the Northwest Passage

By the time he returned home in 1775, Captain Cook was considered Europe's leading navigator. In 1776, he was made a fellow in the Royal Society. That same year, he agreed to search for the Northwest Passage from the Pacific, while the British government sponsored other expeditions to seek the passage from the Atlantic. By this time, many Europeans believed that such a route connecting the Atlantic and Pacific oceans could be found somewhere in the Arctic. And a Russian map circulating at the time depicted Alaska as an island, with a strait between it and the North American mainland.

Cook left England in July 1776 as captain of the *Resolution,* accompanied by the ship *Discovery,* captained by Charles Clark. Cook sailed around the Cape of Good Hope and then eastward across the Indian Ocean and into the Pacific. He journeyed to New Zealand and Tahiti, and reached Hawaii in January 1778.

From Hawaii, he sailed along the coast of California and mapped it. In March, he reached the coast of Oregon and, shortly thereafter, began sailing along the coast of British Columbia, which he also mapped.

On April 1, Cook anchored at Resolution Cove in Nootka Sound and stayed there until late April. At the cove, he conducted scientific observations and made repairs to the ships. He then left Nootka and sailed along the Alaska coast, where he discovered Prince William Sound and sailed into the inlet (today called Cook Inlet) at what is now Anchorage, Alaska. He proceeded to the Bering Strait and onward to the northeast coast of Siberia.

With sea ice closing in, and the *Resolution* leaking and its hull filling with water, Cook pressed on through the Bering Strait. When the ice barrier became impassable, he ordered the *Resolution* and the *Discovery* to turn south. He did not know that he was only 50 miles (80 kilometers) from the Beaufort Sea, the entrance to his goal, the Northwest Passage. (The sea stretches along the northern coast of Alaska.)

Cook circumnavigated the big island of Hawaii from December 1778 to January 1779. He dropped anchor for a while and then set sail, but a storm forced him to turn back to Hawaii, where he arrived on February 11. On the island, tensions developed between Cook's crew and Hawaiians. Cook's men demanded a seemingly endless supply of food and fulfilled their lust with the local women; the Hawaiians stole items from the Europeans. The final straw was when the *Discovery*'s cutter (a small boat used to travel between the ship and the land) was stolen.

On February 14, 1779, Cook went ashore at Kealakekua Bay. A showdown between Cook and a large crowd of Hawaiians resulted in Cook killing one native with his shotgun and some of his sailors killing six more Hawaiians. As Cook turned to leave the scene, a Hawaiian stabbed him in the back with a dagger. The group then descended on the badly wounded Cook as he lay sprawled in the sand and stabbed him repeatedly, until he was dead.

Then, in a ritual reserved for the highest members of Hawaiian society, the natives roasted Cook's body in a pit for six hours. Eventually, some of his bones were recovered by his crew. They buried him in Kealakekua Bay with full military honors; a tiny coffin, carrying his remains, was weighted down with cannonballs. The ships *Resoultion* and *Discovery* returned home under the command of John Gore in October 1780.

Cook was more than a discoverer. His keen observations combined with his mathematical calculations produced maritime charts so accurate that they became the standard for years to come. He greatly expanded the European knowledge of the South Pacific, and through his journals encouraged other expeditions.

Those who read Cook's account were especially intrigued by the northwestern coast of North America. His trade with the Nootka Indians for pelts indicated that a fur trade could prosper there. Indeed, several of Cook's men later were involved in such expeditions. Many historians consider Cook to be England's greatest seaman, navigator, surveyor, and explorer.

Further Reading

Beaglehole, J.C., ed. *The Journals of Captain James Cook on His Voyages of Discovery.* Rochester, NY: Boydell, 1999.

———. *The Life of Captain James Cook.* Stanford, CA: Stanford University Press, 1974.

Dugard, Martin. *Farther Than Any Man: The Rise and Fall of Captain James Cook.* New York: Pocket Books, 2001.

Mackay, David. *In the Wake of Cook: Exploration, Science, and Empire, 1780–1781.* New York: St. Martin's, 1985.

Williams, Glyndwr, ed. *Captain Cook: Explorations and Reassessments.* Rochester, NY: Boydell, 2004.

See also: Pacific Exploration.

COPE, EDWARD DRINKER (1840–1897)

1840: Born on July 28 in Philadelphia
1865: Becomes curator at the Academy of Natural Sciences in Philadelphia
1871: Begins his travels in the American West
1897: Dies on April 12 in Philadelphia

An American paleontologist, Edward Drinker Cope traveled the western United States in search of dinosaur fossils and engaged in a fierce contest with fellow paleontologist Othniel Charles Marsh of Yale University for scientific prominence. He advanced the disputed theory that animal and plants of the same lineages grow bigger in body size over time.

Born into a Philadelphia Quaker family on July 28, 1840, Cope grew up amid wealth. Although his formal schooling ended when he was sixteen, he enrolled in an anatomy class at the University of Pennsylvania School of Medicine taught by Joseph Leidy (considered the father of American vertebrate paleontology) and reorganized the reptile collections at the Philadelphia Academy of Natural Sciences. At age eighteen, he delivered his first scientific paper at the academy, on the reclassification of salamanders. In his lifetime, he would publish more than 1,200 scientific papers.

In 1863, Cope traveled to Europe to study collections in such cities as Berlin, London, Munich, Paris, and Vienna. The following year, he was appointed professor of natural science at Haverford College (near Philadelphia), a post he held until 1867. Cope also served as curator of the Academy of Natural Sciences in Philadelphia in 1865; in 1889, he accepted a professorship of geology and paleontology at the University of Philadelphia.

From 1871 to 1877, Cope traveled the American West in search of dinosaur fossils. In 1872, he traveled to Wyoming as part of a government-sponsored geological survey under prominent geologist Ferdinand Hayden. In 1874 and 1875, he traveled to Montana, New Mexico, Oregon, and Texas as part of another geological survey under George Wheeler, a notable explorer and cartographer. In New Mexico, Cope found evidence of some of the oldest known mammals.

Cope advanced a theory, since challenged, called "Cope's rule," in which he maintained that animal and plants of the same lineages grow bigger in body size over generations, making them more adept at obtaining food and at other ways of surviving. Cope believed that change in the environment causes changes in the needs of organisms, which, in turn, cause changes in their behavior. He was a neo-Lamarckian, following the concept of French scientist Jean-Baptiste Lamarck that changes acquired during an organism's lifetime somehow are transferred into genetic information and passed on to the offspring. The idea embraces evolution as a part of nature but is at odds with the method of evolution proposed by Charles Darwin. (Darwin believed that changes in an organism during its life do not affect the evolution of the species.)

Cope was known for his volatile temper, having once engaged in a fistfight at a meeting of the American Philosophical Society. More famously, he engaged in a long feud with Marsh—a contest sometimes called the Great Bone Wars. They competed for the limelight in American paleontology. Each rushed to outdo the other in collecting fossils, publishing papers, and winning acclaim.

As a result, they often produced mistake-riddled findings. At one point, in 1869, Marsh discovered an error by Cope, who in restoring a 35-foot-long (10-meter-long) plesiosaur had put the skull on the wrong end of the reptile. (Marsh later committed a similar mistake with another dinosaur.)

In the late 1870s, Cope's excavation team dug for fossils at Wyoming's Como Bluff in fierce competition with one of Marsh's teams. The two men even sent spies into each other's camps. Philosophically, Marsh embraced Darwinian evolution, another point of contention with Cope.

In addition to his feud with Marsh, Cope conflicted with administrators at Haverford and with members of the Academy of Natural Sciences. Yet Cope also produced such impressive works as *The Vertebrata of the Tertiary Formations of the West* (1884) and *The Origin of the Fittest: Essays on Evolution* (1887).

In his later years, Cope lost a great deal of money due to bad investments in mining projects. He died on April 12, 1897, in Philadelphia. In the popular mind, he is most often remembered in the context of his feud with Marsh and the selfishness the two men exhibited in their frantic pursuit of science and fame.

See also: Marsh, Othniel Charles.

Further Reading

Jaffe, Mark. *The Gilded Dinosaur: The Fossil War Between E.D. Cope and O.C. Marsh and the Rise of American Science.* New York: Crown, 2000.

Wallace, David Rains. *The Bonehunters' Revenge: Dinosaurs, Greed, and the Greatest Scientific Feud of the Gilded Age.* Boston: Houghton Mifflin, 1999.

COUSTEAU, JACQUES-YVES (1910–1997)

1910: Born on June 11 in Saint-André-de-Cubzac, France
1930: Enters the French naval academy
1950: Converts the *Calypso* into a research vessel
1953: Publishes *The Silent World*
1962: Begins the first of three Conshelf expeditions
1975: Founds the Cousteau Society
1997: Dies on June 25 in Paris

French oceanographer Jacques Cousteau gained fame for his many books and documentaries dedicated to his undersea explorations, including those made from his base ship, the *Calypso*. But Cousteau did more than produce popular works. He developed a self-contained underwater breathing apparatus, showed that human beings could live underwater for extended periods of time, and exposed the threat of pollution to the oceans.

Jacques Cousteau was born on June 11, 1910, in Saint-André-de-Cubzac, in southwestern France. His father, Daniel Cousteau, was a legal advisor to wealthy clients and moved his family about the European continent. Jacques was a sickly child, but he learned to swim at age four and fell in love with the sea.

Invention of Scuba and Voyages of the *Calypso*

While in his teens, Cousteau attended boarding school in Alsace, France, but he had little interest in schoolwork. In 1930, he entered the French naval academy at Brest and, movie camera in hand, spent much of his free time filming scenes of the sea.

In the late 1930s, Cousteau served as an artillery instructor at a naval base in Toulon and experimented with watertight goggles to improve his vision while swimming in the Mediterranean Sea. With his friends, he began using homemade snorkel hoses, insulated body suits, and portable breathing devices in an attempt to dive deeper.

Serving in the French navy during World War II, he continued his underwater experiments. It was during this time that he met Émile Gagnan, a French engineer. Working together, the two men invented the Aqua-Lung, later called a self-contained underwater breathing apparatus, or SCUBA.

In 1950, Cousteau obtained a ferryboat, the *Calypso*, which formerly had been a minesweeper, and converted it into a ship for diving, filming, and oceanographic research. The vessel had been purchased by an Irish millionaire, Thomas Loel Guinness, who subsequently leased it to Cousteau for a nominal fee.

Cousteau strongly believed that undersea exploration would contribute to a better understanding of the world. He developed a motto for his work: "We must go and see for ourselves."

In 1952, he and a team of divers traveled aboard the *Calypso* to a location off the French Mediterranean coast to engage in an archaeological project. There, Cousteau salvaged an ancient Roman shipwreck located some 140 feet (43 meters) down in the water. He called it the most thorough marine salvation ever done, as he and his fellow divers found a collection of items, including amphorae (two-handled earthenware jars).

The popular French oceanographer and undersea explorer Jacques-Yves Cousteau enters the observation chamber of his research ship *Calypso* during the filming of his 1956 documentary, *The Silent World.* *(Granger Collection, New York)*

THE *CALYPSO*

Jacque Cousteau's research ship, the *Calypso,* originally was built as a minesweeper. The J-286—its original designation—was launched on March 21, 1942, at the Ballard Marine Railway Yards in Seattle, Washington. It was transferred to the British navy and assigned to the Mediterranean for duty in World War II.

In 1947, the ship was converted to a civilian ferryboat and named the *Calypso,* after the sea maiden in Homer's *Odyssey* who fell in love with Odysseus. It served a route between the islands of Malta and Gozo in the Mediterranean.

The Irish millionaire Thomas Loel Guinness bought *Calypso* in 1950 and leased it to Cousteau for 1 franc a year. Over the next year, Cousteau proceeded to have the 139-foot-long (40-meter-long) ship gutted and rebuilt to serve his purposes. (He later said that the cost of refurbishing and outfitting the *Calypso* forced him to become an adept fund-raiser.)

An underwater observation chamber was added to the ship's bow, 8 feet (2 meters) below the waterline; a false nose allowed crewmembers to film underwater life through circular windows. Cousteau also installed a high observation platform, which enabled his crew to see far across the horizon to spot whales and other sea life. He enlarged the crew quarters, added a crane, and installed navigational equipment. Finally, the *Calypso* was painted a glistening white.

The *Calypso* began its first mission under Cousteau on November 24, 1951, when it left Toulon, France, for the Red Sea. At one point early in that voyage, the engines failed. But in a larger sense the *Calypso* would never fail Cousteau—it would be an ocean home that would earn him renown and provide his explorations with a historic place in the science of the oceans.

In 1996 (a year before Cousteau's death), the *Calypso* was heavily damaged in a collision with a barge at the port of Singapore. The *Calypso* sank and had to be lifted back to the surface with a crane and have the water pumped from it.

In 1998, the ship was towed to the basin of the Maritime Museum of La Rochelle in France, where it was intended to become an exhibit. But legal claims and a shortage of money kept it from being restored. The *Calypso* since has been purchased by Carnival Cruise Lines, which has promised to fund the restoration and intends to dock the vessel in the Bahamas.

Besides having salvaged the ship, Cousteau had shown the effectiveness of scuba gear. In 1953, his book *The Silent World* brought scuba diving, and Cousteau's name, to a wider audience; it sold more than 5 million copies. In the book, he told of his early diving adventures, provided vivid descriptions of undersea life, and reflected on his findings. For example, he wrote,

> Fish do not like to go up or down, but swim on a chosen level of the reef, like tenants of a certain floor of a skyscraper. . . . The more we experience the sea, the less certain we are of conclusions.

In 1955, with backing from the French government and the National Geographic Society, Cousteau took the *Calypso* on a 13,800-mile

(22,200-kilometer) voyage to the Red Sea and the Indian Ocean. He made a documentary of the exploration done by his divers and by scientists; the film, like his book, is titled *The Silent World.*

Conshelf

In the 1960s, while the first Russian and American astronauts were venturing into outer space, Cousteau wanted to show that humans could live underwater on the continental shelves. In 1962, he launched a project, financed by the oil industry, called Conshelf I. In this study, two men spent a week in the Mediterranean inhabiting a diving saucer that Cousteau had developed, called DS-2.

Conshelf II followed in 1963. In this study, five men lived for a month below the surface of the Red Sea in a pressurized home consisting of several buildings. The headquarters, dubbed Starfish House, could sleep eight and housed a biological lab and a photography room. One building in the complex, called Deep Cabin, housed two explorers 85 feet (26 meters) below the surface. The entire complex was laced with cables that powered a specially designed air-conditioning unit and other devices from the surface and enabled communication with the *Calypso*. Cousteau's documentary film about this expedition, *World Without Sun* (1964), was widely praised—*The New Yorker* said Cousteau's "cameras make everything we behold so ravishing"—and won an Academy Award.

In 1965, Cousteau launched Conshelf III, with the deep-sea living environment now established at 330 feet (100 meters) in the Mediterranean. The expedition involved twelve ships, which carried 150 technical and medical experts. A film about it, shown on television in the United States as a National Geographic Society special, led to a multimillion-dollar contract with the ABC television network.

From the mid-1960s until the mid-1970s, Cousteau produced specials under the title *The Undersea World of Jacques Cousteau*. His documentaries for ABC, and later for the Public Broadcasting System and Turner Broadcasting, extolled the voyages of the *Calypso* and revealed aquatic life to millions of viewers.

During this time, Cousteau also became a crusader against the pollution of the seas he so loved. Gilbert Grosvenor, the chairman of the National Geographic Society, called him "the Rachel Carson of the oceans" (referring to the American author who exposed the dangers of widespread chemical pollution in the 1950s and 1960s). In 1973, Cousteau founded the Cousteau Society (based in the United States) to advocate environmental protection and publicize the effects of pollution. (The Cousteau Society and its French counterpart, l'Équipe Cousteau, continue their work today.)

Recognizing that damage to the oceans was the result of more than industrial chemicals, Cousteau condemned dynamite fishing, fishing in spawning grounds, and landfills that affected wetlands. He warned,

> The ocean floors are being scraped. In the past the sea renewed itself. It was a continuous cycle. But this cycle is being upset.

In 1937, Cousteau had married Simone Melchior, with whom he had two sons, Jean-Michel and Philippe. Both were involved in undersea exploration. (Philippe died in 1979 when his seaplane crashed.) After Simone died in 1990, Cousteau married Francine Triplet, and they had two children. Cousteau died in Paris on June 25, 1997.

Over the years, some critics have assailed Cousteau for having staged underwater scenes to make them appear more dramatic. Others have pointed to his lack of scientific credentials—a "layman explorer," he held no academic degrees in science. Yet he advanced scuba diving and underwater archaeological work, paved the way for extensive undersea research, exposed environmental threats, and raised the public's understanding of the world's oceans.

Further Reading

Berne, Jennifer. *Manfish: The Story of Jacques Cousteau.* San Francisco: Chronicle, 2008.

Cousteau, Jacques, with Frédéric Dumas. *The Silent World.* New York: Harper, 1953.

Munson, Richard. *Cousteau: The Captain and His World.* New York: William Morrow, 1989.

D

DARWIN, CHARLES (1809–1882)

1809: Born on February 12 in Shrewsbury, England
1831: Graduates from Cambridge and boards the HMS *Beagle*. captained by Robert FitzRoy, for a scientific expedition
1835: Reaches the Galápagos Islands and makes observations that will prove crucial to his theory of natural selection
1857: Writes letter to American botanist Asa Gray, in which he expresses his theory of natural selection

1858: With Alfred Russel Wallace, a fellow British naturalist, publicly presents the theory of natural selection
1859: Publishes *On the Origin of Species*
1871: Publishes *The Descent of Man*
1872: Publishes *The Expression of the Emotions in Man and Animals*
1882: Dies in London on April 19

Based on evidence from his expedition to the Galápagos Islands and from other locations to which he traveled on the brig-sloop *Beagle* in the 1830s, British naturalist Charles Darwin proposed the theory of evolution through natural selection, which revolutionized scientific thought and, in many ways, modern thought.

Charles Robert Darwin was born on February 12, 1809, in Shrewsbury, Shropshire, England, into a wealthy and distinguished family. His maternal grandfather, Josiah Wedgwood, had earned a fortune in pottery by industrializing the craft. His paternal grandfather, Erasmus Darwin, had helped run the Wedgwood pottery firm and had earned prominence as a physician, thinker, and inventor. Charles's father, Robert Waring Darwin, also was a physician. His mother was the first child of Josiah Wedgwood and married Robert in 1796; she died when Charles was eight years old.

Charles Darwin grew up at the Mount, his family's spacious three-story home, with a greenhouse and an observatory, set on a hill in Shrewsbury. He graduated from the elite Shrewsbury School in 1825 and then attended the University of Edinburgh to study medicine. He soon lost interest in the subject, however, and transferred to Cambridge University, from which he expected to get a degree and become an Anglican clergyman.

Charles Darwin began formulating his theory of evolution by natural selection during the voyage of the *Beagle* in the early 1830s. It would not be until 1858, however, that he would publish his revolutionary views—jointly with Alfred Russel Wallace. *(Science & Society Picture Library/Getty Images)*

At Cambridge, Darwin was greatly influenced by the geologist Adam Sedgwick, with whom he went on a geological excursion in 1831, and the naturalist John Stevens Henslow, who taught Darwin to investigate natural phenomena and collect specimens with an eye to careful, detailed study. Darwin was an industrious student, known for his insightful mind, attention to detail, and willingness to question accepted ideas and reconsider his own views. He later said that he loved science and liked "reflecting over any subject."

One of Darwin's favorite pastimes as a young man was collecting beetles, and the measure of his seriousness became evident when his collection was recognized in J.F. Stephens's compendium *Illustrations of British Entomology* (1828–1835). In his autobiography, Darwin wrote that he had "invented two new methods" for collecting the bugs:

> I employed a labourer to scrape during the winter, moss off old trees and place [it] in a large bag, and likewise to collect the rubbish at the bottom of the barges in which reeds are brought from the fens, and thus I got some very rare species.

He also recounted how one day he grabbed two beetles and placed one in each hand, only to spot another one he wanted. Since he did not want to lose any of them, he took the one in his right hand and popped it into his mouth. The bug, however, secreted a liquid that burned his tongue, forcing him to release it and lose one of the others as well.

The *Beagle*

The year 1831 would prove to be momentous for Darwin. After earning his degree from Cambridge in the spring, he secured a place on the *Beagle* for a scientific expedition that would last five years and provide the foundation of his life's work and scientific legacy. A young and largely untested naturalist when he graduated from Cambridge, Darwin nevertheless was recommended for the expedition by Professor Henslow. He persuaded his father to allow him to make the journey and agreed to serve without pay in the study of geological formations, flora, and fauna.

The *Beagle* departed Devonshire on December 27, 1831, and reached the Cape Verde Islands in January 1832 and South America in April. From then until September 1835, Darwin explored the natural wonders of Argentina, Brazil, and Chile, with an excursion to the Falkland Islands. He traversed the coasts and journeyed inland, captivated by the beauty and diversity of life. In Brazil, he wrote in his journal, his mind was "a chaos of delight." The forest was "a most paradoxical mixture of sound & silence."

While in South America, he traveled from the coldest mountain climates to tropical forests, and from the Pampas to Tierra del Fuego. He was constantly observing, taking notes, and collecting specimens. In March and April 1835, he journeyed from Santiago, Chile, over the Andes Mountains to Mendoza in Argentina. Geological hammer in hand, he traversed the Andes with two guides, ten mules, and a mare, chipping away at the rocks as he went, gathering fossils.

At Valdivia on the south Chilean coast, on February 20, 1835, Darwin suddenly felt a trembling beneath his feet. Then the earth shook. He had experienced an earthquake whose intensity he did not fully realize until he reached what had been its epicenter at the port of Talcahuano, where he observed houses that had collapsed, uprooted trees, and boulders that had fallen from the hillsides. Soon after the earthquake began, an enormous wall of water had surged up from the ocean through the bay and pounded the town; it was followed by two more gigantic waves. Inland, the town of Concepción had been completely destroyed.

Darwin was stunned and saddened by the devastation, but he also made an important scientific observation. As a result of the catastrophe, the level of the land had risen several feet. If the land could rise by that amount as a consequence of a single event, Darwin wondered, why could it not rise by a significant amount—even as much as 10,000 feet (3,000 meters)—over a longer period of time? Perhaps such transformations might explain why he had found seashells high in the Andes.

The Galápagos

On September 16, 1835, Darwin reached the Galápagos Islands, a small, rocky chain some 600 miles (950 kilometers) west of Ecuador in the Pacific Ocean. Only a few people lived on the islands, mainly exiled prisoners. Darwin and the crew of the *Beagle* arrived first at Chatham Island. No waving coconut palms greeted them; no beautiful sandy beaches. The landscape was stark, black, and dotted with volcanic cones. Roaming lizards seemed to be everywhere. Uninviting as they were, the islands provided the young naturalist with a window to the past. He wrote,

> Nothing could be less inviting. [The islands were] a broken field of black basaltic lava, thrown into the most rugged waves, and crossed by great fissures. Here, both in space and time, we seem to be brought somewhat near to that great fact—that mystery of mysteries—the first appearance of new beings on this earth.

The *Beagle* cruised the islands for more than a month, during which time Darwin camped for a week with four other men on James Island. There, he again saw lizards—marine iguanas, really—crowded along the shoreline. They had enormous mouths, spiny ridges down their backs, and long, flat tails. Darwin picked one up and flung it into a pool of water to see if it would come back to the land; it did. He flung it a second time; again, it came back to land. Curious to find out what the lizards ate, he dissected one and found seaweed in its stomach.

Inland from the beach, Darwin came across two giant tortoises, so big that he was unable to turn one of them over. Hopping on the back of one and riding it for a distance, he calculated that the tortoise could travel 60 yards (55 meters) in 10 minutes. He came upon other tortoises on a long procession, a seemingly endless back-and-forth journey up a hill to a fresh-

DARWIN'S FINCHES KEEP EVOLVING

To this day, the finches observed by Darwin on the Galápagos Islands display the distinct traits he said they had developed in relation to their environments. The sharp-beaked ground finch steals the eggs of boobies (a type of seabird) and uses its beak to slam the egg into a rock to break it open. The woodpecker finch uses its beak to drill holes in trees and to carry a twig or cactus spine as a tool to get at grubs and insects.

But one of the questions that has perplexed scientists is whether any of the Galápagos finches still show signs of evolving. According to an article by Mason Inman published in *National Geographic News* in 2006, scientists indeed have found such evidence.

In 1982, the large ground finch was observed for the first time on Daphne Island. The resident medium ground finch faced competition from the intruder, and, over time, it developed a smaller beak to acquire food—namely, smaller seeds—that the large ground finch was not interested in.

According to Peter Grant, a scientist who observed and first reported this development, "It is a very important one in the studies of evolution, because it shows that species interact for food and undergo evolutionary change which minimizes further competition."

Moreover, according to David Pfennig, a scientist at the University of North Carolina at Chapel Hill, the change challenges the widely held view that evolutionary developments take many years to unfold. In fact, he said, they may occur so rapidly that "we may actually miss the process taking place."

water spring and back down again. Hundreds of the tortoises had been killed by sailors who had come to the island; the animals, he noted, were good eating if roasted in their shells.

A British official stationed on the Galápagos, Nicholas Lawson, called Darwin's attention to an important fact: Each island supported its own form of tortoise. Just by looking at one of them, Lawson explained, an observer could determine which island the tortoise came from. Darwin, for his part, noticed how the finches of the Galápagos showed wide variations in the shapes and sizes of their beaks from one island to another.

Only later would the pieces of the Galápagos puzzle come together in Darwin's mind. The beaks on the finches, he hypothesized, varied to allow each species to take better advantage of the food supply in its locale. A thin, sharp beak, for example, allowed the bird to eat insects and grubs; a large, claw-shaped beak allowed it to eat buds, fruits, and nuts, where those forms of food prevailed.

Darwin concluded that the finches that adapted better to the environment were more likely to survive. Moreover, he proposed, over time, they passed on the beneficial change, or mutation, from generation to generation, with the new characteristic eventually replacing the older, outmoded one. For Darwin, all living things were in competition—for space, food, mates—

and mutation allowed for the species' survival. The process amounted to one of "natural selection"; the organisms that survived were the ones best suited to their environments and to reproducing in them.

As did the process itself, Darwin's thoughts about natural selection and evolution took shape gradually. Aboard the *Beagle*, he continued his journey, traveling to Tahiti, New Zealand, and Australia. He returned to England in October 1836, completing what he considered to be the most important event in his life, a milestone in his career. Later that year, he discussed his thoughts about species change in his *Notebooks on the Transmutation of Species*. Still, he had yet to fully formulate his theory of evolution through natural selection.

Darwin and Malthus

Then, he read *An Essay on the Principle of Population* (published in 1798 as a pamphlet and later revised and expanded) by the British economist Thomas Malthus. Darwin later recounted this experience:

> In October 1838, that is fifteen months after I had begun my systematic inquiry, I happened to read for amusement Malthus on *Population*, and being well prepared to appreciate the struggle for existence which everywhere goes on from long-continued observation of the habits of animals and plants, it at once struck me that under these circumstances favourable variations would tend to be preserved and unfavourable ones destroyed. The result of this would be the formation of a new species. Here, then, I had at last got a theory by which to work.

In his recollection, Darwin condensed the time frame of his "systematic inquiry"—it actually had been going on quite a bit longer than he stated, and it would take another twenty years for him to refine it. Clearly, however, his reading of Malthus had eliminated many of his doubts and propelled him toward the theory of natural selection.

In 1842, Darwin put down on paper his first sketch of the theory of evolution. He was not the first to discuss evolution; others in the scientific community had pondered and discussed various possibilities before. Darwin's master stroke was to offer the theory of natural selection as a coherent scientific explanation for the entire process—in other words, a theory of evolution through natural selection.

As for Malthus, he had stated in his work that the geometric growth in human population taxed food supplies to the point that only famine, disease, and war could keep the number of human beings from becoming unmanageable. This, he contended, was how human populations remained in balance.

Darwin took Malthus's theory and used it to shape his own. In doing so, he challenged the leading theory of the time regarding geological change, the catastrophic theory. According to this view, changes to the Earth come about only through catastrophes of nature. The last had been Noah's flood, during which only those life-forms taken aboard Noah's ark had survived.

Challenges to the "Catastrophes"

Even before Darwin, many had posed challenges to the catastrophe theory. Thus, Darwin later said, "The only novelty in my work is the attempt to explain *how* species became modified."

In 1830, Sir Charles Lyell, in his *Principles of Geology,* wrote that the Earth's geological features change gradually and that changes occurring over time can be understood by studying current geological processes. Although Lyell later would reject Darwin's theory of natural selection, the young naturalist took a copy of Lyell's book with him on the *Beagle,* ready to measure Lyell's findings and soon to add more ammunition to the assault on the catastrophe theory.

Another pre-Darwinian challenger was Charles Darwin's own grandfather, Erasmus Darwin, who advocated biological evolution. In 1770, he affixed the motto "Everything from shells" on his carriage and bookplates. (A skeptical clergyman responded in verse: "Great wizard be! By magic spells, Can all things raise from cockle shells.") In 1800, Jean Baptiste Lamarck, a French naturalist who has been called "the founder of the doctrine of evolution," proposed that species change over time in reaction to their environments.

On the popular front, a book appeared in 1845 titled *Vestiges of the Natural History of Creation,* in which the Scottish journalist Robert Chambers went so far as to argue that human beings derived from monkeys and apes. Although the book sold widely—Prince Albert reportedly read it aloud to Queen Victoria—it was vilified by those who were appalled by the idea and those who found in it a sloppy use of facts and little to support the outlandish claim. Darwin reacted to the book by calling its geology "bad" and its zoology "far worse."

Nevertheless, *Vestiges* contributed to a delay in the publication of Darwin's own work. In the aftermath of Chambers's work, Darwin proceeded cautiously. He did so in part to avoid having his research come out amid all the controversy over *Vestiges,* and in part because he wanted to be sure that he had his facts straight and that his claims were fully corroborated.

Wallace and *On the Origin of Species*

In any event, skepticism regarding the catastrophe view had appeared before Darwin proposed his theory of natural selection. Indeed, the foundation had been laid for a more thorough and systematic alternative to the idea

THE DESCENT OF MAN

In publishing *The Descent of Man* in 1871, Darwin took his theory of evolution through natural selection a step farther than he had in *On the Origin of Species,* focusing on the relationship between human beings and other primates.

Essentially, he says, there are basic similarities between the physical structure of humans and that of other primates. These include likenesses in the bones of the skeleton, the muscular system, and the brain. Even the embryos of humans resemble those of related animal species. Finally, Darwin observes, the basic organs of human physiology evolved from predecessors who used and shaped them, moving them toward the state they are in today.

The process of natural selection permeates Darwin's thought. He even applies it to intellectual development. "We can see . . . in the rudest state of society," he asserts, "the individuals who were the most sagacious, who invented and used the best weapons and traps, and who were best able to defend themselves, would rear the greatest number of offspring" and thereby multiply. Darwin concludes,

> Thus, we can understand how it has come to pass that man and all other vertebrate animals have been constructed on the same general model . . . and why they retain certain rudiments in common. Consequently we ought frankly to admit their community of descent: to take any other view, is to admit that our own structure, and that of all the animals around us, is a mere snare laid to entrap our judgment.

of catastrophe, supported by extensive empirical evidence—the very kind to which Darwin, as a rigorous scientist, was committed. In 1857, Darwin wrote a letter to the American botanist Asa Gray in which he provided an abstract of his forthcoming book:

> I think it can be shown that there is such an unerring power at work, or *Natural Selection* . . . which selects exclusively for the good of each organic being. . . . This little abstract touches only on the accumulative power of natural selection, *which I look at as by far the most important element in the production of new forms.* [italics added]

As Darwin continued to work on his theory, he soon encountered a startling development. In 1858, Alfred Russel Wallace, an English naturalist who had been working independently, sent Darwin an essay in which he proposed the theory of natural selection (although he did not use that phrase). Like Darwin, Wallace had been influenced by Malthus. After reading the *Essay on the Principle of Population,* Wallace began asking about animals, "Why do some die and some live?" In considering the question, he realized that "in every generation the inferior would inevitably be killed off and the superior would remain—that is, the fittest would survive."

Although Wallace had previously informed Darwin about the progress he had made in investigating the relationship of species to their environments, Darwin was amazed by Wallace's essay and how it dovetailed with his own. He wrote Lyell, "If Wallace had my MS. [manuscript] sketch written out in 1842, he could not have made a better short abstract!"

Darwin offered to get Wallace's paper published in any journal of the latter's choosing. He then sent Wallace's essay, along with an outline of his own similar views, to the Linnean Society in London.

On July 1, 1858, their joint presentation, "On the Tendency of Species to Form Varieties; and on the Perpetuation of Varieties and Species by Natural Means of Selection," was read publicly at Burlington House, the home of the Linnean Society. Darwin attended, Wallace could not. The two men, who had established a friendship years earlier, remained close friends; Wallace never felt slighted by the greater attention paid to Darwin.

Wallace's work encouraged Darwin to finally publish his book *On the Origin of Species* in 1859. In it, he presented his theory of natural selection in full detail. According to this view, the young in a species compete with each other for survival and pass on to the next generations any variations that might help them succeed. The variations constitute adaptations to the environment, which are communicated through heredity. Sometimes, Darwin recognized, only the slightest variations could mean the difference between the survival and extinction of a species. Beyond natural selection, Darwin also suggested that related organisms come from common ancestors.

On the Origin of Species sold widely and quickly went through several printings. A reviewer for *The New York Times* wrote,

> We are persuaded that the doctrine of progressive modification by Natural Selection will give a new direction to inquiry into the real genetic relationship of species, existing and extinct—will, in fact, make a revolution in natural history.

In a similar vein, botanist H.C. Watson wrote in a letter to Darwin,

> Your leading idea will assuredly become recognized as an established truth in science, i.e. "Natural Selection." It has the characteristics of all great natural truths. . . . You are the greatest revolutionist in natural history of this century, if not of all centuries.

Other scientists criticized Darwin for failing to present the proof behind the hereditary transfer of variations. Religious opponents attacked him for undermining orthodox belief by seeming to equate human beings with animals and denying the creation story as recounted in the Bible. Yet Darwin had been careful to avoid advancing any theory concerning the origin of life, and not to deny that there was a supreme creator. Indeed, the text of his book referred to "laws impressed on matter by the Creator."

Darwin elaborated on various aspects of his theory and offered new ones in three subsequent works: *The Variation of Animals and Plants Under Domestication*, published in 1868; *The Descent of Man*, published in 1871; and *The Expression of the Emotions in Man and Animals*, published in 1872.

In his personal life, Darwin had wed a first cousin, Emma Wedgwood, in January 1839. The couple had ten children, two of whom died in infancy.

Charles Darwin died on April 19, 1882, in London. He was given a state funeral and buried at Westminster Abbey. He has been recognized as a giant of modern science who revolutionized the field of biology and unleashed an enduring challenge to age-old assumptions about the nature of life, humanity, religion, and society.

Further Reading

Bowleb, Peter. *Charles Darwin: The Man and His Influence.* New York: Cambridge University Press, 1996.
Brown, Janet. *Charles Darwin: Voyaging.* New York: Alfred A. Knopf, 1995.
Desmond, Adrian, and James Moore. *Darwin.* New York: Warner, 1991.

See also: Wallace, Alfred Russel.

DISCOVERY, AGE OF

1420: Under Prince Henry the Navigator, the Portuguese explore and settle the Madeira Islands in the Atlantic Ocean, west of Morocco
1487: Portuguese explorer Bartholomeu Dias sails around the southern tip of Africa
1492: Sailing for the Spanish crown, Christopher Columbus reaches America, landing in the Bahamas
1497–1499: Portuguese explorer Vasco da Gama sails around the southern tip of Africa and reaches India
1519: Ferdinand Magellan, a Portuguese navigator sailing for Spain, begins a journey that culminates in the first voyage around the world
1521: Spanish conquistador Hernán Cortés captures the Aztec capital of Tenochtitlán (site of modern-day Mexico City)
1532: Francisco Pizarro conquers the Inca Empire for Spain
1534: French explorer Jacques Cartier discovers the St. Lawrence River, one of the major waterways of North America
1540: Spanish conqueror Francisco Coronado begins his search for the fabled Golden Cities of Cíbola
1610: English explorer Henry Hudson enters and explores Hudson Bay in Canada
1616: English sea pilot William Baffin maps the entire shore of Baffin Bay in Canada
1682: René-Robert de La Salle of France descends the Mississippi River to the Gulf of Mexico

From the mid-fifteenth through the seventeenth centuries, Europeans sailed the world's oceans to discover unseen lands, peoples, and natural resources in the farthest reaches of Africa, Asia, and the Western Hemisphere. Their far-flung explorations constituted the Age of Discovery, whose motivation was part materialistic and part scientific.

Historians debate the extent to which the Age of Discovery—also known as the Age of Exploration—was truly scientific in purpose and orientation. According to some, the overseas expeditions were guided, at least in part, by the quest for empirical evidence to support fledgling scientific theories. Others insist that evidence of scientific curiosity as a primary motivation is, at best, scant.

Prince Henry the Navigator

Sailors from Portugal began voyaging southwest into the Atlantic during the 1300s; however, it was not until Prince Henry the Navigator (1394–1460)—the son of Portugal's King John I—sponsored such explorations that they ventured far south along the coast of Africa, across the equator, and finally around the southern tip of the continent.

Prince Henry the Navigator of Portugal, whose sponsorship of ocean voyages in the first half of the fifteenth century launched the Age of Discovery, is portrayed in an illuminated travel chronicle of 1453. *(Granger Collection, New York)*

Numerous obstacles worked against ocean voyagers journeying to the equator. The lack of sophisticated navigational equipment made it difficult for sailors to determine their location; storms buffeted their ships and often carried them away at will; and legend had it that the water near the equator would boil travelers to death or that sea monsters would swallow them whole. Latitude 29° north was recognized as a point from beyond which no one had ever returned.

It was Prince Henry who envisioned expeditions far south to determine if it were possible to journey around Africa. Neither a navigator nor a sailor himself (except for his participation in one brief naval engagement), Prince Henry earned his place in history by encouraging voyages of discovery in the first half of the fifteenth century. Certainly, his motivation was less a matter of scientific curiosity than one of filling Portugal's coffers and spreading the Christian faith.

For one thing, Prince Henry sought to open trade routes with the Far East that would enable Portugal to bypass the small independent states on the northern Italian peninsula (called "city states") that dominated passage through the eastern Mediterranean Sea. In addition, he also dreamed of converting pagans to Christianity and of containing Islam by linking Europe with a mythical Christian kingdom that he thought real. Finally, he sought to fulfill the prophecy of his horoscope, which foretold that he would make important discoveries.

Thus, under a charter from Prince Henry, Portuguese sailors explored and settled the Madeira Islands in 1420. Gil Eannes, on a voyage sponsored by Prince Henry in 1434, navigated the dangerous shoals (referred to by Arabs as the "father of danger") off the west coast of Africa and rounded Cape Bojador (today part of Western Sahara); Nuno Tristão reached Cape Blanc (in what is now Mauritania) in 1441; Dinis Dias reached the Cape Verde Islands (off of modern-day Senegal) in 1444; and Tristão reached the mouth of the Gambia River in 1446.

When Spain began its own expeditions to Africa, the Portuguese felt pressured to sail farther yet. In 1487, Bartholomeu Dias (ca. 1450–1500) and his crew were blown past the southern tip of Africa (later called the Cape of Good Hope) by a storm and thereby discovered that it was possible to sail around the continent.

Ten years later, Vasco da Gama (ca. 1469–1524) rounded Africa and landed at Mozambique, where Arabs told him of rich ports to the north. Da Gama proceeded across the Indian Ocean and reached Calicut on the southwest coast of India in May 1498, returning to Portugal the following year. He lost two of his four ships and half of his men along the way, but he proved that it was possible to sail south and east from Europe to Asia.

Christopher Columbus

By this time, another idea had been advanced by a part-time weaver and sailor from Genoa, Italy, Christopher Columbus (1451–1506). Long interested in maps and mapmaking, Columbus knew of the findings of ninth-century Muslim geographer Alfragan, who had calculated that one degree of the Earth's circumference is equal to 66 nautical miles (122 kilometers). Columbus, however, made the mistake of misreading Alfragan's figure as 45 nautical miles (83 kilometers). In actuality, one degree is equal to 60 nautical miles (111 kilometers); thus, for *each degree* Columbus miscalculated (shortened) the circumference of the Earth by 15 nautical miles (28 kilometers). Since the Earth is divided into 360 degrees, this meant that he had shortened the total circumference by 5,400 nautical miles (10,000 kilometers).

Moreover, Columbus agreed with the Italian mathematician Paolo Toscanelli who, influenced by the findings of the explorer Marco Polo, had determined that Asia extended much farther east than it actually does. With Toscanelli's numbers in hand, Columbus insisted that he could sail west from the Canary Islands for about 2,400 miles (3,900 kilometers) and reach Asia (Japan)—a miscalculation that left him more than 8,000 miles (13,000 kilometers) short. Nevertheless, even at the distance calculated by Columbus, he proposed a daring journey, for he would have to sail far into the open sea with no coastal markers to guide him.

Columbus set about seeking a sponsor for his expedition. He met with rejection until the Spanish monarchs, Ferdinand and Isabella, finally agreed to back him. The Italian was promised 10 percent of all profits, governorship over any newfound lands, and the title Admiral of the Ocean Sea. The rest would belong to Spain.

On August 3, 1492, Columbus and his crew set sail from Palos, Spain. Their expedition consisted of three ships, the *Niña*, the *Pinta*, and the *Santa Maria*. The largest, the flagship *Santa Maria*, measured only about 100 feet (30 meters) long and carried thirty-nine crewmembers.

Upon reaching the Bahamas on October 12, Columbus believed that he had made it to the outer islands of Asia. He claimed that he had found a land resplendent with gold and spices and a people—"Indians"—who could be converted to Christianity. He imprisoned several dozen of these native people, of whom only a few survived the journey back to Europe the following year. Thus began the long, dismal treatment of Native Americans by Europeans.

Indeed, Columbus's treatment of native peoples, as well as the unintended consequences of European contact, later ignited ongoing controversy among historians and others over how to evaluate the famous mariner. For example, in his classic work *Admiral of the Ocean Sea: A Life of Christopher*

LIFE ABOARD THE *NIÑA, PINTA,* AND *SANTA MARÍA*

As Columbus and his crew crossed the Atlantic Ocean on the *Niña,* the *Pinta,* and the *Santa María,* life on board followed a routine. Columbus's crew worked in four-hour shifts, performing such duties as cleaning the deck, working the sails, and checking the ropes and cargo.

The sailors' diet was largely made up of salt meat, dried peas, and hardtack (a saltless hard biscuit). Also on board was some rice, cheese, and figs, with a few live pigs and hens to be slaughtered and eaten along the way. The men cooked on deck, in a wooden firebox with a base of sand to protect the ship and a hood to protect the flames from the wind. For liquids, they drank wine and water that was stored in casks but sometimes went bad.

Only the ship captains and pilots had cabins with bunks. The other sailors slept where they could, some of them on the deck.

The Lord's Prayer was recited at sunrise, the sailors chanted during the day, and another prayer was said after sunset. At night, a boy would recite the following every half hour:

To our God let's pray
To give us a good voyage,
And through the Blessed Mother,
Our advocate on high,
Protect us from the waterspout
And send no tempest nigh.

Columbus (1942), Samuel Eliot Morison praises Columbus for his bravery and navigational talent. In *A People's History of the United States* (1980), Howard Zinn accuses the explorer of committing genocide.

Columbus ultimately made three subsequent voyages across the Atlantic (1493–1496, 1498, and 1502–1504), but it was another Italian who became the namesake of the lands he had discovered. In 1499, and again in 1501, the Florentine navigator Amerigo Vespucci sailed to the coast of Brazil, and he concluded that Columbus had discovered a "new world." In 1507, a German publisher, influenced by Vespucci's account, placed the Italian's name on a map of the new continent, thereby designating it "America."

Other Spanish and Portuguese Expeditions

In the wake of Columbus's voyages, several other Spaniards sailed west to explore the Americas, prompted by a mix of motivations. Scientific inquiry was part of the story, but a relatively minor part.

On February 19, 1519, Hernán Cortés (1485–1547) sailed from Cuba with a force of some 600 men with the purpose of conquering and colonizing Mexico. In May 1521, Cortés and his well-armed soldiers laid siege to the Aztec capital of Tenochtitlán; by August 3, upon the capture of the Aztec emperor, Montezeuma II, Tenochtitlán fell. Cortés consolidated Spanish control over the land and people of Mexico, treating some natives brutally and forming alliances with others.

In similar fashion, Francisco Pizarro (ca. 1476–1541) conquered the Incas of Peru. In 1532, on his third expedition to the west coast of South America, Pizarro arrived with a force of 180 men, including several dozen cavalry, and proceeded inland through Peru. Although the expedition provided valuable information about the Inca Empire, Pizarro's main goal was to conquer the native peoples and get from them as much gold as he could. Solidifying the Spanish conquest, Pizarro and his army defeated the Inca leader Atahuallpa on November 16, 1532, and captured the capital, Cuzco, a year later.

In the meantime, Ferdinand Magellan (ca. 1480–1521), a Portuguese navigator in the service of Spain, received a royal commission to find a westward route to the Spice Islands of Asia. The expedition, consisting of five ships and 270 men, set sail west across the Atlantic Ocean in 1519, journeying around South America and into the Pacific Ocean. Magellan was killed in a skirmish with an indigenous tribe in the Philippines in April 1521, but one of his ships, with a crew of eighteen men, reached Spain in September 1522, completing the first voyage around the world.

Another Spanish conquistador, Francisco Coronado (ca. 1510–1554), who had conquered territories in northwest Mexico, set out across the Rio Grande in February 1540 in search of cities said to be laden with gold. As it turned out, however, the Golden Cities of Cíbola turned out to be a group of Zuni pueblos in Arizona and contained no particular riches at all.

From there, Coronado dispatched a small party westward under Garcia López de Cárdenas, who became the first Europeans to see the Grand Canyon of the Colorado River. In the spring of 1541, Coronado pushed farther north and east, through and beyond what is now Texas, in search of yet another wealthy kingdom, called Quivira. Arriving in what is today central Kansas, he found only a village of the Wichita people and, again, no riches. Despite his failure to find gold, Coronado had discovered vast tracts of land previously unknown to Europeans.

French and English Expeditions

For the French, Jacques Cartier (1491–1557) discovered the St. Lawrence River in 1534 and made two other expeditions to North America in the 1530s and 1540s. The French based their claim to Canada largely on Cartier's findings. In 1673, the French-Canadian explorer Louis Jolliet (1645–1700) joined with Father Jacques Marquette (1637–1675) on an expedition across Lake Michigan and along the Fox and Wisconsin rivers.

On June 17, they entered the Mississippi River and followed it south to just below the mouth of the Arkansas River before turning back. Their exploration opened the Great Lakes and Mississippi Valley region to European settlement and influence.

René-Robert Cavelier, the Sieur de La Salle (1643–1687), explored the region south of lakes Ontario and Erie from 1669 to 1670; he later claimed to have discovered the Ohio River the following year. With the Italian-born explorer Henri de Tonti (ca. 1650–1704) and a large party of French and Indians, La Salle descended the Mississippi River to the Gulf of Mexico in 1682. Claiming all the land drained by the river for France, he named the region Louisiana.

Among English explorers, Henry Hudson (?–ca. 1611) undertook four expeditions to North America in search of the Northwest Passage. In 1607,

THE MARINER'S ASTROLABE

As navigators began referring to the positions of their ships according to degrees of latitude, the astrolabe became an important instrument. Used first by astronomers, the device was adapted for maritime use in the fifteenth century.

Most astrolabes were small, measuring only 6–10 inches (15–25 centimeters) in diameter. Rather than being held in the hand, like an astronomer's astrolabe, the mariner's astrolabe usually was hung in a convenient spot on deck for taking sightings.

The mariner's astrolabe consisted of a disk or ring made of brass and marked off in degrees, with a movable arm at the center. By taking the zero point on the disk and orienting it with the horizon, a sailor could measure the altitude of any celestial object by sighting it along the arm.

Using this procedure, a mariner could determine the latitude of a ship at sea during the day by measuring the altitude of the Sun; at night, he could measure the altitude of a star of known declination when it was on the meridian. (Declination is similar to latitude; it is the position of a star relative to the celestial equator.) Despite the advances in instrumentation, however, most astrolabes still were inaccurate and commonly were off by four or five degrees.

The mariner's astrolabe, a vital instrument of navigation beginning in the fifteenth century, made it possible to determine the latitude of a ship at sea. This Portuguese bronze astrolabe dates to 1555. *(Granger Collection, New York)*

aboard the *Hopewell,* he reached Greenland. Then in September 1609, aboard the *Half Moon* on an expedition sponsored by the Dutch East India Company, he entered New York Bay. He spent the following month exploring the Hudson River to a point about 150 miles (240 kilometers) from its mouth, about where Albany is located today.

In 1610, Hudson sailed for an English company in the ship *Discovery.* That summer, he entered Hudson Bay, in Canada. He spent three months exploring the eastern islands and shores while trying to find an outlet to the northwest. No outlet was ever found, and those aboard the *Discovery* spent the winter in Hudson Bay. In the spring, the crew mutinied. Hudson, his son, and several others were set adrift in a small boat; they were never heard of again.

As part of another expedition searching for the Northwest Passage, the famed British navigator William Baffin (1584–1622), sailing on the ship *Tiger* as part of a fleet under the command of Captain Benjamin Joseph in 1615, explored the Hudson Strait and part of Southampton Island in Canada, compiling highly accurate maps and notes on the local tides. Baffin also determined longitude by comparing the altitude of the moon with another body in space and measuring the angular distance between them, purportedly making him the first person to take such a lunar measurement at sea.

In 1616, Baffin journeyed again to North America, this time aboard the ship *Discovery* with Robert Bylot as captain. Sailing farther north than any previous European explorers, they mapped the entire shore of Baffin Bay, including Lancaster Sound. Baffin mistakenly concluded that the bay lacked the outlet he was looking for; he failed to realize that Lancaster Sound would take him west to other channels and eventually to the Pacific Ocean.

Taken together, these and the many other expeditions during the Age of Discovery made the western European countries dominant in conquering overseas lands, unleashed a migration of Europeans across the oceans, and either inadvertently or purposefully advanced the scientific knowledge of the world. In doing so, Western society underwent an important transition from the medieval emphasis on superstition to the application of rational thought.

Further Reading

Barden, Renardo. *The Discovery of America: Opposing Viewpoints.* San Diego, CA: Greenhaven, 1989.

Morison, Samuel Eliot. *Admiral of the Ocean Sea.* New York: MJF, 1997.

———. *The Great Explorers: The European Discovery of America.* New York: Oxford University Press, 1978.

Parry, J.H. *The Age of Reconnaissance, 1450–1650.* London: Phoenix, 1963.

DUNBAR-HUNTER EXPEDITION

ca. 1750: William Dunbar is born in Scotland
1755: George Hunter is born in Scotland
1771: Dunbar emigrates to America
1774: Hunter emigrates to America
1792: Dunbar builds his plantation, the *Forest*, near Natchez, Mississippi
1796: Hunter journeys to St. Louis
1804: The Dunbar-Hunter expedition begins on October 16, on the east bank of the lower Mississippi River
1805: The expedition ends on January 27 in Natchez
1810: Dunbar dies on October 16 at the *Forest*
1832: Hunter dies on February 23 in New Orleans

With William Dunbar as leader and George Hunter as second in command, the Dunbar-Hunter Expedition of 1804–1805 explored the Ouachita River, which flows through the present-day cities of Hot Springs, Arkansas, and Monroe, Louisiana, and the nearby hot springs of the Old Southwest, in territory gained by the Louisiana Purchase. The expedition's scientific accomplishments were second only to those of the more famous Lewis and Clark expedition in the northern and far western part of the territory.

William Dunbar

Prior to his expedition with Hunter, William Dunbar compiled an impressive record in business and science. He was born circa 1750 near Elgin, Scotland, to Sir Archibald Dunbar and Anne Bayne. An inquisitive young man, William was directly influenced by the Scottish Renaissance, with its emphasis on science, then in full swing. In 1767, he graduated from King's College at Aberdeen, where he had embraced professor Alexander Rait's belief that the cultivation of higher mathematics would advance civilization.

Dunbar emigrated to America in 1771, largely because he saw it as a land of opportunity. He arrived with goods he used in the Indian trade at Fort Pitt in Pennsylvania, and he entered into a long and lucrative partnership with Philadelphia merchant John Ross and his son, Alexander. In the mid-1770s, Dunbar founded a plantation near the lower Mississippi River, at Manchac, in what was then British West Florida (today Louisiana). Working with the Rosses, he used slave labor to make barrel staves, which he then shipped to the Caribbean. During the American Revolution, however, the plantation was plundered and many of his slaves ran away.

After rebuilding his plantation at Manchac and establishing a mercantile house in New Orleans, Dunbar built another plantation, near Natchez, in 1792. The Forest, as he called it, became his home. Dunbar and his wife, Dinah Clarke, raised nine children there. By this time, West Florida had come under the control of Spain, and Dunbar formed a close relationship with the new government.

While accumulating wealth by raising and selling indigo and cotton, again an industry based on using slave labor, Dunbar also became widely known for his scientific interests. He invented new types of plows and employed innovative agricultural practices on his land. In addition, he invented an improved iron-screw press designed to pack cotton into square bales for shipment; studied Indian languages and paleontology; described trees, recorded their locations, and listed their uses for new settlers; catalogued flowers; wrote about fish and wildlife; and kept detailed daily weather observations.

Later, Dunbar built an astronomical observatory, equipped with what he described as a "Gregorian reflector [telescope] of 5½ or 6 feet in length in the great tube with 9 inch aperture possessing 6 magnifying powers from 100 to 525." As he noted in his diary: "The small fortune which I have acquired cultivating the earth alone enables me to procure many instruments of moderate expense which might facilitate my researches." With his extensive scientific studies, the Forest became a gathering point for fellow scientists, and his many visitors included the leading American botanist of the time, William Bartram.

In 1798, Dunbar represented Spain on the boundary commission that drew the 31st parallel between Spanish West Florida and the United States (and placed Natchez within the latter). The American representatives were led by land surveyor Andrew Ellicott, who was known for his mathematical and astronomical studies. Dunbar and Ellicott became fast friends.

It was through Ellicott, who had done work for Thomas Jefferson, that Dunbar struck up a correspondence with the president—himself an accomplished naturalist. In their letters, Dunbar and Jefferson discussed flora and fauna, as well as various scientific ideas. When Dunbar began writing articles for *Transactions*, the journal of the American Philosophical Society, Jefferson reviewed Dunbar's writings before they went to publication. The articles covered topics ranging from weather and fossils to eclipses of the sun and the flow of the Mississippi River.

The Expedition

In 1804, Meriwether Lewis and William Clark stopped at the Forest on their way to St. Louis and the launch of their own historic expedition to explore the newly purchased Louisiana Territory. Dunbar was immediately impressed with their knowledge and determination.

A short time thereafter, President Jefferson invited Dunbar to head an expedition to explore the Red and Arkansas rivers. Despite his relationship with the president, Dunbar, at age fifty-four, had never expected a chance to lead such an important expedition. But Jefferson recognized Dunbar as the leading scientific expert on the Old Southwest and wanted him to collect information on the landscape, plant and animal life, and native peoples of the region.

Dunbar agreed, and Jefferson appointed George Hunter of Philadelphia to assist him on the expedition. Born in Edinburgh, Scotland, in 1755, Hunter had come to America in 1774. He served in a Continental Army hospital during the American Revolution and was imprisoned for a time by the British. By the 1790s, he was part owner of a distillery and trading successfully in pharmaceuticals.

Although Hunter had a reputation for being opportunistic and slow moving, his background in chemistry lent a solid background in science to the expedition. More important, he had traveled extensively in the American wilderness. In 1796, he journeyed from Philadelphia to Pittsburgh and then along the Ohio and Mississippi rivers, eventually reaching the Spanish outpost at St. Louis. In 1802, he traveled to Kentucky and took extensive notes about the region's mineral wealth.

Dunbar handled most of the planning and organization for the proposed journey. Hunter did not arrive in Natchez until August 1804; he brought with him his medicines, geological tools, and mathematical instru-

HOT SPRINGS

Part of the goal of the Dunbar-Hunter Expedition was to explore the hot springs of Arkansas. Hot springs are found in many parts of the United Sates, especially the West, and throughout the world, including such otherwise frigid locations as Greenland and Siberia.

Hot springs are caused by geothermal heat—that is, heat from the Earth's interior. In general, the interior of the Earth gets hotter as depth increases. When water enters a crack in the Earth's surface, it can force out water that has collected beneath a fault and has been heated by hot rocks deeper in the Earth's interior, thereby creating a hot spring.

Important to the creation of such a spring is the ability of the heated water to move quickly to the surface, before it cools. Thus, many hot springs are found amid porous limestone formations. In volcanic zones, such as Yellowstone National Park, water may be heated by coming into contact with molten rock.

The hot springs Dunbar and Hunter explored in Arkansas are now part of Hot Springs National Park, which was established as a federal reservation in 1832. It includes forty-seven thermal springs with a total water flow of about 750,000 gallons (2.8 million liters) to 950,000 gallons (3.6 million liters) per day. Water from the springs remains near 143 degrees Fahrenheit (62 degrees Celsius). The park attracts more than a million visitors per year, who relax and find relief for weary bodies at bathhouses that collect and store the spring water, allowing it to cool to a comfortable temperature.

ments. Before they departed, however, opposition from the Spanish and from Native American tribes, combined with Dunbar's enthusiasm for exploring the region's hot springs, led to a change in plans: The expedition would be limited to exploring the Ouachita River and the nearby hot springs in west-central Arkansas.

The Dunbar-Hunter Expedition debarked from St. Catherine's Landing, near Natchez, on October 16, 1804. Dunbar, Hunter, and their team of fifteen explorers, including soldiers, would travel a total of about 1,000 miles (1,600 kilometers) over 103 days. During the course of the journey, Dunbar made astronomical observations and collected plants and rocks for study upon returning home.

The expedition ascended the Ouachita River from Louisiana into Arkansas and then continued on to the hot springs. Dunbar noted one spring with a temperature of 140 degrees Fahrenheit (60 degrees Celsius) and collected water samples for further analysis. Despite spending several days at the spring, he failed to determine what caused the waters to be heated.

The expedition landed back at Natchez on January 27, 1805. Dunbar sent specimens to Jefferson to share with scientists and wrote a report that the president submitted to Congress on February 19, 1806. In his introduction to the report, Jefferson stated that the expedition had been led by "Mr. Dunbar, of Natchez, a citizen of distinguished science, who had aided, and continues to aid us, with his disinterested and valuable services in the prosecution of these enterprises."

Also in 1806, Dunbar contributed to a book on the exploration of the Louisiana Territory titled *Discoveries Made in Exploring the Missouri, Red River, and Washita by Captains Lewis and Clark, Doctor Sibley, and William Dunbar.* Included in the work were lists and descriptions of flowers, vegetables, and trees, along with meteorological information about the region.

Although poor health forced him to decline an invitation from President Jefferson to lead another expedition into the Old Southwest, Dunbar did play a major role in planning it. In 1806, a party led by surveyor and astronomer Thomas Freeman and medical student Peter Custis traveled 600 miles (950 kilometers) up the Red River, until they were turned back by Spanish troops.

Having served in the Mississippi territorial legislature before his expedition with Hunter, Dunbar was chosen as speaker of the house in 1803 and served in the position for two years, until losing interest in politics. He became seriously ill in 1808, recovered, and then died from unknown causes at the Forest on October 16, 1810.

In the meantime, Hunter journeyed to Kentucky in 1809; six years later, he settled in New Orleans with his family. He worked as a druggist there until his death on February 23, 1832.

Further Reading

DeRosier, Arthur H., Jr. *William Dunbar: Scientific Pioneer of the Old Southwest.* Lexington: University Press of Kentucky, 2007.

Rowland, Eron, ed. *Life, Letters, and Papers of William Dunbar of Elgin, Morayshire, Scotland, and Natchez, Mississippi: Pioneer Scientist of the Southern United States.* Jackson: Mississippi Historical Society, 1930.

E

EARLE, SYLVIA (1935–)

1935: Born on August 30 in Gibbstown, New Jersey
1948: Moves to Dunedin, Florida
1966: Earns doctorate in botany from Duke University
1976: Begins studying sperm whales in the Pacific Ocean
1979: Makes her "JIM Dive" in a suit of armored plating
1982: With Graham Hawkes, founds Deep Ocean Engineering
1990: Becomes chief scientist at the National Oceanic and Atmospheric Administration
1998: Begins leading the Sustainable Seas Expeditions to study the U.S. National Marine Sanctuaries

An American botanist, oceanographer, deep-sea explorer, author, and lecturer, Sylvia Earle has been dubbed "Her Royal Deepness" for the time she has spent in the water and the discoveries she has made there.

Sylvia Alice Earle was born on August 30, 1935, in Gibbstown, New Jersey, to Lewis Earle, an electrician, and Alice Freas Richie. She was raised on a farm near Camden, New Jersey, where her mother taught her to study animals and respect their habitats. Earle later recalled how she spent much time at the pond in her backyard, filling jars with fish, frogs, and tadpoles.

In 1948, when Earle was thirteen, her family moved to Dunedin, Florida, on the Gulf Coast near Clearwater. Earle immediately was attracted to the sea. "On my first visit to the shore," she later wrote, "a great wave knocked me off my feet. I've been irresistibly drawn to the ocean ever since." At age seventeen, she began scuba diving and from then on preferred being in the ocean to being on land.

Intelligent and hardworking, Earle graduated from Florida State University in 1955. She earned her master's degree from Duke University the following year and immediately began studying for her doctorate there.

Botanist and deep-sea explorer Sylvia Earle, who led scores of research expeditions and spent extended periods in an undersea habitat, has also been the chief scientist at NOAA, a prolific author, and a staunch advocate for the world's oceans and marine life. *(John Shearer/WireImage/Getty Images)*

Her graduate studies were interrupted by the first of her three marriages, the births of her two children, and her need to take a job outside academia. Nevertheless, in 1964, she found time to join an expedition to the Indian Ocean sponsored by the National Science Foundation.

Upon returning home, she resumed her graduate studies and conducted research on marine flora in the Gulf of Mexico. Earle was one of the few botanists at the time who actually went into the water to study specimens; most had them collected by others and then studied them onshore. Earle obtained her doctorate from Duke in 1966; her dissertation stood out for the details it provided about aquatic life.

In the summer of 1970, Earle became a U.S. aquanaut when she took part in Tektite II, a scientific underwater project sponsored by the U.S. Navy, the Department of the Interior, and the National Aeronautics and Space Administration (NASA). In the program, scientists lived on the ocean floor near the Virgin Islands for an extended period; Tektite I was for male aquanauts, Tektite II for women.

Earle lived with four other scientists in two large tanks joined by a cylindrical passageway, 50 feet (15 meters) beneath the surface. During the two weeks of the project, Earle alone cataloged twenty-six plants previously unknown to those waters. NASA applied what was learned about living in restricted, close quarters to its human space flight program.

Tektite II brought Earle national publicity and a visit to the White House. She recalled,

> Tektite lifted me from the realm of pure science to communicating with a broad audience. Suddenly there were microphones in front of me and millions of people were hearing what I had to say. I felt a strong obligation to educate them about the oceans.

From 1976 to 1980, Earle studied sperm whales in the Pacific Ocean as part of a research team. Her work resulted in a show on public television titled "Gentle Giants of the Pacific."

During this time, she made a historic deep-sea dive in 1979. For this dive, she donned a "JIM suit," bulky armor plating made of plastic and metal that resembled the suits worn by astronauts on the moon. In the JIM suit,

Earle dove to a depth of 1,250 feet (381 meters) in the Pacific Ocean off the coast of the Hawai'ian island of Oahu. It was a dangerous dive, because even a slight tear in the suit would create so much pressure that she would be crushed to death, and because she walked the ocean floor untethered from the expedition's submarine.

It was the deepest solo dive ever made to that time without using a cable connected to a surface vessel. Earle was on the seabed for more than two hours, collecting numerous specimens along the way. She wrote about her adventure in a book titled *Exploring the Deep Frontier*, published in 1980.

From 1980 to 1984, Earle served on the National Advisory Committee on Oceans and Atmosphere. In 1982, she founded a company called Deep Ocean Engineering (later Deep Ocean Technologies) with the designer of the JIM suit, her husband, Graham Hawkes. The company produced submersibles, including the *Deep Rover*, a one-person vessel much more compact and less expensive than other subs. In 1985, Earle took *Deep Rover* to a depth of 3,000 feet (900 meters).

By this time, Earle had become an outspoken environmentalist who advocated protection of the oceans. She warned,

> If the sea is sick we'll feel it. If it dies, we die. Our future and the state of the oceans are one.

THE JIM SUIT

Named after test diver Jim Garrett, the JIM suit was preceded by an atmospheric diving suit (ADS) developed in 1930 by British engineer Salim Joseph Peress. As a young man living in the Middle East, Peress had watched men dive for pearls in the Persian Gulf, and he resolved to develop a suit that would ease the problem of the bends (decompression sickness).

Years later, working at a company in Byfleet, England, Peress began developing a suit that would keep divers warm and dry, while at the same time maintaining atmospheric pressure in deep water. His first attempt, in the early 1920s, proved too heavy to be viable and had stiff arm and leg joints. In 1930, he completed a somewhat lighter version, the Tritonia, with more flexible joints. Innovative as it was, the Tritonia stirred little interest and found minimal use.

In the mid-1960s, oil companies working in the North Sea began looking for innovative ways to help divers prowl the ocean floor. The original JIM suit, made in 1971, incorporated Peress's Tritonia joint design and featured four Plexiglas portholes and experimental hand-like devices for gripping objects. The first deepwater test dive in the JIM suit was held off the north coast of Scotland, at a depth of about 400 feet (120 meters).

Divers found that the joints based on Peress's design had the drawback of pinching their skin, requiring a series of technological improvements. The JIM suit used by Sylvia Earle in 1979 incorporated improved, oiled joints, a large acrylic dome (which replaced the portholes), and pincers for collecting specimens.

In 1989, Earle studied the effects of the *Exxon Valdez* oil spill at Prince William Sound in Alaska. Two years later, she surveyed the oil that spilled into the Persian Gulf after Iraq destroyed oil wells during its 1990–1991 invasion of Kuwait and war with the United States.

In 1990, Earle had become the first woman to serve as chief scientist of the National Oceanic and Atmospheric Administration (NOAA). She left that post in 1992 over political conflicts. From 1998 to 2002, she led the Sustainable Seas Expeditions to study the U.S. National Marine Sanctuaries, federally protected areas encompassing some 18,000 square miles (47,600 square kilometers) of coastal waters.

During the course of her long career, Earle has cataloged more than 20,000 marine plant specimens. She has written approximately 125 books and articles on marine science, has led some 60 expeditions, and has spent more than 6,000 hours underwater. In addition, she has held several academic jobs, including staff researcher at the Farlow Herbarium at Harvard University from 1967 to 1981.

Above all, she has worked incessantly to generate public interest in marine life and the fate of the world's oceans. In 1999, the president of the National Wildlife Federation, Mark Van Putten, praised her achievements:

> Sylvia Earle has earned tremendous credibility among her peers in the scientific community. But perhaps her greatest accomplishment is her ability to popularize the mysteries of the oceans for nonscientists all over the world.

Further Reading

Earle, Sylvia. *Dive! My Adventures in the Deep Frontier.* Washington, DC: National Geographic Society, 1998.

———. *Sea Change: A Message of the Ocean.* New York: Putnam, 1995.

Earle, Sylvia, and Al Giddings. *Exploring the Deep Frontier.* Washington, DC: National Geographic Society, 1980.

EVEREST EXPEDITIONS

1921: British explorer George Leigh Mallory leads a reconnaissance expedition up the north slope of Mount Everest, from Tibet

1953: On May 29, New Zealand climber Edmund Hillary and Tibetan Sherpa Tenzing Norgay become the first to reach the summit

1963: An American scientific expedition, led by Swiss climber Norman Dyhrenfurth, reaches the summit for the first time

1975: Junko Tabei of Japan becomes the first woman to reach the summit

The initiative to reach the summit of Mount Everest—located in northeastern Nepal along the border with China, it is the highest mountain in the world, at 29,035 feet (8,850 meters)—began in the late 1800s with European explorers, who first contemplated an ascent on foot.

Traditionally, area residents believed that the Himalayas were the home of gods. Mount Everest, the highest among them, was therefore to be revered, not conquered. While most of the efforts to reach the top of Mount Everest have had few scientific benefits and even less scientific motivation, a number of the expeditions have contributed to the understanding of regional topography and climate, as well as of the effects of extreme conditions on human survival.

In England at the turn of the twentieth century, the Royal Geographical Society and the Alpine Club began promoting the idea of climbing Mount Everest. The chief obstacles were getting to the mountain—since Nepal and Tibet were closed to foreigners at the time—and overcoming its hostile terrain and weather conditions.

Edmund Hillary of New Zealand (left) and Nepalese Sherpa guide Tenzing Norgay (right) were the first climbers to reach the peak of Mount Everest, the highest point on Earth. They reached the summit on May 29, 1953. *(Granger Collection, New York)*

Mount Everest, named in the mid-1800s for George Everest, a surveyor general of India, is covered by enormous glaciers and buffeted by howling winds, and heavy snowstorms. At the summit, the temperature never rise above freezing and can drop as low as -76 degrees Fahrenheit (-24 degrees Celsius).

With Tibet briefly open to foreigners in 1921, George Leigh Mallory—who famously declared that he wanted to climb Mount Everest "because it's there"—led a British expedition up the north side of the mountain; however, the group had to turn back due to high winds and avalanches. A second British expedition, in which Mallory also took part, reached a record altitude in 1922 before having to turn back. On his third attempt, in 1924, Mallory and fellow climber Andrew Irvine disappeared on the northeast ridge. (Mallory's body was found in 1999 just 800 feet, or 240 meters, from the summit.) On these attempts, and others to come, Sherpas (people of Tibetan descent who lived near the Himalayas) proved important as guides and porters.

Attempts to reach the summit in the 1930s and 1940s also failed, though an important breakthrough came in 1933 with the first airplane photography of the summit and the surrounding landscape. This contributed to what some have called the "Golden Age of Mount Everest Exploration" in the 1950s and 1960s.

During the spring and autumn of 1952, two Swiss expeditions reached the South Col, a major mountain pass (and today the most popular route to the top). But they failed to advance more than a short distance beyond it.

Then on May 29, 1953, Edmund Hillary of New Zealand and Tenzing Norgay, a Sherpa from Nepal, climbing as part of a British expedition led by John Hunt, traversed beyond the South Col and reached the summit. To do so, they had to navigate what came to be called the "Hillary Step," a 55-foot (17-meter) formation of rock and ice so steep that just one slip could cause a climber to plunge to certain death. They made the ascent without the ropes commonly used by climbers today.

In 1960, a Chinese and Tibetan team led by Shih Chan-chun made the first summit of Everest by traversing the North Col and Northeast Ridge. Three years later, an American expedition led by the Swiss climber Norman Dyhrenfurth reached the summit. The team consisted of nineteen mountaineers and scientists from throughout the United States, along with thirty-seven Sherpas.

A key purpose of the U.S. expedition was scientific research in the fields of physiology, psychology, glaciology, and meteorology. One of the expedition's more interesting assignments was to record how climbers reacted to the extreme stresses at high altitudes, where oxygen deprivation was unavoidable. Information from these findings proved useful in the U.S. manned space flight program.

In 1975, Junko Tabei of Japan became the first woman to reach the summit, as part of an all-female expedition (accompanied by male Sherpas). Three years later, Austrians Reinhold Messner and Peter Habeler climbed to the summit without the use of oxygen tanks. And in 2003, a Sherpa named Lakpa Gelu climbed the southern route from Base Camp to the summit in a record 10 hours, 56 minutes.

Over the years, more than 200 people have lost their lives trying to reach the summit of Mount Everest. Those who traverse the mountain today may encounter remnants of tents, empty oxygen canisters, and even frozen corpses. Climbing Mount Everest in the twenty-first century has become heavily commercialized, with guided trips costing $65,000 or more.

Further Reading

Bernbaum, Edwin. *Sacred Mountains of the World.* Berkeley: University of California Press, 1997.

Johnston, Alexa. *Reaching the Summit: Sir Edmund Hillary's Life of Adventure.* New York: DK, 2005.

EXPLORERS CLUB

1904: The Explorers Club is formally organized on May 28
1921: The *Explorers Journal* is first published
1981: The club opens membership to women for the first time
2000: The club sponsors an expedition to the world's highest plateau, the Chang-Tang

The Explorers Club was founded in New York City in 1904 to promote and support scientific expeditions throughout the world. Today, its mission remains much the same. The Explorers Club defines itself as "an international multidisciplinary professional society dedicated to the advancement of field research and the ideal that it is vital to preserve the instinct to explore."

The organization was founded in New York City by Henry Collins Walsh, who had engaged in an Arctic expedition in the mid-1890s, as well as several other men prominent in the sciences and journalism. Among them were Frederick Dellenbaugh, an American explorer who had journeyed to the western United States with John Wesley Powell; Adolphus Greely, an American polar explorer; Carl Lumholtz, a Norwegian discoverer and ethnographer; Marshall Saville, an American archaeologist; and Donaldson Smith, a British explorer. After meeting in early May 1904, they held a dinner on May 28 at the Aldine Association, where the Explorers Club was formally organized.

The club was incorporated on October 25, 1905, whereupon regular meetings were initiated. In 1912, the club established its headquarters in a building on Amsterdam Avenue, where it housed its books, documents, trophies, and artifacts. It also began inviting explorers and natural scientists to present lectures about their experiences and findings. The same year, the Arctic Club of America merged with the Explorers Club.

In 1921, the club began publishing the *Explorers Journal.* It contains articles about the organization and its activities along with timely scientific information. In 1961, the club purchased the site of its present headquarters, a townhouse on East Seventieth Street in Manhattan named for famed journalist Lowell Thomas.

Another major landmark came in 1981, when the Explorers Club opened its membership to women. The first female members included Sylvia Earle, the world-renowned American oceanographer; Dian Fossey, the American zoologist known for her studies of the mountain gorillas in East Africa; Anna Roosevelt, the daughter of Franklin and Eleanor Roosevelt; and Kathryn Sullivan, an oceanographer who would become the first American woman to walk in space.

Over the years, several club members have been involved in momentous explorations. When astronaut Neil Armstrong journeyed to the moon on board *Apollo 11* in 1969, he brought with him the Explorers Club flag. The ranks of notable members include Roald Amundsen, Robert Ballard, Edmund Hillary, Charles Lindbergh, Robert Peary, Ernest Shackleton, Chuck Yeager, and thousands of others.

In the year 2000, the club sponsored an expedition to the world's highest plateau, the Chang-Tang, in Tibet. Today, the Explorers Club has more than thirty U.S. and international chapters, with member scientists and explorers from more than sixty countries.

Further Reading

The Explorers Club. http://www.explorers.org.

Plimpton, George, ed. *As Told at the Explorers Club: More Than Fifty Gripping Tales of Adventure.* Guilford, CT: Lyons, 2003.

F

FLINDERS, MATTHEW (1774–1814)

1774: Born on March 16 in Donington, England
1789: Joins the Royal Navy
1795: Explores Botany Bay in Australia and George's River

1798: With George Bass, circumnavigates Van Damien's Land (Tasmania)
1803: Explores southern Australia's Unknown Coast
1814: Publishes *Voyage to Terra Australis;* dies in London on July 19

In his journeys to Australia, the English naval commander, explorer, and hydrographer Matthew Flinders proved that Tasmania is an island, charted the Unknown Coast, and led a team of scientists in collecting valuable information about the largely unexplored continent.

Matthew Flinders, Jr., was born on March 16, 1774, in Donington, Lincolnshire, England, to Matthew Flinders, a surgeon, and Susanna Ward. Young Matthew was a bright boy who was particularly attracted to mathematics. He attended a free school run by the local parish and a grammar school run by the Reverend John Shinglar.

Located in eastern England's fenlands, Donington was tied to the sea for its livelihood. Matthew was fascinated by the sea and relished the stories of an older cousin who served in the Royal Navy. At the nearby port of Boston, he walked amid the wharves and watched the ships as they sailed into the harbor. He read Daniel Defoe's novel *Robinson Crusoe* (1719) and, many years later, wrote that he had gone to sea "against the wishes of friends from reading [it]."

Flinders joined the Royal Navy at age fifteen. Two years later, in 1791, he journeyed to Australia, New Zealand, and Tahiti under Captain William Bligh aboard the HMS *Providence.* During these journeys, Flinders was the most junior of the midshipmen aboard and likely was involved in only limited navigational work.

Down Under

Flinders next served on the HMS *Reliance,* which in 1795 sailed from England to Port Jackson, Australia, near Sydney. The journey greatly expanded his experience and furthered his reputation.

With George Bass, the ship's surgeon, he explored the area around Sydney in a small, open boat. Captain James Cook had previously navigated the coastline, but Flinders wrote,

> [T]he intermediate portions of the coast, both north and south, were little further known than from captain Cook's general chart; and none of the more distant openings, marked but not explored by that celebrated navigator, had been seen.

Flinders and Bass sailed into Botany Bay and then up George's River before abandoning their boat to travel by foot for another 20 miles

(32 kilometers). They mapped the river's course more extensively than had been done before and noted the richness of the soil in the area.

The adventure excited Flinders and made him determined to seek further discoveries. Several weeks later, in another small boat, the *Tom Thumb*, Flinders and Bass explored Providential Cove, located 22 miles (35 kilometers) south of Port Jackson. Flinders engaged in hydrographical research, likely his first time doing so, before rejoining the *Reliance* to sail for the Cape of Good Hope.

In 1798, as a lieutenant on the sloop *Norfolk*, Flinders studied the waters at the Furneaux Group, islands north of Van Damien's Land (today Tasmania). From October 1798 to January 1799, he and Bass circumnavigated Van Damien's Land, passing through what is now known as Bass Strait and proving the territory to be an island. Bass took detailed notes on the plants, animals, and geography.

Back in England in 1801, Flinders published a memoir, *Observations on the Coast of Van Diemen's Land*, which he dedicated to the great British botanist Joseph Banks. Later that year, Flinders was given command of the *Investigator*, with the assignment to explore the coastline of southern Australia, called the "Unknown Coast." The *Investigator* had been built in

NICOLAS BAUDIN

The Frenchman Nicolas Baudin (1754–1803) had an accomplished record as an explorer before he met Matthew Flinders at Encounter Bay in April 1802. Born on the Île-de-Ré off the west coast of France, Baudin fought in the French navy against Great Britain during the American Revolution. In the mid-1780s, as a commander of merchant ships, he became friends with Franz Boos, the head gardener and botanist for the emperor of Austria. Boos taught Baudin about botany and how to preserve specimens. On one trip, they collected live plants and seedlings, as well as ostriches and zebras.

Baudin returned to France in 1795 and convinced Professor Antoine de Jussieu at the Muséum National d'Histoire Naturelle (National Natural History Museum) to support a botanical voyage to the Caribbean. Baudin journeyed to the Virgin Islands and Puerto Rico and came back with an impressive collection of plants, insects, and birds, along with seven cases of corals, crabs, sea urchins, and starfish, and 200 specimens of wood. Crowds turned out in Paris to see his strange collection of coconut palms and other exotic plants.

In 1800, Baudin convinced Napoleon to back him in exploring Australia and New Guinea. Baudin's goals were to map the coast of Australia, gather specimens, and make scientific studies of the area. He reached the continent in May 1801 with a team of astronomers, geographers, mineralogists, botanists, and zoologists aboard two ships, *Le Géographe* and *Le Naturaliste*.

Le Naturaliste returned to France in 1802 loaded with specimens, while Baudin continued exploring the Pacific region. He died of tuberculosis on September 16, 1803, en route home, on the island of Mauritius in the Indian Ocean.

1795 and purchased by the Royal Navy in 1798. Flinders later described it as "three-hundred and thirty four tons . . . newly coppered and repaired" and evaluated it as "the best vessel which could, at that time, be spared for the projected voyage to Terra Australis."

Joseph Banks, who would remain in England, appointed most of the ship's scientific staff of six men: Robert Brown, England's leading botanist; Ferdinand Lukas Bauer, botanical painter; William Westall, landscape painter; Peter Good, gardener (whose chief duty was to help transport plants); John Allen, miner (who served as the mineralogist); and John Crosley, astronomer. Good and Bauer often gathered plants while Brown was busy processing them.

The *Investigator* sailed from England on July 16, 1801, and reached Cape Leeuwin, on Australia's southwest coast, in December. From then into May 1803, Flinders conducted a detailed exploration of the Unknown Coast, chartering the shoreline and sending scientists ashore to collect specimens.

In February, he entered Spencer Gulf; the following month, he discovered Kangaroo Island, observing the vast number of kangaroos feeding on the grass. The kangaroos were so unafraid, Flinders wrote, that "the poor animals suffered themselves to be shot in the eyes with a small shot, and in some cases to be knocked on the head with sticks." Flinders himself shot ten kangaroos and used the meat for stew.

At the eastern end of the Unknown Coast, in April 1802, Flinders unexpectedly met Nicolas Baudin, captain of the French ship *Le Géographe*. Flinders named the meeting site Encounter Bay.

Flinders arrived at Port Jackson, on June 9, 1803. His exploration made him the first person to provide a detailed outline of Australia's south coast. While at Port Jackson, Robert Brown took measures to preserve the plants he had collected. The *Investigator* then completed a circumnavigation of Australia, including a study of the Great Barrier Reef and the Gulf of Carpentaria.

During the course of the journey, however, Flinders discovered that the *Investigator* was severely rotted and desperately in need of repair. While he searched for a substitute ship, he traveled as a passenger on the *Porpoise*. In August 1803, the *Porpoise* struck a reef and sank about 700 miles (1,100 kilometers) north of Port Jackson. Flinders escaped on a small boat and managed to get others who had been aboard the ship rescued from Wreck Reef, which jutted just 3–4 feet (about 1 meter) above sea level.

Sailing on the *Cumberland*, Flinders entered Torres Strait in October 1803. Beginning the trip back to England, he sailed west across the Indian Ocean and arrived in French-controlled Mauritius that December. Flinders was promptly arrested, as France had gone to war with England months earlier. Although he was imprisoned only briefly, he was detained on the island for nearly seven years. Although it was a bitter experience, it gave Flinders the opportunity to work on his journals. The governor of the island finally granted Flinder's release in June 1810.

Writings and Reputation

Returning to England in October 1810, Flinders published his description of the near circumnavigation of Australia—titled *Voyage to Terra Australis: Undertaken for the Purpose of Completing the Discovery of that Vast Country, and Prosecuted in the Years 1801, 1802, and 1803, in His Majesty's Ship the Investigator*—in July 1814. In addition to recounting the voyage, this work provided extensive information on meteorology, hydrography, magnetism, and navigation. Having been ill for some time, Flinders died on July 19, 1814, in London, at the age of forty.

In his years at sea, he had made major contributions to the mapping of the Australian coast, especially the Unknown Coast. The accuracy of his charts was a result of his often sailing twice over explored coastlines in order to check his work. In addition, he had researched the tides and shown how iron in ships affected compasses. His report, *Magnetism on Ships,* was circulated throughout the Royal Navy. By the late 1800s, a "Flinders Bar" of soft, unmagnetized iron in a brass container was being used to correct the effect of shipboard metals on compass readings.

Flinders suggested the names Australia and Terra Australis for the large continent he had circumnavigated, which previously had been identified on maps as "New Holland." His scientific curiosity and intellectual commitment were well summarized in a letter from Joseph Banks in April 1803:

> The Frequent opportunities you have Given to the naturalists to investigate does you Great Credit both as a navigator & as a considerate man. Natural history is now a study so much in Repute by the Public & in its self is so interesting, that the Good word of the Naturalists when you come home will not fail to interest a large number of People in your Favor.

See also: Banks, Joseph; Pacific Exploration.

Further Reading

Estensen, Miriam. *The Life of Matthew Flinders.* Crows Nest, Australia: Allen and Unwin, 2002.

G

GOBI DESERT

366: The Cave of a Thousand Buddhas, a religious temple, is first created
1971: A Mongolian-Polish expedition finds the remains of a 6-foot-long (1.83-meter-long) dinosaur, *Protoceratops*
2002: A new species of sauropod, a long-necked dinosaur, is found at Bor Guve

Straddling Mongolia and China, the Gobi Desert has been the site of several major scientific expeditions, most notably those in pursuit of fossils and ancient Buddhist ruins. The largest desert in Asia, the Gobi covers approximately a half-million square miles (1.3 million square kilometers), extending about 1,000 miles (1,600 kilometers) from east to west and about 600 miles (950 kilometers) from north to south.

The Gobi is largely an arid plateau that ranges in elevation from 3,000 feet (900 meters) above sea level in the east to 5,000 feet (1,500 meters) in the west. It is ringed by mountains: the Da Hinggan Ling to the east; the Altun Shan and Nan Shan to the south; the Tian Shan to the west; and the Altay Shan, Hangayn Nuruu, and Yablonovyy to the north. Most of the Gobi is covered with grass or scrub and has enough food and water for nomadic herders to raise animals; however, the southeastern Gobi has no water.

Trade routes—preeminently the fabled Silk Road—have crisscrossed the Gobi since ancient times. The first European to cross the Gobi was the Venetian explorer Marco Polo in the thirteenth century.

In the twentieth century, several modern scientific expeditions sought the Buddhist cave-temples near the Chinese city of Dunhuang. Among them is the Cave of the Thousand Buddhas, which dates back to 366 C.E. The entire complex, called the Mogao Caves, contains Buddhist art created over a period of about 1,000 years.

In the early 1900s, a Chinese Taoist named Wang Yuanlu searched for the caves and discovered 60,000 documents walled up among them. Many of the documents were religious in nature; some were secular, such as administrative records and dictionaries. Other expeditions to the caves followed, including ones from France, Japan, and Russia.

At the turn of the twentieth century, the Swedish explorer Sven Anders Hedin discovered the ruins of the ancient oasis city of Loulan in remote northwestern China. Also discovered there have been the remains of Paleolithic, Neolithic, and Bronze Age civilizations.

As evidenced by this fossilized dinosaur skull, discovered in the windswept Bayanzag Valley of Mongolia, the Gobi Desert continues to provide fertile ground for paleontological research. *(DEA/Christian Ricci/De Agostini/Getty Images)*

In a series of expeditions during the 1920s and 1930s, the American naturalist Roy Chapman Andrews discovered a trove of dinosaur bones and eggs in the Gobi Desert. The Gobi is particularly abundant in fossils from the late Cretaceous period, from about 98 million to 65 million years ago. The Flaming Cliffs site in Mongolia has been an especially rich source of dinosaur fossils.

Dinosaur remains have continued to turn up in the Gobi. In 1971, a Mongolian-Polish expedition uncovered the remains of a *Protoceratops,* a dinosaur about 6 feet (1.83 meters) long and 2 feet (61 centimeters) tall, with a thick neck and horns, and a *Velociraptor,* a long-tailed carnivore about the same size as *Protoceratops.* In the 1990s, a team led by American paleontologist Mark A. Norell discovered the Ukhaa Tolgood fossil field, which *The New York Times* described as the "richest vertebrate site in the world," in Mongolia.

And in 2002, anthropologists discovered a new species of sauropod, *Erketu ellisoni,* an extremely long-necked creature, at Bor Guve, a recently excavated site also located in Mongolia. The expedition was sponsored by the American Museum of Natural History in New York City and the Mongolian Academy of Sciences, which continue to sponsor joint fossil expeditions to the region.

See also:
Hedin, Sven.

Further Reading

Man, John. *Gobi: Tracking the Desert.* New Haven, CT: Yale University Press, 1999.

H

HAKLUYT SOCIETY

1582: English geographer and writer Richard Hakluyt publishes *Divers Voyages Touching the Discoverie of America,* advocating settlement of North America
1589: Hakluyt publishes *Discoveries of the English Nation,* considered the most comprehensive geography of his time
1846: The Hakluyt Society is founded on December 15 in London

Founded in 1846 to publish primary and secondary works pertaining to early expeditions, the London-based Hakluyt Society took its name and inspiration from sixteenth-century geographer Richard Hakluyt.

The Hakluyt Society held its first meeting on December 15, 1846, in the London Library at St. James's Square. The society was organized largely through the efforts of geographer and historian William Desborough Cooley.

In Cooley's view, it was important that the scientific study of geography be placed in historical context. Cooley himself wrote several works supporting this approach, among them *The Negroland of the Arabs Examined and Explained; Or, an Inquiry into the Early History and Geography of Central Africa* (1841) and *Inner Africa Laid Open* (1852), which described the geographic features of the little-known African interior.

Cooley had wanted to name the society for Christopher Columbus, but the governing council, whose members in the first year included Charles Darwin, decided on naming it for Richard Hakluyt, an early advocate of English overseas expansion. Hakluyt was born about 1552 and attended Westminster School, then Christ Church School at Oxford University. He graduated from Oxford with a bachelor's degree in 1574 and a master's degree in 1577.

While at Westminster, Hakluyt had discovered a map in his cousin's library and been intrigued by how it was compiled and by his cousin's stories about explorers. From that point on, Hakluyt had devoted his studies to geography.

As a lecturer on the subject at Oxford, he discussed the changing nature of maps and called attention to the possibilities for English overseas expansion. He insisted that, because of the explorations of John Cabot—who, in 1497, while sailing under the English flag, landed near Labrador, Newfoundland, and explored the coast of northeastern Canada—England had a rightful claim to America that preceded the Spanish claim to the continent. Hakluyt insisted that England had been remiss in failing to press

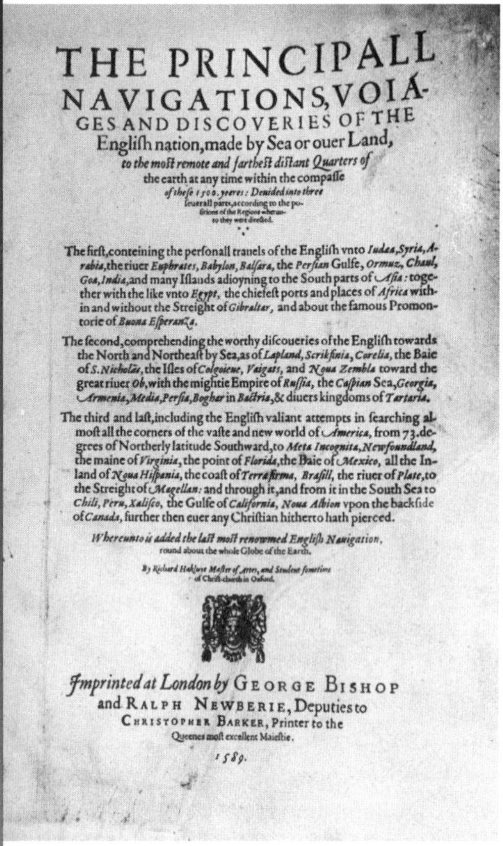
THE PRINCIPALL NAVIGATIONS, VOIAGES AND DISCOVERIES OF THE English nation, made by Sea or ouer Land, *to the most remote and farthest distant Quarters of* the earth at any time within the compasse *of these 1500. yeeres: Deuided into three* seuerall parts, according to the positions of the Regions whereunto they were directed.

The first, conteining the personall trauels of the English vnto *Iudaea, Syria, Arabia*, the riuer *Euphrates, Babylon, Balsara*, the *Persian* Gulfe, *Ormuz, Chaul, Goa, India*, and many Islands adioyning to the South parts of *Asia*: together with the like vnto *Egypt*, the chiefest ports and places of *Africa* within and without the Streight of *Gibraltar*, and about the famous Promontorie of *Buona Esperanza*.

The second, comprehending the worthy discoueries of the English towards the North and Northeast by Sea, as of *Lapland, Scrikfinia, Corelia*, the Baie of *S. Nicholas*, the Isles of *Colgoieue, Vaigats*, and *Noua Zembla* toward the great riuer *Ob*, with the mightie Empire of *Russia*, the *Caspian* Sea, *Georgia, Armenia, Media, Persia, Boghar* in *Bactria*, & diuers kingdoms of *Tartaria*.

The third and last, including the English valiant attempts in searching almost all the corners of the vaste and new world of *America*, from 73. degrees of Northerly latitude Southward, to *Meta Incognita, Newfoundland*, the maine of *Virginia*, the point of *Florida*, the Baie of *Mexico*, all the Inland of *Noua Hispania*, the coast of *Terra firma, Brasill*, the riuer of *Plate*, to the Streight of *Magellan*: and through it, and from it in the South Sea to *Chili, Peru, Xalisco*, the Gulfe of *California, Noua Albion* vpon the backside of *Canada*, further then euer any Christian hitherto hath pierced.

Whereunto is added the last most renowmed English Nauigation, round about the whole Globe of the Earth.

By Richard Hakluyt Master of Artes, and Student sometime of Christ-church in Oxford.

Imprinted at London by GEORGE BISHOP and RALPH NEWBERIE, Deputies to CHRISTOPHER BARKER, Printer to the Queenes most excellent Maiestie.

1589.

English geographer Richard Hakluyt, namesake of the London-based scholarly society and publisher, produced his landmark work—*The Principall Navigations, Voiages, and Discoveries of the English Nation*—in 1589. *(Eliot Elisofon/Time & Life Pictures/Getty Images)*

its rights and argued that great benefits would accrue from developing the eastern North American coast south of the French settlements in Canada and north of the Spanish settlements in Florida. In addition, he called for the English to search for the Northwest Passage.

In advocating for North American settlement, Hakluyt made contact with many sea captains, merchants, and sailors. In 1582, he published a work, *Divers Voyages Touching the Discoverie of America,* in which he advocated the colonization of America. Two years later, he wrote the tract *Discourse of Western Planting,* which he presented to Queen Elizabeth I in support of a plan by Sir Walter Raleigh to settle North America.

About this time, Hakluyt was appointed chaplain to the English ambassador to France. He lived in Paris for five years. There he collected information for the English government on French overseas expeditions as well as those of other countries. As Hakluyt put it, he made "diligent inquriie of such things as might yield any light unto our western discoverie in America."

Hakluyt published his greatest work, *The Principall Navigations, Voiages, and Discoveries of the English Nation,* in 1589. The compendium included the firsthand accounts of sea captains and explorers, stories about strange lands and sea monsters, and, in a later edition, a plea for the colonization of Virginia. Hakluyt died on November 23, 1616.

The declared mission of the Hakluyt Society today is "to advance knowledge and education by the publication of scholarly editions of primary records of voyages, travels and other geographical material." Toward that end, it has published more than 200 works of scientific findings from expeditions around the globe, focusing on geography, ethnology, and natural history. In addition to publishing scholarly texts, the society organizes meetings, symposia, and conferences to promote exploration, cultural encounters, and specific organizational goals.

Further Reading

The Hakluyt Society. http://www.hakluyt.com.

Mancall, Peter C. *Hakluyt's Promise: An Elizabethan's Obsession for an English America.* New Haven, CT: Yale University Press, 2007.

HANBURY-TENISON, ROBIN (1936–), AND MARIKA HANBURY-TENISON (1938–1982)

1936: Robin Hanbury-Tenison is born on May 7 in Cornwall
1938: Marika Hanbury-Tenison, née Hopkinson, is born in London
1971: The Hanbury-Tenisons live among the Xingu people in Brazil
1974: The couple travels to the outer islands of Indonesia
1982: Marika dies of cancer
1998: Robin returns to Mulu on the island of Borneo

Cornish explorer, conservationist, and writer Robin Hanbury-Tenison and his wife, English explorer and food writer Marika Hanbury-Tenison, focused their scientific efforts on the ethnographic study of indigenous peoples, whom they worked to save from the displacement caused by modern developments.

Robin was born on May 7, 1936, in Cornwall and educated at Oxford University. Marika was born in London in 1938 to John and Alexandra Hopkinson. Robin and Marika were wed in 1959 and eventually had two children.

By the time of their marriage, Robin had engaged in two expeditions, one to South Asia and one to South America. The latter included the first land crossing of the continent at its widest point. To make this crossing, he traversed mountains and muddy swamps, attaching pieces of wood to his jeep in order to keep from sinking. In the mid-1960s, he journeyed across the Sahara Desert by camel; he also made the first river crossing of South America from north to south, beginning at the Orinoco River in Venezuela and finishing at Buenos Aires, Argentina.

Marika, meanwhile, began her career writing about cooking and went on to author several cookbooks and magazine articles. Beginning in 1968, and continuing until her death in 1982, she was the food editor at a London newspaper, the *Sunday Telegraph*. In 1971, not long after the birth of their second child, Marika accompanied her husband on a three-month trip to live among the Xingu people of Brazil and record their way of life.

The expedition was sponsored by Survival International, an organization Robin had helped found. At the time, the Xingu were being forced from their native land by development, and the Hanbury-Tenisons recorded how the tribe was faring in the encampments in which it had been placed. Survival International was formed to help protect indigenous people from such dislocation and thereby protect their cultural practices.

Upon the couple's return, Marika published a book about the expedition, titled *Tagging Along* in the United States and *For Better, For Worse: To the Brazilian Jungle and Back Again* in England (both 1972). In this book, she wrote,

> For me, the expedition to South America had been an awakening, I had met and lived with the Amerindian tribes who form so large a part of the work of Survival International. . . . These beautiful, fine, intelligent, amazing people should be saved from the kind of degradation, loss of pride, and the straight wiping out of their kind which will inevitably occur unless something revolutionary happens—and happens fast.

In 1973, Robin published a follow-up book, a plea on behalf of indigenous peoples titled *A Question of Survival for the Indians of Brazil.*

The couple set out again the following year, this time to the outer islands of Indonesia. Again, they lived with the native tribes and, as in Brazil, studied the effects of displacement. Their ethnographic findings and plea for the protection of threatened native peoples were captured in Malika's book *Slice of Spice* (1974) and Robin's *A Pattern of Peoples: A Journey Among the Tribes of Indonesia's Outer Islands* (1975).

From 1977 to 1978, Robin Hanbury-Tenison led the largest expedition ever organized by the Royal Geographical Society, taking a group of 115 scientists to the interior of Sarawak in Borneo. Out of this expedition came his groundbreaking book, *Mulu: The Rain Forest* (1980); this work played a major role in focusing world attention on the threat to tropical rain forests.

Back at the couple's farm in Cornwall, Marika was diagnosed with cancer. She died in 1982, at age forty-four. Robin was remarried the following year, to Louella Williams Edwards, who accompanied him on several subsequent expeditions.

In 2009, Robin Hanbury-Tenison published *The Land of Eagles,* a book about his travels through Albania. The *London Times,* meanwhile, dubbed him "the greatest explorer of the past 20 years." After a return trip to Mulu in 1998, he wrote,

> The rate of destruction of the world's forests has accelerated so dramatically that the end is in sight. My return to Mulu . . . showed me that the time has come to stop tilting at windmills and feel[ing] better by protesting without success at all that has gone wrong. Now our only hope is to take part in helping to save what is left, restore what has been damaged and make sure that, if we are not too late, it never happens again.

Further Reading

Hanbury-Tenison, Marika. *Tagging Along.* New York: Coward, McCann and Geoghegan, 1972.

Hanbury-Tenison, Robin. *A Pattern of Peoples: A Journey among the Tribes of Indonesia's Outer Islands.* New York: Charles Scribner's Sons, 1975.
———, ed. *The Seventy Great Journeys in History.* New York: Thames and Hudson, 2006.
———. *Worlds Apart: An Explorer's Life.* Boston: Little, Brown, 1984.

HEDIN, SVEN (1865–1952)

1865: Born on February 19 in Stockholm, Sweden
1890: Begins serving as an interpreter for a Swedish diplomatic mission to Persia
1894–1897: Makes his first major expedition to Central Asia
1900: Discovers the ancient Chinese city of Loulan
1904: Publishes *Scientific Results of a Journey in Central Asia, 1899–1902*
1906–1908: Undertakes his third expedition to Central Asia
1926: Organizes the Sino-Swedish expedition to northwestern China
1952: Dies on November 26 in Stockholm

A geographer, explorer, and prolific researcher and writer, Sven Anders Hedin of Sweden led several expeditions into Central Asia, compiling extensive scientific data about the region and its history. In addition to providing essential information for the detailed mapping of Central Asia, Hedin is known for his explorations of the Gobi Desert and the discovery of several important archaeological sites.

Hedin was born on February 19, 1865, in Stockholm, Sweden, to Ludvig Hedin, the chief architect of the city, and Anna Berlin Hedin. As a boy, Sven was attracted to exploration through the exploits of Finnish-Swedish mineralogist and explorer Adolf Erik Nordenskjöld, who had traversed the Northeast Passage along the Arctic shores of Europe and Siberia. When Nordenskjöld returned to Sweden in 1880, Sven's father took the boy to see him. Hedin later said that he remembered the scene, with its huge crowds and jubilant celebration, for the rest of his life.

Hedin's first journey of any distance came after his graduation from high school, when he traveled to the Russian city of Baku to tutor a Swedish boy. Located at the foot of the Caucasus Mountains on the Caspian Sea, Baku gave Hedin his first taste of Central Asia, which became another lifelong attraction. Hedin entered Stockholm University in 1886, followed by Uppsala University, where he took up the study of geography. From 1889 to 1890, he attended the University of Berlin for advanced studies under Germany's leading geographers.

Bookish and small in stature, Hedin appeared to be more the scholar than the adventurer, but he proved effective at combining both interests.

Swedish explorer and travel writer Sven Hedin made a host of notable discoveries, including the Trans-Himalaya Mountains and the ancient city of Loulan in northwestern China, on three major expeditions to Central Asia. *(Time & Life Pictures/ Getty Images)*

From 1890 to 1891, he served as an interpreter for a Swedish diplomatic mission to Persia (now Iran). From Tehran, he was able to travel to Mount Damāvand, where he measured the elevation of the peak (his figures turned out to be inaccurate) and recorded the weather patterns and vegetation.

Leaving Tehran again in September 1890, Hedin traveled east across northern Persia and then turned north, reaching Kashgar, the westernmost town in China, in December. From there, he traveled to Lake Issyk Kul in Russia, where he visited the grave of Nikolai Przhevalsky, a famous Russian explorer whom the young Swede greatly admired; two years earlier, Hedin had translated Przhevalsky's works.

From this trip, Hedin learned much about how to organize a major expedition, including the bringing together of equipment, servants, guides, and the necessary animals.

Central Asian Expeditions

Hedin went on to organize and lead three major expeditions to Central Asia. During the first, which lasted from 1894 to 1897, he attempted to climb Muztagata in the Pamir Mountains, but failed. (Known as "the roof of the world," the Pamirs of Tajikistan, Kyrgyzstan, Afghanistan, and Pakistan are among the highest mountains anywhere.) Nevertheless, he made valuable observations of the region's lakes, streams, and glaciers and became the first to map the Muztagata massif.

The highlight of Hedin's second expedition, from 1899 to 1902, was his discovery of the remains of the ancient oasis city of Loulan in the Gashun Gobi desert of northwestern China. The expedition had found an old riverbed called Kuruk Daria and followed it for more than 150 miles (240 kilometers), when a guide inadvertently came across the remains of Loulan, an important outpost on the ancient Silk Road well before the Christian era. At the site, Hedin uncovered the ruins of houses, ancient Chinese writings, and other remains and sent them to archaeologists for further study.

Returning to Loulan in 1901, Hedin discovered a dried-up lake bed. Research led him to conclude that in approximately 330 C.E. there had been a dramatic change in a northern lake, called Lop Nur, and the Tarim River, whose lower branch was Kuruk Daria. The river's water no longer flowed in the same bed, and the northern Lop Nur had dried up; in the meantime, two new lakes had formed, creating a southern Lop Nur. The shift in the river, he concluded, had caused the inhabitants to abandon Loulan.

According to Hedin, the Tarim and its tributaries had changed course because of the collection in their waters of silt from windblown desert sand over hundreds of years. Because the desert regions to the north had been decimated by windstorms, he maintained, the elevation of the land had declined and the bottoms of the southern Lop Nur lakes were rising. Thus, he predicted, the water eventually would return to its previous beds. Hedin's theory was proven accurate in 1921, when Kuruk Daria again filled with water and the northern Lop Nur was restored. (Kuruk Daria dried up again in 1976 after being dammed for irrigation; this caused both the northern and southern Lop Nur to dissipate.)

In 1903, Hedin published a travel book, *Central Asia and Tibet,* about his first expedition. The work proved highly popular and was translated into a number of foreign languages. The expedition, and in particular the discovery of Loulan, earned Hedin widespread acclaim from the scientific

THE SILK ROAD

Founded in the second century B.C.E., the town of Loulan sat astride the Silk Road in what is now the Xinjiang Autonomous Region of northwestern China. The Silk Road was not a single thoroughfare, but a shifting network of trade routes—established around 100 B.C.E.—that connected China with the Middle East. The main route extended thousands of miles from Chang'an (modern Xi'an) in China west to Antioch in Turkey.

Although the network was named for the precious commodity of silk, which was carried on it from one continent to another, many other items were transported along its vast distances. Seldom, though, did one merchant or caravan travel the Silk Road's entire length. Rather, a series of caravans would be used to transport goods.

The various routes of the Silk Road traversed deserts and high mountains, forcing travelers to overcome a wide range of terrain and weather conditions ranging from sandstorms to frigid temperatures. Looters who lived in the deserts and steppes would raid the caravans, and towns along the route demanded payments for passage. All in all, it was a dangerous and expensive way to trade.

Nevertheless, the Silk Road thrived for some 1,500 years, until it was superseded by sea travel. For even though traders risked their lives and fortunes along the road, the traffic between the East and the West was highly profitable. The wealthy of Europe and western Asia were willing to pay handsome prices for desired Chinese products, such as silk and porcelain.

The trade did little to enrich the empires of the time, but it did enrich individual merchants and communities. Moreover, trade along the Silk Road encouraged the exchange of ideas, art, and technology. Among other things, the Silk Road helped spread Buddhism from northern India to China.

community. Britain's Royal Geographical Society awarded him its Victoria Medal for "the highest record of geographical research."

Hedin's next major publication, from 1904 to 1907, was *Scientific Results of a Journey in Central Asia, 1899–1902*, totaling six volumes (the last two were compiled by contributors). The set included a map showing the physiographic features of the Chechen and Lop deserts—the sand, clay, and water sources—along with detailed information about the Tarim River and the formation and movement of sand dunes in the surrounding desert. The third and fourth volumes focused on Tibet. Again, the Royal Geographical Society singled out the Swede for his fortitude in exploring Central Asia and his thoroughness in reporting the results.

Hedin's third expedition began in 1906 and ended in 1908. With a caravan of camels, servants, and two cavalrymen, he journeyed across Persia. In the course of this expedition, Hedin located the sources of the Indus, Brahmaputra, and Sutlej rivers in western Tibet. For the Indus, he pinpointed the springs from which the headwaters flowed. He recounted his journey in *Transhimalaya* (1909), a two-volume work (later supplemented by a third volume) containing maps of the region and a detailed narrative of what he had found in the Tibetan highlands. In it, he wrote,

> Among the results of my voyage are two hundred specimens of rocks, fossils from two places, 68 panoramas, 162 sheets of maps, over 100 portraits of natives, and between 400 and 500 photographs.

During the period 1913–1918, Hedin immersed himself in national conservative politics, advocating the rearmament of Sweden. He also found time to write *Southern Tibet* (1917–1922) a multivolume work on the physical geography of a large part of Central Asia published between 1917 and 1922. It was a land, he noted, that had been inadequately explored before his journey. He wrote,

> As to the Central Transhimalaya, it was absolutely unknown. . . . I went out to fill up the blanks, so far as my forces allowed.

Notable details included the altitude of each of the 482 camps made by Hedin in western Tibet. Contributors to volume six analyzed Hedin's 1,200 rock samples. Other contributors analyzed Hedin's meteorological observations—such as air pressure, humidity, and wind speed—and his astronomical data. The London *Times* stated, "For our latter-day geographical knowledge of Tibet, we owe more to the author of this work than to any other explorer."

Sino-Swedish Expedition

Resuming his explorations, Hedin organized and led the Sino-Swedish Expedition of 1926–1935, which focused on the northwestern provinces of China. This was much more of a group effort than his previous expeditions. Different teams of scientists established weather stations and collected archaeological, botanical, geological, and ethnographic information.

Their work was hampered, however, by failure to obtain permission from the Chinese government to conduct airplane flyovers. Hedin himself was taken captive by a Chinese general and briefly detained as an enemy spy. Nevertheless, the work of the scientific staff yielded several major reports—fifty-four volumes published between 1937 and 1982, with others still in progress.

Between 1931 and 1940, Hedin wrote four books for general readers, mainly about the Gobi Desert. Perhaps because of his affinity for German culture and conservative politics, or perhaps out of his desire to see Soviet communism contained, Hedin was a firm supporter of Nazi Germany, and he maintained personal contacts with Adolf Hitler and other high German officials. He did use his correspondence with them to request pardons for those condemned to death and the release of concentration camp prisoners.

In his last years, Hedin, who lived with three family members in a house in Stockholm, wrote his political memoirs and an autobiography. He died from a viral infection on November 26, 1952. He left behind a massive collection of published works totaling about 30,000 pages and a legacy of having scientifically revealed "the heart of Asia."

Further Reading

Haslund, Henning. *Men and Gods in Mongolia.* London: K. Paul, Trench, Trubner, 1935.

Hedin, Sven. *My Life as an Explorer.* New York: Kodansha International, 1996.

Kish, George. *To the Heart of Asia: The Life of Sven Hedin.* Ann Arbor: University of Michigan Press, 1984.

See also: Nordenskjöld, Adolf Erik.

HENSON, MATTHEW (1866–1955)

1866: Born on August 8 in Charles County, Maryland
1891: Arrives in Greenland with American explorer Robert E. Peary
1906: With Peary, comes within 175 miles (280 kilometers) of the North Pole
1909: With Peary, reaches the North Pole on April 6
1912: Publishes autobiography, *A Negro Explorer at the North Pole*
1955: Dies on March 10 in New York City

An African American explorer known for his technical skills, Matthew Henson provided crucial leadership during Robert E. Peary's historic expedition to the North Pole in 1909. Henson accompanied Peary on all eight of the latter's Artic voyages and was selected, along with four Eskimos, for the final run to the North Polar regions in April 1909.

Matthew Henson was born on August 8, 1866, in rural Charles County, Maryland, about 40 miles (65 kilometers) south of Washington, D.C. His parents, who had been free blacks in the era of slavery, struggled to make ends meet as tenant farmers. When Matthew was still a child, the family moved to Washington, where jobs were more available. After the death of his mother, however, Matthew and his siblings were sent to live with a nearby uncle. Matthew completed the sixth grade and then dropped out of school. When his uncle could no longer support him, twelve-year-old Henson obtained work as a cabin boy on the merchant ship *Katie Hines*. He had been attracted to the sea by stories he had heard from sailors who ate at a restaurant where he worked.

Henson worked on the *Katie Hines* for five years, during which time he traveled to such lands as Japan, China, the Philippines, France, and Spain—exotic locales for a young American. The captain of the ship took a special liking to him, taught him about navigation, and encouraged him to read. When the captain died, however, Henson left the ship. He worked at a variety of jobs for the next several years.

While employed at a men's clothing store, Henson met Robert E. Peary, who was planning to lead an engineering team to Nicaragua to survey a route for a canal through Central America. Peary asked Henson to accompany him as his servant, and Henson agreed. Before long, he was managing Peary's labor camp of nearly 150 men.

Peary next asked Henson to join him on an expedition to Greenland. They arrived there with a team of explorers in 1891. Their goal was to cross the island's northern ice cap. Henson learned from the local Inuit people how to hunt, drive a dogsled, and otherwise survive in the harsh terrain. As Peary later said, "He was more of an Eskimo than some of them."

Upon their return to New York in 1892—having crossed the ice cap—Peary praised Henson's role in the mission (in somewhat condescending terms): "Henson, my faithful colored boy, hard worker and apt at anything . . . showed himself . . . the equal of others in the party."

Henson accompanied Peary on a succession of subsequent expeditions to Greenland, including one to retrieve the three Cape York meteorites, which collided with Earth more than 10,000 years ago and whose total known weight is 58.2 tons. In 1886, they sledged deep into the interior of Greenland. In 1891 and 1892, they mapped the northern coast of Greenland. On the expedition of 1898–1902, their fourth, Peary, Henson, and four Inuits were overwhelmed by harsh conditions and were able to travel only 82 miles (130 kilometers) in sixteen days. On the expedition of 1905–1906, they came within 175 miles (280 kilometers) of the North Pole before blizzards and cracking ice sheets forced them to quit.

Peary and Henson set out once again on March 1, 1909, leaving Ellesmere Island in northern Canada accompanied by four Inuits. On April 3, Henson and his dog team hit thin ice. He fell into the frigid ocean but was saved by one of the Inuits. Peary, who could no longer continue on foot, completed the journey on dogsled. Friction between the two men developed in the latter part of the expedition, most likely over who had reached the North Pole first. The two men apparently had agreed that Peary would arrive first, but Henson and his Inuit companions inadvertently traveled ahead and arrived some forty-five minutes before Peary—who seethed.

From that point on, Peary said little to Henson and kept him at a distance. On the three-week return trip to New York, Henson later wrote,

Matthew Henson, who accompanied Robert Peary on the first successful expedition to the North Pole in 1909, had a falling out with his fellow explorer over who arrived first. It took years for Henson to win recognition for his crucial role in the mission. *(Granger Collection, New York)*

Peary said little to him: "Not a word about the North Pole or anything connected with it." At a special ceremony in Washington, D.C., the National Geographic Society awarded medals to Peary and his white colleagues but ignored Henson (and, for that matter, the Inuits).

Ultimately, however, Henson received the recognition he was due. The prestigious Explorers Club invited him to join in 1937, and the National Geographic Society awarded him the Hubbard Medal in 2000. Peary himself offered words of praise in the foreword to Henson's autobiography, *A Negro Explorer at the North Pole*, which was published in 1912.

Matthew Henson died in New York City on March 10, 1955. His body was removed to Arlington National Cemetery in 1988 and interred near the monument to Peary there. Although some have claimed that Peary and Henson never reached the North Pole, but got lost en route and missed it by hundreds of miles, most historians accept their claim to being the first there. And clearly, Henson's contribution was essential. Peary's comments before their final assault on the North Pole proved correct. "Henson must go with me," Peary said. "I cannot make it without him."

Further Reading

Counter, Allen S. *North Pole Legacy: Black, White and Eskimo*. Amherst: University of Massachusetts Press, 1991.

Henson, Matthew. *A Negro Explorer at the North Pole*. New York: Cooper Square, 2001.

See also:
Peary, Robert E.

HEYERDAHL, THOR (1914–2002)

1914: Born on October 6 in Larvik, Norway
1936: Travels to the Marquesas Islands in the South Pacific
1939: Makes archaeological discoveries in British Columbia
1947: Sails on the balsa raft *Kon-Tiki* from Peru to Polynesia
1950: Publishes best-selling account of the journey, *Kon-Tiki*
1970: Sails the Sumerian-style papyrus boat *Ra II* from Morocco to Barbados
1977–1978: Journeys aboard the *Tigris*, a reed boat, from Iraq to Pakistan
2002: Dies on April 17 in Italy

A Norwegian anthropologist, ethnologist, and adventurer, Thor Heyerdahl challenged conventional wisdom by asserting—and attempting to demonstrate—that ancient civilizations spread through extended transoceanic expeditions. Heyerdahl gained international fame for his 4,300-mile (6,900-kilometer) raft voyage from South America to the Polynesian

Islands in 1947 to support his theory that native South Americans could have settled the South Pacific.

Norwegian anthropologist Thor Heyerdahl gained international renown for a series of transoceanic expeditions to support his theory—based on myths, language, and archaeologcal remains—that ancient civilizations spread by long-distance sea travel. *(ullstein bild/ Granger Collection, New York)*

Thor Heyerdahl was born on October 6, 1914, in Larvik, Norway. His father, also named Thor, owned a brewery; his mother, Alison Lyng, studied anthropology, enthusiastically endorsed Darwinism, and was the chairwoman of the Larvik Museum. She encouraged Thor to read books about the South Sea Islands and animals, and often took him on trips to an isolated cabin in the mountains above Lillehammer. Whether acquainting him with the outdoors or directing his reading, his mother was a dominating force; according to one biographer, she "took charge of his upbringing."

Interestingly, Heyerdahl grew up fearing water after the drowning death of a schoolmate. He did not overcome his fear until age 22, when he fell into a raging river in Tahiti and swam to safety.

At the University of Oslo from 1933 to 1936, Heyerdahl studied zoology and geography. He also made friends with Bjarne Kroepelin, a wealthy Oslo wine merchant who had once lived on Tahiti and had compiled a large library. Heyerdahl pored over Kroepelin's books and papers on native society and culture on the island.

A New Theory

In 1936, Heyerdahl decided to leave the University of Oslo before graduating so he could undertake a study of the Marquesas Islands in the South Pacific. His goal was to investigate indigenous animal species to determine their origins and methods of survival.

Shortly after arriving with his bride, Liv Coucheron, on Fatu Hiva, Heyerdahl found himself more interested in the native human culture than in animal life. He learned the local language and legends, including the story of an ancient god-king named Tiki who was said to have brought the settlers of the Marquesas from "the east."

Heyerdahl began to consider how the Polynesian people might have arrived on the remote Pacific islands. His research, including a study of stone monuments, suggested that the islands had been settled by people from pre-Inca Peru. In 1937, after spending a year with Liv on Fatu Hiva—"living as Adam and Eve," as he put it—she and Heyerdahl returned to Norway where he published a book about his experience, *On the Hunt for Paradise* (1938). With his work now heavily oriented toward anthropology, in 1939

Heyerdahl discovered rock carvings made by prehistoric Pacific Northwest Indian tribes in British Columbia that bore a striking resemblance to those of the ancient Polynesians. The discovery lent support to a theory he had been working on: that members of these Indian tribes had settled in Polynesia. Heyerdahl had hypothesized that Polynesia had been settled partly by people from pre-Inca Peru and partly by Indian fishing people from the Pacific Coast of North America.

Heyerdahl's emerging theory ran counter to the prevailing scientific view, according to which Polynesia had been settled by Asians who had journeyed slowly—island by island—from west to east across the expanse of the Pacific Ocean. As he put it in a manuscript written shortly before he traveled to British Columbia,

> Only in the islands farthest to the east—Easter Island and the Marquesas group—were they [the Northwest Indians] forced to conquer an earlier culture—people, probably offshoots from the highly civilized Indo-American branch in Peru.

Heyerdahl next conducted research in Peru and found more evidence to support his theory. He heard the legend of a fair-skinned people who, in the time before the Incas, had worshipped a sun god named Kon-Tiki. A competing tribe was said to have killed most of the fair-skinned people in about 500 C.E., though a few of the latter escaped. Heyerdahl surmised that it was these fair-skinned survivors who set out west across the ocean and colonized several uninhabited Polynesian islands. He theorized that they sailed on rafts made of balsa logs and, after arriving, carved stone statues (such as the ones he had seen in the Marquesas) similar to those found in Peru.

When the Spanish arrived in Peru in the sixteenth century, Heyerdahl learned, the Incas told them that colossal monuments there had been built by "white gods" who once had lived in the region. And when Europeans arrived in the Polynesian Islands in the mid-1700s, Heyerdahl was told, they were shocked to find fair-skinned people living among those with golden brown skin. Indeed, when Jakob Roggeveen discovered Easter Island in 1722 he was surprised to find fair-skinned natives.

Voyage of the *Kon-Tiki*

With the outbreak of World War II, Heyerdahl served as a parachutist for the free Norwegian forces. When the war ended, he tried to get a publisher interested in his manuscript about the connection between Polynesian society and the Americas, but found no interest. He resolved to demonstrate how ancient peoples could have made just such a connection.

BUILDING THE *KON-TIKI*

When Thor Heyerdahl set out to build the *Kon-Tiki,* he wanted it made from balsa logs, as rafts in pre-Inca America had been. Getting the logs was not easy.

First, Heyerdahl traveled to a jungle town called Quivedo, at the foot of the Andes in Ecuador, where he harvested the logs from a plantation. The logs then were transported downriver to the harbor of Guayaquil. From there, they were taken by coastal steamer to the seaport town of Callao, Peru.

At Callao, Heyerdahl found himself in a crowded harbor with no room for building the raft. Fortunately, Peru's president allowed the *Kon-Tiki* to be built on a naval base. Heyerdahl later described the construction of the raft:

> Nine of the thickest logs were chosen. . . . Deep grooves were cut in the wood to prevent the ropes which were to fasten them and the whole raft together from slipping. Not a single spike, nail or wire rope was used in the whole construction. . . . The longest log, 45 feet long, was laid in the middle and projected a long way at both ends.

The sides of the raft measured 30 feet (9 meters) long. Once the thickest logs were bound together, thinner logs were placed and fastened crosswise over them, and a deck was attached atop part of the surface. There also was a small, open cabin and, forward of it, two masts made from mangrove wood. As Heyerdahl wrote,

> The whole construction was a faithful copy of the old vessels in Peru and Ecuador except for the low splash-boards in the bows, which later proved to be entirely unnecessary.

The 45-foot (14-meter) balsa raft *Kon-Tiki,* modeled after sailing vessels used by the ancient Inca, carried its six-member crew across the Pacific Ocean from Peru to Polynesia in 101 days. *(Keystone/Stringer/Hulton Archive/Getty Images)*

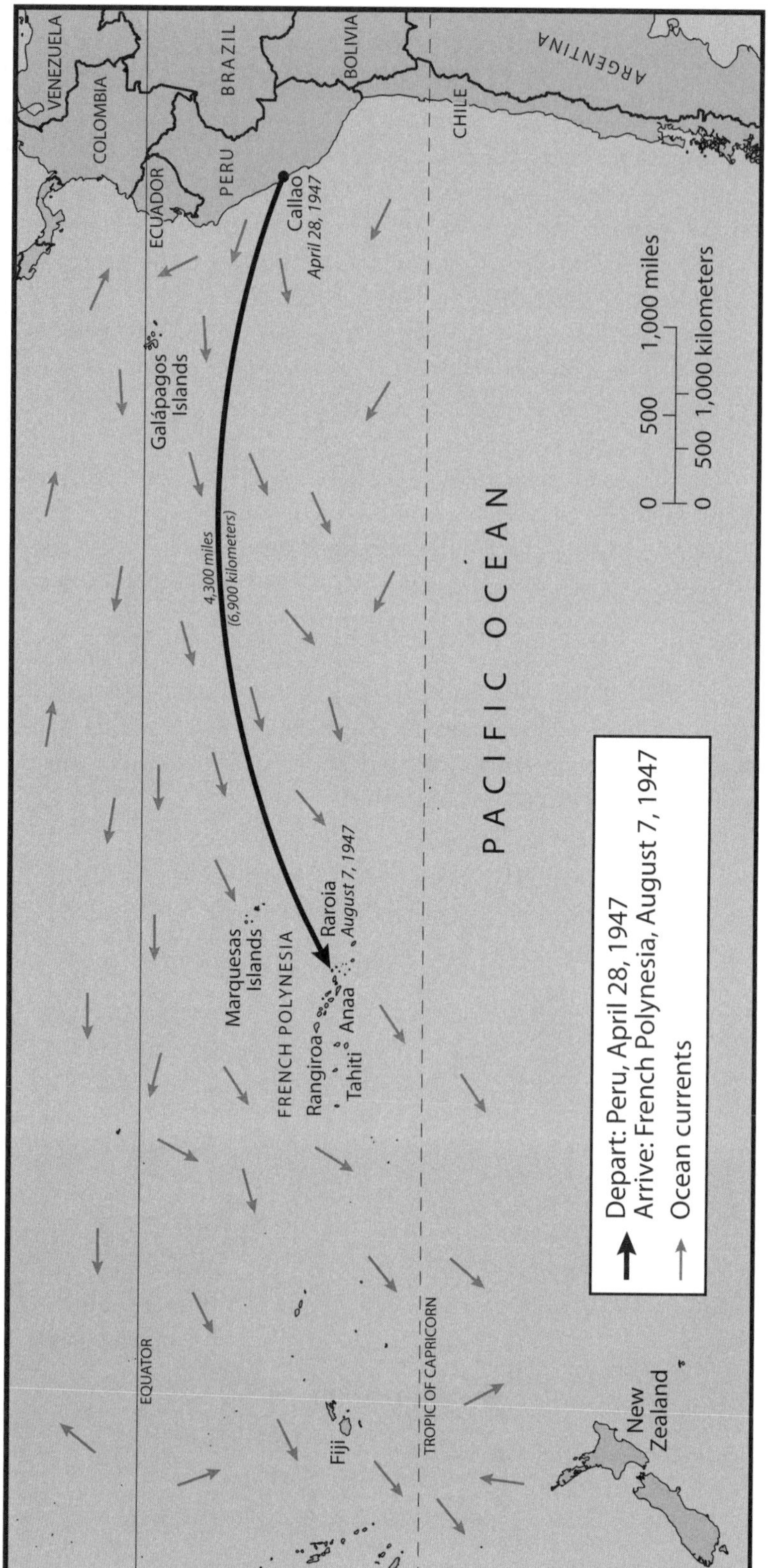
VENEZUELA
COLOMBIA
ECUADOR
PERU
BRAZIL
BOLIVIA
CHILE
ARGENTINA
Callao
April 28, 1947
Galápagos Islands
4,300 miles
(6,900 kilometers)
Marquesas Islands
FRENCH POLYNESIA
Raroia
August 7, 1947
Rangiroa
Tahiti
Anaa
Fiji
New Zealand
EQUATOR
TROPIC OF CAPRICORN
PACIFIC OCEAN
0 500 1,000 miles
0 500 1,000 kilometers
Depart: Peru, April 28, 1947
Arrive: French Polynesia, August 7, 1947
Ocean currents

To do so, Heyerdahl and his team built a raft like those known to have been used by pre-Inca Indians and determined to sail it west from Peru across the Pacific Ocean. Coconut juice in hand, he christened the raft *Kon-Tiki* and set sail on April 28, 1947, from Callao, Peru, with five fellow adventurers. On August 7, having sailed 4,300 miles (6,900 kilometers) in 101 days, the team landed safely on a reef at Raroia in the Tuamotu Islands.

Their exercise in what has come to be called "experimental archaeology" thus proved that ancient peoples could have made just such a journey and dispelled the long-held notion that a balsa-log raft would absorb too much water on an extended voyage and sink. Based on the expedition, Heyerdahl wrote a book titled *Kon-Tiki* (1950), which became a best seller and was printed in fifty languages. A documentary film of the same name, compiled from footage shot by the crew, won an Academy Award in 1951.

With the end of the *Kon-Tiki* expedition, Heyerdahl reiterated and expanded his thesis about the settlement of Polynesia. The region, he claimed, was settled by a people who had sailed from Peru aboard rafts like the *Kon-Tiki*. Sometime around 1100 B.C.E., he surmised, they were overrun by American Indians from the Pacific Northwest.

Heyerdahl's research into the oral history of people on Easter Island was said to support his view, as did archaeological evidence. Moreover, he stressed, ocean currents lent further support, sweeping from the Pacific Northwest, along the coasts of the Americas, and into the South Pacific. Contrary to the claims of some scientists, Heyerdahl never denied that Polynesians came from Asia. But they did so, he said, via the Pacific Northwest—first sailing east across the far Northern Pacific, following the ocean currents to North America, and then following the ocean currents south and west into the South Pacific.

In 1953, Heyerdahl journeyed with two anthropologists to the Galápagos Islands, located in the Pacific Ocean some 600 miles (950 kilometers) off the coast of South America. There they found nearly 2,000 ceramic sherds from pottery created before the arrival of the Spanish and resembling pottery made in South America before the Incas.

Easter Island and Voyages of the *Ra* and *Ra II*

From 1955 to 1956, Heyerdahl organized and led a team called the Norwegian Archaeological Expedition to Easter Island, where they engaged in excavations that led to three massive scientific reports and a popular book by Heyerdahl titled *Aku-Aku* (1958). One anthropologist described the new book as "science, adventure, human warmth, excitement, drama on a high level."

From his research, Heyerdahl theorized that Easter Island was originally settled by the "Long Ears" from South America, who were later displaced by the "Short Ears," or Polynesians. According to Heyerdahl, this explains why Roggeveen found fair-skinned people living among the Polynesians, but when James Cook arrived in 1774 he found almost all Polynesians.

In 1969, Heyerdahl built another ancient-style vessel, a papyrus ship called the *Ra,* which he intended to sail across the Atlantic Ocean from Morocco to the Americas. The purpose was to demonstrate the seaworthiness of reed boats and thereby show how ancient mariners, such as those from Egypt, could have crossed the ocean, settled the Americas, and founded the Aztec and Inca civilizations. Such a migration, Heyerdahl believed, could explain why the temples of ancient Peru resemble those of ancient Egypt.

Although the *Ra* collapsed about 600 miles (950 kilometers) short of its destination of Barbados, a sturdier vessel the following year, the *Ra II,* successfully completed the journey. While in the Atlantic, Heyerdahl sampled the ocean waters for signs of pollution. He became an outspoken critic of the industrial pollution of the world's oceans, especially from oil. "We seem to believe the ocean is endless," he said, "but we use it like a sewer." Heyerdahl recounted the reed boat voyage in *Ra Expeditions* (1971).

Aboard the *Tigris*

In late 1977, Heyerdahl undertook another expedition, this one to show how the ancient Sumerians of Mesopotamia could have engaged in trade and migration with the civilizations of the Indus River Valley. In another reed boat, the *Tigris,* he made his way from Iraq to Pakistan through the Persian Gulf and then headed southwest across the Arabian Sea toward the African coast. In April 1978, however, entry into the Red Sea was blocked due to wars in the Horn of Africa. Heyerdahl declared the expedition over, burned the *Tigris* at Djibouti in an act of protest, and wrote an open letter to the secretary-general of the United Nations "against the inhumane elements in the world."

In his book *Early Man and the Ocean* (1978), Heyerdahl directly challenged the assumptions of mainstream academics about early sea travel. A watertight hull, he wrote, was in fact less secure than a wash-through bottom, a feature on the *Kon-Tiki.* Moreover, he contended, a bigger ship with greater height above sea level was not necessarily more secure than a small one, and coastal travel was more dangerous than sailing across the open ocean.

Heyerdahl later investigated mounds on the Maldive Islands and theorized that people from Sri Lanka had settled there. He stirred controversy yet again in 2002, claiming in his book *Jaketen pa Odin (The Search for Odin)* that a tribe from Azov in Russia had migrated to Denmark and

PACIFIC OCEAN CURRENTS

Of all the world's oceans, the Pacific is by far the largest—indeed, it is larger than all of the others combined. Coursing through it, moreover, is a complex of currents that are crucial in determining the routes taken by early European explorers and, according to Thor Heyerdahl, were important in the ancient settlement of Polynesia.

When European explorers sailed across the Pacific Ocean, they generally traveled from east to west, following the prevailing currents. If, upon reaching the western Pacific, the explorers wanted to return to the Americas, they generally took a northern route that coincided with the Kuro Shiro (Japan) Current. This flowed from Japan east to the Aleutian Islands and then southeast to the Pacific Northwest. Bucking such currents was difficult in the sailing vessels of the time.

According to Thor Heyerdahl, ancient Asians would have taken the Kuro Shiro Current to North America. From there, they would have followed the North Equatorial Current into what is called the "Polynesian Triangle," whose apex is Hawaii in the north and whose base is formed by New Zealand to the west and Easter Island to the east.

Pre-Inca peoples journeying from South America would have followed the South Equatorial Current into the heart of the triangle occupied by the Marquesas, Tuamotu, Society, and Fuji islands. It was this current that Heyerdahl followed in his voyage on board the *Kon-Tiki.*

settled Sweden in the first century C.E. This conclusion was based on an archaeological expedition he conducted in 2001, but critics called the research "pseudoscience."

Thor Heyerdahl died of cancer on April 17, 2002, while vacationing in Italy. His findings remain controversial, and modern genetic research has called into question his theory regarding American Indian settlement of Polynesia. According to Heyerdahl, though, his expeditions proved that early human beings could have traveled thousands of miles across open oceans with the vessels they had at hand. He said, "I feel that the burden of proof now rests with those who claim the oceans were . . . a factor in isolating civilizations."

Further Reading

Evensberget, Snorre. *Thor Heyerdahl: The Explorer.* Oslo, Norway: J.M. Stenersens Forlag A/S, 1994.

Heyerdahl, Thor. *Green Was the Earth on the Seventh Day.* New York: Random House, 1996.

Kon-Tiki Museum. http://www.kon-tiki.no.

Ralling, Christopher. *The Kon-Tiki Man: Thor Heyerdahl.* London: BBC Books, 1990.

HORNER, JOHN R. (1946–)

1946: Born in Shelby, Montana, on June 15
1977: Finds a dinosaur egg in Montana
1978: Finds a nest at Willow Creek, Montana, that contains eggshell fragments and 3 foot-long (1-meter-long) dinosaur bones
1986: Receives a "genius grant" from the MacArthur Foundation
2000: Finds the largest collection of *T. Rex* fossils to date at Fort Peck Reservoir in Montana

The American paleontologist John R. "Jack" Horner has revolutionized his field with a massive number of fossil discoveries and the conclusions he has drawn from them. Among other breakthrough accomplishments, he discovered a new dinosaur genus, *Maiasaura,* and was the first to suggest that some dinosaurs cared for and fed their young.

Horner was born on June 15, 1946, in Shelby, Montana, to John and Miriam Horner. He did poorly in school because of dyslexia, a condition undiagnosed until after his childhood. As Horner later recalled,

> No one had any expectations of me becoming a scientist on account of my being so bad in school. Every year my mother called the teachers to see if I was passing to the next grade. I really don't think anyone had any expectation that I would be anything more than a gas station attendant.

At any early age, however, he had a strong interest in dinosaurs. "My mother took me on trips to visit areas where dinosaurs came from because she just liked to sightsee," he later wrote. At age eight, he discovered his first dinosaur bone.

Horner was drafted into the U.S. Marines in 1966 and spent the next two years in Vietnam. Upon his return, he attended the University of Montana for seven years, attempting to complete a college degree in geology and zoology. Having a hard time maintaining his grades, he finally gave up on college in 1973 and entered the family gravel and sand business. Two years later, however, largely on the strength of his senior thesis in college, the Museum of Natural History at Princeton University hired Horner to clean and assemble fossils collected from digs. That job turned out to be a crucial turning point in Horner's life because it allowed his talent for paleontology to be recognized and provided him with an important entry into the field of science.

Then, in 1977, while back in Montana, Horner found what his colleagues at the museum confirmed to be a dinosaur egg. The following year, he and a friend, Bob Makela, made a monumental discovery. While searching the Two Medicine Formation at Willow Creek in Montana, they unearthed a bowl-shaped nest complete with eggshell fragments and 3 foot-long (1-meter-long) dinosaur bones. This was the first such nest, or egg clutch, ever found in the Americas, and the fossils turned out to be a new species of hadrosaurs, a duck-billed dinosaur from about 75 million years ago. With funding from the Princeton museum, Horner resumed his exploration at Willow Creek, where he found more nests and the remains of numerous adult hadrosaurs. He then received additional funding from the National Science Foundation.

While Horner was adept at finding fossils, he also proved skillful at interpreting them. He concluded that hadrosaurs stayed in their nests for several months and that their movement within the nests explained the crushed shells. Furthermore, Horner maintained, the young hadrosaurs were raised and fed by one or both parents, 30-foot-long (9-meter-long) creatures he designated *Maiasaura peeblesorum*.

At the same site, which he called Egg Mountain, Horner also found intact hypsilophodontid eggs with fully formed fetuses in them.

THE QUESTION OF DINOSAUR GROWTH

The long-held view that dinosaurs were cold-blooded, slow-growing reptiles has been challenged by more recent research such as that of John Horner.

In fact, Gregory Erickson, an evolutionary biologist and paleontologist at Florida State University, has hypothesized that dinosaurs grew quite rapidly. "All dinosaurs, primitive and advanced, large or small, grew at rates accelerated beyond those of typical reptiles today," Erickson claimed in 2001. The growth rates in dinosaurs, he maintained, are linked to size, with small dinosaurs likely to have grown more slowly than large ones.

In 2008, paleontologists at the University of California at Berkeley tied dinosaur growth rates to life cycles. According to one researcher, Robert Sanders, dinosaurs grew throughout their lives but, much like mammals, grew most rapidly during adolescence. As one paleontologist stated,

> This is an exciting finding because age at reproductive maturity is related to so many things. It also shows that you can't use reptiles as a model for dinosaur growth, as many scientists still do.

The Berkeley researchers agreed with Erickson that growth rates were linked to dinosaur size. They disagreed, however, on the correlation between size and growth rate; they speculated that smaller creatures grew more rapidly than larger ones.

Despite the presumed close relationship between dinosaurs and reptiles, dinosaurs grew faster than living reptiles do, and their bones had a larger blood supply. Moreover, among living vertebrates, only birds and mammals exhibit growth rates such as those of dinosaurs, another factor supporting the theory that these ancient ancestors were indeed warm-blooded.

Hypsilophodontids were small, gazelle-like dinosaurs, possibly the ancestors of hadrosaurs. This discovery was another first in the annals of paleontology. Horner called this new species *Orodromeus makelai.*

In 1986, Horner received a "genius grant" from the MacArthur Foundation and an honorary doctorate from the University of Montana. In 2000–2001, working at Fort Peck Reservoir in Montana, Horner found the largest *Tyrannosaurus Rex* to date. The giant meat eater is estimated to have weighed between 10 and 13 tons (9 and 12 metric tons). Since then, Horner has joined with French paleontologists in studying fossilized dinosaur tissue. His findings have helped confirm the theory of some paleontologists, beginning with John Ostrom, that certain dinosaurs were warm-blooded. Horner has become especially known for his research on dinosaur growth. He has been trying to figure out how quickly dinosaurs grew and how long they lived.

Horner has published more than 100 professional papers, six popular books, and numerous articles. He was the technical advisor for three Hollywood movies: *Jurassic Park, The Lost World (Jurassic Park II),* and *Jurassic Park III,* ensuring that the dinosaurs looked as accurate as possible based on the scientific evidence of the time. He teaches at Montana State University in Bozeman and is the curator of paleontology at the Museum of the Rockies. In fact, Horner has compiled an impressive list of accomplishments for someone who said of his early years, "When I was a kid I thought I was a real idiot, and I'm sure everybody else thought so, too."

Further Reading

Horner, John, and Edwin Dobb. *Dinosaur Lives: Unearthing an Evolutionary Saga.* San Diego, CA: Harcourt Brace, 1998.

Patent, Dorothy Hinshaw. *In Search of the Maiasaurs.* New York: Benchmark Books, 1999.

HUMBOLDT, ALEXANDER VON (1769–1859)

1769: Born in Berlin, Germany, on September 14
1790: Travels to England with George Forster, who had sailed the Pacific with British explorer James Cook
1792: Hired by the Prussian government as a mine inspector
1799: With botanist Aimé Bonpland, sets sail for South America
1800: Explores the Orinoco River in Venezuela
1804: Returns to Paris and begins work on a thirty-volume account of his expedition
1827: Becomes an advisor to the king of Prussia

1829: Travels to Russia for geological studies of Siberia and the Ural Mountains
1845: Publishes his highly acclaimed five-volume work, *Cosmos*
1859: Dies on May 6 in Berlin

A giant in the field of natural history, the German scientist and explorer Alexander von Humboldt made notable contributions to a variety of disciplines and, at the same time, pioneered a holistic view of nature. He was also an active advocate of the popularization of science and among the first to represent rigorous scientific data in graphic form.

Alexander von Humboldt was born in Berlin on September 14, 1769, to Alexander George von Humboldt and Maria Elizabeth von Colomb, who had inherited considerable wealth from a previous marriage. His father was a major in the Prussian army and died when the youngster was only nine years old. As a child, Alexander liked to collect plants, shells, and insects but was frail and showed little indication he would be able to withstand the rigorous expeditions he would engage in as an adult.

As a student at Göttingen University beginning in 1789, Humboldt studied physics, chemistry, and geology. His interest in botany and exploration was piqued as well by his friendship with George Forster, who had sailed with British explorer Captain James Cook as the scientific illustrator on Cook's second voyage to the South Pacific. The friendship with Forster only intensified Humboldt's desire to travel, and in 1790 he traveled with Forster to England.

Mine Inspector

Two years later, Humboldt was hired as government mines inspector in Franconia, Prussia. This proved to be a life-defining event for the young man, helping to shape his scientific interests and expertise. In his capacity as an inspector, he traveled extensively, studied vegetation and geographic stratification, and designed improved breathing equipment for miners. In 1795, Humboldt traveled privately to the Swiss and French Alps, where he studied geomagnetism and the effects of altitude and climate on plant life.

In 1796, at age twenty-seven, Humboldt inherited a significant sum of money from his mother, which enabled him to quit his job and devote himself to scientific exploration. From the start, he set his sights on creating a science that would reflect the unity and diversity of nature. This type of study, he believed, required exploration.

Humboldt had come to believe that the distribution of plants in a particular location depends on environmental influences and that these, in turn, shape human life. To understand how plants grow, he maintained, they

The great German naturalist Alexander von Humboldt is portrayed on his five-year expedition to South America (1799–1804), collecting specimens along the Orinoco River. *(Granger Collection, New York)*

have to be studied in their natural state. His research in plant geography, moreover, was to be based on a holistic perspective. He wrote,

> [The] observation of individual parts of trees or grass is by no means to be considered plant geography. Rather plant geography traces connections and relations by which all plants are bound together among themselves, designates in what lands they are found, in what atmospheric conditions they live . . . and describes the surface of the earth in which humus is prepared.

Ultimately, Humboldt no longer classified plants merely on the basis of their outward appearance, as had been the case since the time of Linnaeus. Instead, he followed the recommendation of German philosopher Immanuel Kant to classify plants based on their appearance in nature and how they relate to other plants.

Journey to the Americas

With French botanist Aimé Bonpland, Humboldt sailed to South America in 1799, equipped with the latest in scientific instruments. By the time they sailed, expeditions of discovery had become wedded with those of science, with an ever-greater emphasis on recording and measuring natural phenomena accurately and collecting specimens for study. In 1769, for example, the year of Humboldt's birth, the French naval officer and explorer Louis-Antoine de Bougainville had brought discovery and science together in his voyage to the South Pacific. Such was the case, too, with James Cook, whose voyage was clearly a powerful inspiration to Humboldt.

As he and Bonpland readied to leave Europe, Humboldt wrote,

> In a few hours we sail around Cape Finisterre. I shall collect plants and fossils and make astronomic observations. But that's not the main purpose of my expedition—I shall try to find out how the forces of nature interact upon one another and how the geographic environment influences plant and animal life. In other words, I must find out about the unity of nature.

Humboldt and Bonpland reached Venezuela on July 16, 1799. From there they sailed to Havana, Cuba, then back to Venezuela and overland to Colombia, Ecuador, and Peru in a journey of five years' duration. While in South America in 1800, they traversed the Orinoco River and traveled through a remote inland delta called the Casiquiare Canal. It was a dangerous trip through virtually unknown land teeming with alligators, jaguars, and biting insects. Humboldt nevertheless mapped some 1,700 miles (2,750 kilometers) of the river, and the two explorers showed that the Orinoco and the Amazon form a unified river system.

Humboldt climbed Mount Chimborazo (in modern-day Ecuador) to an elevation of about 19,000 feet (5,800 meters), and at Quito he studied several volcanoes, concluding that they were linked to subterranean fissures. When he and Bonpland sailed to Mexico in 1803, Humboldt discovered and traced the ocean current—which today bears his name—off the Peruvian coast. From Mexico, he traveled again to Havana and then to Washington, D.C., where he met President Thomas Jefferson, a fellow naturalist. He and Jefferson exchanged scientific views and became good friends.

Humboldt and Bonpland returned to Paris in 1804, carrying a vast amount of scientific information about the Americas. Humboldt had measurements of the geomagnetic field, temperatures, and barometric pressure; he had extensive maps; and he had a collection of 60,000 plants, many of them previously unknown. Not long after his return, Humboldt told the Paris Institute of his discovery that the earth's magnetic force decreases in strength from the poles to the equator.

Scientific Publications and Journey to Russia

Humboldt's house in Paris became a gathering place for intellectual discussions. As much could be learned from a one-hour conversation with the German naturalist as from reading several books. His renown spread around the world, and he spent the next twenty-one years compiling thirty volumes of material from his expedition to the Americas. The work was published in sections between 1807 and 1825, under the title *Personal Narrative of Travels to the Equinoctial Regions of the New Continent.* It was packed with tables, diagrams, maps, and measurements, testimony to his exacting attention to detail. The breadth and depth of his observations are reflected in these varied statements:

> I have just given a list of more than 200 tribes spread over a space a little larger than France; these tribes believe themselves to be at least as foreign to each other as the English, the Danes, and the Germans.

> Venezuela is one of the countries in which the parallelism of the strata of gneiss-granite, mica-slate and clay-slate, is most strongly marked. The general direction of these strata is N. 50° E., and the general inclination from 60° to 70° north-west.

> The movement of the barometer at Bogotá is of surprising regularity. . . . [And] in the town of Mexico . . . the barometric heights scarcely differ from 2 to $2^{1/2}$ millimeter during whole months.

Between 1814 and 1825, Humboldt also published a three-volume work on his expedition for popular audiences. At the same time, he pioneered the use on maps of isothermal lines (or isolines), which connect places that have the same atmospheric pressure or temperature. This makes it possible to compare climates across regions.

Humboldt preferred living in Paris to Berlin, which he thought too provincial, but in 1827 he returned there to serve as an advisor to the king of Prussia. The position provided him with a much-needed income, as his travels and the expense of publishing his works had consumed much of his wealth. Berliners welcomed Humboldt enthusiastically, packing the halls where the scientist presented a series of lectures in 1827 and 1828. In the latter year, Humboldt organized an international scientific conference.

In 1829, at the invitation of the czar of Russia, Humboldt explored east into Siberia and followed up the trip with his three-volume *Asie Centrale.* He advised the Russian government to set up weather stations to gather climate data and data on magnetism. From the information collected, he

HUMBOLDT'S INSTRUMENTS

When Alexander von Humboldt traveled to South America in 1799, he took with him a variety of scientific instruments that reflected new developments in manufacturing, as well as the increasing focus of expeditions of discovery on rigorous scientific research. Among the instruments Humboldt carried were:

1. Chronometer—a precision timepiece used in determining longitude.
2. Theodolite—used to measure horizontal and vertical angles in surveying, it had just become a modern instrument, in terms of accuracy, in the 1780s.
3. Dipping needle—a magnetized needle designed to rotate freely in a vertical plane in order to measure the Earth's magnetic field.
4. Hygrometers—two thermometers, one with a wet bulb and the other with a dry one, in order to measure humidity.
5. Eudiometer—a long glass cylinder invented in 1775 to measure the change in the volume of gas following a chemical reaction; it was used by Humboldt to measure the quantity of oxygen in the atmopshere.

In addition to these instruments, Humboldt took with him telescopes, sextants, quadrants, compasses, a pendulum, and devices for measuring electrical charges and the color of the sky.

formulated his "principle of continentality," in which he stated that the interiors of continents have more extreme climates than coastal regions because they are removed from the moderating influences of the oceans.

In 1845, at age seventy-six, Humboldt published the first book of his five-volume masterwork, *Cosmos*, which was critically acclaimed and translated into nearly every European language. The first four volumes appeared during his lifetime (1845–1862) and the last posthumously. He coined the word *cosmos* to represent what he understood as the "ordered system of the global environment." Thus, a recurring theme of *Cosmos* is the link among diverse environments; for example, he wrote, plants and animals are all affected by the same laws of temperature as they relate to altitude and latitude. In a letter to a friend before starting to write, Humboldt outlined his purpose:

> I have the crazy notion to depict in a single work the entire material universe, all that we know of the phenomena of heaven and earth, from the nebulae of stars to the geography of mosses and granite rocks—and in a vivid style that will stimulate and elicit feelings.

Cosmos presented the universe as an orderly, natural world consisting of interconnected environments. This view made Humboldt, in many ways, an environmentalist. He warned about the implications of exploiting natural resources and emphasized how effects on one part of the natural world can affect other parts. Even as a consummate scientist, however, Humboldt also allied himself with the Romantic movement of his time, recognizing a beauty in nature that science could never measure. Or, as he put it,

> The stars as they sparkle in the firmament fill us with delight and ecstasy, and yet they all move in orbit marked out with mathematical precision.

An inspiration to the work of many later scientists—and a direct supporter of several, including Charles Darwin—Alexander von Humboldt died on May 6, 1859, in Berlin.

Although scientific research has become increasingly specialized since his time, Humboldt's holistic approach reshaped modern thinking about the natural world. Perhaps his method was best represented by an engraving he produced shortly after his return from South America. It was a cross-sectional profile of the Andes from the Atlantic to the Pacific at the latitude of Mount Chimborazo, showing where plant and animal species lived, the zone of vegetation, geological structure and rock types, temperatures, and other meteorological facts. In short, it was a visual tour de force of the mutual reliance in the natural world that complemented the tour de force of Humboldt's own scientific life.

"What a man he is!" said the great German intellectual Johann Wolfgang von Goethe of Humboldt. "He is everywhere at home."

Further Reading

Botting, Douglas. *Humboldt and the Cosmos.* New York: Harper and Row, 1973.

De Terra, Helmut. *The Life and Times of Alexander von Humboldt.* New York: Alfred A. Knopf, 1955.

Helferich, Gerard. *Humboldt's Cosmos: Alexander von Humboldt and the Latin American Journey That Changed the Way We See the World.* New York: Gotham, 2004.

Sachs, Aaron. *Humboldt Current: A European Explorer and His American Disciples.* Oxford, UK: Oxford University Press, 2007.

I

INTERNATIONAL GEOPHYSICAL YEAR

1950: The idea for the International Geophysical Year (IGY) is discussed at a meeting of American scientists
1957: The IGY begins on July 1
1957: The Soviet Union launches the world's first artificial satellite, *Sputnik*, on October 4
1958: The United States launches its first satellite, *Explorer I*, on January 31
1958: The IGY ends on December 31

The International Geophysical Year (IGY; 1957–1958) was a coordinated effort by countries around the world to scientifically study the Earth's polar regions and equator.

The idea for the IGY came from a meeting of American scientists at Silver Spring, Maryland, in August 1950. In a discussion about recent methods and devices developed for geophysical studies, such as radar, rockets, and computers, the scientists began considering how an international effort could be launched to study physical phenomena on the planet. This led to a proposal to establish the IGY to coordinate with a series of eclipses and an expected upsurge in sunspot activity.

The IGY was formally sanctioned by the International Council of Scientific Unions and scheduled to run for eighteen months, from July 1, 1957, through December 31, 1958. Scientific organizations from more than seventy nations took part in IGY committees and activities. IGY research focused primarily on the polar regions and equator in such areas as geomagnetism, ionospheric physics (the study of the uppermost part of the Earth's atmosphere), mapping, meteorology, oceanography, seismology, and solar studies.

As part of the program, a permanent research station was built at Antarctica and instruments were readied for use, along with the rockets and balloons that would carry them. Concerned that data from these explorations might be lost—as had happened when World War II disrupted the analysis of information from the International Polar Year of 1932–1933—participating countries established the World Data Center System to collect and store the data. One World Data Center was set up in the United States, a second in the Soviet Union, and a third was shared by Western Europe, Australia, and Japan. Arrangements also were made to make public any and all information collected as part of the initiative, an impressive commitment in a world divided by cold war suspicions.

As part of the IGY, on October 4, 1957, the Soviet Union launched *Sputnik,* the first man-made satellite to orbit the Earth. The launch raised considerable fear and controversy, as the satellite was carried into space aboard a military rocket, which seemed to violate the peaceful emphasis of the IGY. Despite these concerns, *Sputnik* contributed valuable information to the IGY data by detecting meteoroids and measuring the density of high atmospheric layers and the distribution of radio signals in the ionosphere. In late January 1958, the United States launched its own first satellite, *Explorer I,* which measured cosmic rays.

Among other notable accomplishments, IGY efforts included the discovery of the Van Allen radiation belts (based on Geiger counter data ob-

Space scientists William Pickering, James Van Allen, and Wernher von Braun (left to right) celebrate the successful launch of *Explorer I,* America's first Earth satellite, in January 1958. It was the signature U.S. accomplishment of the International Geophysical Year. *(Rue des Archives/ Granger Collection, New York)*

tained from *Explorer I*), confirmed the existence of underwater mid-ocean ridges, charted ocean depths and currents, measured atmospheric winds, and studied Antarctica's ice sheets. The work in Antarctica convinced several participating countries that continued scientific research there required peaceful cooperation; this, in turn, led to the signing of a treaty to keep the continent a military-free zone and to encourage additional scientific work.

See also: Space Exploration, Unmanned.

Further Reading

Marshack, Alexander. *The World in Space: The Story of the International Geophysical Year.* New York: Thomas Nelson, 1958.

The National Academies, International Geophysical Year. http://www.nas.edu/history/igy.

Sullivan, Walter. *Assault on the Unknown.* New York: McGraw-Hill, 1961.

INTERNATIONAL POLAR YEAR

2007: The International Polar Year (IPY) begins in March
2008: Scientists from the University of Dresden measure the effects of glacial melting on Greenland
2008: The research vessel *Knorr* investigates the Arctic haze
2009: International Polar Year ends in March

The International Polar Year (IPY) was a collaborative scientific effort to study the Arctic and Antarctic. Organized through the International Council for Science and the World Meteorological Organization, IPY 2007–2009 was the fourth polar year. It followed those in 1882–1883, 1932–1933, and 1957–1958; the latter was broadened in scope to become the International Geophysical Year.

Beginning in March 2007, IPY enlisted the efforts of an estimated 50,000 scientists from more than sixty nations, conducting more than 200 projects to investigate physical, biological, and social issues associated with the polar regions. In one project, scientists from the University of Dresden in Germany measured the Greenlandic mainland in 2008 to see how much the landmass was rising, as glaciers on it were melting. Another team of scientists sailed to the Orkney Islands in the North Atlantic to study the makeup of the toxins jellyfish release in attacking their prey.

Scientists working for the National Oceanic and Atmospheric Administration (NOAA) in the United States researched the "Arctic haze." This reddish-brown haze began appearing over the Arctic in the 1950s. Its origins were unknown at the time. It has now been determined that it is a mix of dust, black carbon, and chemical pollutants from factories, vehicles, and other sources in Europe and Western Asia.

Heads of world environmental and meteorological organizations gather in Paris for the opening of International Polar Year in March 2007. This global scientific effort focused on the role and plight of the Arctic and Antarctic environments. *(Stephane de Sakutin/Stringer/AFP/Getty Images)*

In March and April 2008, the *Knorr,* a specially equipped research vessel operated by the Woods Hole Oceanographic Institution in Massachusetts, sailed nearly 7,400 nautical miles (13,700 kilometers) on expeditions to study Arctic air and water. On trips to the west coast of Norway and into the ice-free waters of the Arctic Ocean, researchers studied how industrial particles influence the destruction of the ozone and measured the air quality near smelters located in Norway and Russia. In all, the *Knorr* collected seventy sets of air filter samples to be analyzed by scientists.

For example, researchers measured particulate sulfate in the Arctic haze and found that the sulfate had originated in Eastern Europe, perhaps from the burning of crops. According to Patricia Quinn, a chief scientist of the project,

> Our goal . . . will be to determine the climate impact of these pollutants and how they, in addition to greenhouse gases, are contributing to the warming of the Arctic.

The International Polar Foundation, headquartered in Belgium, was responsible for building the first zero-emission polar science station for use in Antarctica. The prefabricated station, which cost more than $16 million, was intended to contribute to data on climate change.

Finally, in an effort to involve laypersons, the IPY undertook a number of educational projects. These included interactive programs on the Internet and connections to blogs reporting on developments at the poles.

Further Reading

International Polar Year. http://www.ipy.org.

J

JONES, ALBERT JOSÉ (CA. 1935–)

ca. 1935:	Born in Washington, D.C.
1950:	Begins service in U.S. Army, where he starts his diving career
1959:	Founds the all-black Underwater Adventure Seekers scuba diving club in Washington, D.C.
1972:	Begins teaching at the University of the District of Columbia
1973:	Earns Ph.D. in marine biology from Georgetown University
1989:	Explores Moroccan coast in northern Africa
1992:	Studies marine life in the Red Sea as part of his research into marine ecosystems

An African American scuba diver and marine scientist, José Jones has been called the "Black Jacques Cousteau" because of his accomplishments in undersea exploration.

Albert José Jones was born in Washington, D.C., about 1935. (He has refused to divulge the exact date of his birth to biographers.) Orphaned at an early age, he was raised by an aunt. As a teenager, he developed a strong interest in teaching, which remains central to his life's work.

From 1950 to 1953, Jones served in the U.S. Army during the Korean War and earned a Purple Heart. While in Korea, he was attracted to the martial art Tae Kwan Do. Over the years, he became an expert in it, earning a sixth-degree black belt and winning the U.S. heavyweight championship.

Jones's interest in scuba diving and oceanography also began during his years in the service, when he took a combat swimming course at Fort Campbell in Kentucky. Returning to his native Washington, he obtained a B.S. degree in biology from the District of Columbia Teachers College in 1959 and began a career as a high school teacher. During his senior year in college, he founded an all-black dive club, the Underwater Adventure Seekers (UAS), training members at a swimming pool at Howard University; they became perennial champions in scuba rodeo and spearfishing tournaments. Jones twice won the Mid-Atlantic Scuba Diving Championship.

In 1960, Jones began two years of study at the University of Queensland in Australia as a Fulbright Scholar, devoting his efforts to photographing and collecting marine specimens. Upon returning to Washington, he continued to teach high school and began working on a master's degree in aquatic biology, which he obtained from Howard University in 1968.

Jones began teaching marine science at the University of the District of Columbia (UDC) in 1972; he earned his doctorate in marine biology from Georgetown University the following year. In 1975, he was named one of the Outstanding Educators of America. During his more than twenty-five years at UDC, he served as chairman of the Environmental Science Department and held several administrative positions, including acting provost.

His research in the 1970s focused on reef fishes in the Caribbean Sea, including barracuda, and invertebrates such as sponges. In his ongoing exploration of the world's oceans, he noticed a decline in marine life, which he attributed largely to pollution. He began consulting with various nations on protecting their marine ecosystems.

In 1989, he explored the entire coast of Morocco, and, in 1992, he studied marine life in the Red Sea. In 1993, he led a team of divers in exploring the *Henrietta Marie*, a slave ship from the 1600s, which sunk about 35 miles (55 kilometers) southwest of Key West, Florida. The divers placed a plaque at the underwater site to commemorate the many Africans who had been hauled across the Atlantic Ocean in bondage.

In the meantime, Jones, along with Ric Powell, founded the National Association of Black Scuba Divers (NABS) in 1991. Under Jones's presidency and chairmanship, the NABS has formed more than fifty affiliated clubs in the United States and other countries.

Jones has published numerous scholarly articles and has made more than 6,000 dives around the world. He is married to Paula Cole Jones, who also is an accomplished diver.

Further Reading

National Association of Black Scuba Divers. http://www.nabsdivers.org.
Reef, Catherine. *Black Explorers*. New York: Facts On File, 1996.

K

KINGDON-WARD, FRANK (1885–1958)

1885: Born on November 6 in Manchester, England
1908: Makes his first trip to the Far East, travels to western China
1911: Collects 200 plant species in China and Tibet
1924: Finds the blue poppy of Tibet, or *Meconopsis betonicifolia*
1958: Dies April 8 in London

English horticulturalist Francis ("Frank") Kingdon-Ward is known for his explorations of the Far East, from which he brought back hundreds of previously unseen varieties of plants and shrubs. He has been referred to as the "last of the great plant hunters."

He was born on November 6, 1885, in Manchester, England, to Harry Marshall Ward, a distinguished botanist, and Selina Mary Kingdon, taking his mother's maiden name and his father's surname as a hyphenated last name. In 1904, Kingdon-Ward began his higher education in Christ's College at Cambridge, where his father was a professor of botany.

Two years later, after the death of his father, Frank left school to find work. In 1908, he was recruited for a zoological expedition to western China—the first of his more than twenty-five trips to the Far East. There, he discovered a new species of mouse and began collecting plant specimens.

Kingdon-Ward returned to China in 1911 under commission from a commercial seed company to collect plants. From his travels through Yunnan Province and Tibet, he brought back to England some 200 species, of which twenty-two had been unknown, along with seeds for cultivation. Two years later, he published a book, *Land of the Blue Poppy,* which recounted the expedition. In the account of his journey to the Yangtze River, he wrote,

> Just below A-tun-tsi, I found a purple-flowered Morina . . . and growing on a limestone cliff at 13,000 feet [4,000 meters] was a small Pmguicula [an insect-eating plant known as the bog violet]. . . . I also came across a pretty twining Codonopsis convolvulacea with large mauve flower. . . . One day we made the complete circuit of the high mountainous ridge to the west, Kin [a guide] having discovered what he considered a practicable route. However, before I knew what was coming he had led me to the brink of a clear drop of some thirty feet high. . . . In my descent, I stuck half way down in fear of my life, while Kin, standing on the screes [broken rock] below, encouraged me with shouts of "Don't be afraid! Don't be afraid!" Finally I got down.

In 1924, Kingdon-Ward returned to Tibet to gather plants and to look for the falls of the Yarlung Zangbo River (the highest major river in the world); according to local folklore, the falls were large enough to hide all the people of Tibet. He did find a waterfall, Rainbow Falls, but at 40 feet high (10 meters) it was much less impressive than legend had it. (Years later another waterfall was found nearby; it combined with Rainbow Falls to form a cascade of about 120 feet, or 35 meters.)

More notably, Kingdon-Ward brought back with him the blue poppy, *Meconopsis betonicifolia.* The plant had been discovered in 1866, and a specimen was collected by an Englishman in 1922 and pressed into a book. But Kingdon-Ward returned with the first seeds that were able to be cultivated. The poppy became a main attraction at horticultural shows in England. Its stunning beauty attracted botanists and gardeners alike: its large petals, measuring 3–4 inches (8–10 centimeters), displayed a vivid blue in a silky, cup-shaped form, topped by golden anthers in the center. Kingdon-Ward said, "Never before have I seen a poppy which held out such hopes of being hardy, and of easy cultivation in Britain."

In 1950, during an expedition to the Lohit gorge on the border of Assam (northeastern India) and Tibet, Kingdon-Ward experienced a massive earthquake. The rockslides trapped him and his wife, Jean Rasmussen, for several days. They escaped by crossing a flooded river on a temporary bridge. In the early 1950s, on a trip to Burma, he collected thirty-seven species of rhododendrons and found a honeysuckle called *Lonicera hildebrandiana.*

Kingdon-Ward wrote a total of twenty-five books, most of them accounts of his plant-hunting expeditions. He received numerous honors, including medals from the Royal Horticultural Society and the Royal Scottish Geographical Society.

He died in London on April 8, 1958, and was buried near Cambridge. At his gravestone was planted a flowering, evergreen shrub, *Berberis calliantha,* a specimen he had collected during his Yarlung Zangbo expedition and a testament to his botanical contributions.

Further Reading

Christopher, Tom, ed. *In the Land of the Blue Poppies: The Collected Plant Hunting Writings of Frank Kingdon Ward.* New York: Modern Library, 2003.

Lyte, Charles. *Frank Kingdon-Ward: The Last of the Great Plant Hunters.* London: J. Murray, 1989.

KINGSLEY, MARY (1862–1900)

1862: Born on October 13 in Islington, England
1892: Undertakes an expedition to West Africa along the Gulf of Guinea
1894: Journeys again to West Africa and studies the Bube people
1895: Begins living with the Fang tribe in French Congo
1897: Publishes *Travels in West Africa*
1899: Publishes *West African Studies*
1900: Dies on June 3 in Simonstown, Cape Colony (South Africa)

Taking part in two dangerous expeditions to West Africa, Mary Kingsley became the most famous English woman explorer of the late 1800s. Her writings and lectures on African culture, which she staunchly defended against Europeans who categorized it as inferior, proved highly popular and changed Western views.

Mary Henrietta Kingsley was born on October 13, 1862, in Islington, England. Her father, George Kingsley, was a wealthy physician and travel writer who tended to the ills of dukes and earls but spent most of his time globetrotting. Her mother, Mary Bailey, was a servant whom George married only because she was pregnant with their daughter. George never accepted his wife into his circle of society, and she lived a largely isolated existence, an invalid bedridden by psychological stress. Their daughter Mary was thus isolated as well, for she was expected to take care of her mother and did so from childhood until she was thirty years of age.

Mary saw her father only infrequently; he spent long periods overseas. She was educated by private tutors and sequestered herself in her father's library, where she found her best friends to be books. There, she later wrote, "I had a great world of my own."

She especially loved books about travel, adventure, and foreign lands. Notable among these was *Two Trips to Gorilla Land* (1876), by the explorer Richard Burton, which she found fascinating for his recollection of the Fang people in Africa—among whom Kingsley later lived. She also was attracted to stories about the English explorer David Livingstone and the respect he showed for African culture; the French-American explorer Paul Belloni Du Chaillu; and Pierre Savorgnan de Brazza, sometimes called "the greatest French explorer of his time," who wrote about his perilous forays into West and Central Africa.

She became increasingly interested in chemistry, ethnography, and anthropology, as well. When she moved with her family to Cambridge in 1884, she befriended and exchanged ideas with a number of university professors.

African Expeditions

Mary Kingsley's father and mother died within weeks of each other in 1892. Freed from the lonely and stressful days under her parents and enriched by money inherited from her father, she decided to journey to West Africa.

The exact reasons for her decision remain obscure. At one point, Kingsley said that she wanted to finish a book on African culture begun by her father. At another point, she insisted that she wanted to go there to die but instead became interested in African society. If she wanted to die, it may well have been because of what she discovered shortly before leaving England: evidence among her father's papers that she was conceived out of wedlock and born just four days after her parents married. The news embarrassed her.

In 1893, at the age of thirty-one, Mary Kingsley set sail aboard the *Lagos* and arrived first in Sierra Leone and then in Angola. From there, she traveled north, mostly by land, to several locations along the Gulf of Guinea: Cabinda, French Congo, Cameroon, and Calabar. Kingsley usually traveled alone and lived with the local tribes, from whom she learned about

On two bold journeys to west-central Africa in the 1890s, Mary Kingsley lived with a variety of local tribes, became familiar with their customs, and returned to England with a unique collection of insights, artifacts, and natural history specimens. *(Granger Collection, New York)*

the native culture and how to survive. Insects were a recurring problem; driver ants were especially nettlesome, traveling in vast armies, invading houses and tents, eating food supplies, and attacking people.

During her travels, she collected several specimens of exotic fish, which she later shared with Albert Charles Gunther, head of the zoological department at the British Museum. He, in turn, advised her on methods of collecting and preserving her specimens.

Of all the places she visited, Kingsley was most attracted to the equatorial forest of the French Congo. Of it, she wrote,

> On first entering [its] . . . grim twilight regions you hardly see anything but the vast column-like grey tree stems in their countless thousands around you. . . . But day by day, as you get trained to your surroundings, you see more and more, and a whole world grows up gradually out of the gloom before your eyes. Snakes, beetles, bats, and beasts people the region that at first seemed lifeless.

Upon returning home later in 1893, Kingsley felt a deep emptiness; she felt unattached to life in London and began pining for Africa. The African continent, she said, gives pain "by calling you." The following year, she listened to the call and returned to West Africa.

On the island of Fernando Po in Equatorial Guinea she studied the Bube people, who lived in small villages. Then, she journeyed down the Ogowe River in the French Congo. Setting out on June 5, 1895, she became an expert canoeist and collected specimens of fish, shells, and insects along the way.

ON AFRICAN INTELLIGENCE

In her book *Travels in West Africa* (1897), Mary Kingsley marshaled anthropological evidence to refute those who considered African tribal peoples inferior to Europeans:

> You will frequently meet with the statement that the negro child is as intelligent, or more so, than the white child, but that as soon as it passes beyond childhood it makes no further mental advance. [The explorer Richard] Burton says: "His mental development is arrested and thenceforth he grows backwards instead of forwards. . . ." A man [the African] is, but not of the same species; and his cranial sutures do, I agree, close early; indeed I have seen them almost obliterated in skulls of men who have died quite young; but I think most anthropologists are nowadays beginning to see that the immense value they have a few years since set upon skull measurements and cranial capacity, &c., has been excessive and not to have so great a bearing on the intelligence as they thought. There has been an enormous amount of material carefully collected, mainly by Frenchmen, on craniology . . . I think you will see for practical purposes such considerations as weight of brain, or closure of sutures, &c., are negligible and so we need not get paralysed with respect for "physiological causes."

Entering a dangerous area of the lower Ogowe, Kingsley encountered the Fang tribe, with whom she lived for a time. To this day, it remains uncertain whether the Fang practiced cannibalism, but Kingsley believed they did. In any event, she admired them for holding on to their culture in the face of European influence, and she considered them smart and brave. She wrote of them,

> I have been considerably chaffed . . . about my partiality for this tribe, but as . . . these Africans have more of the qualities I like than any other tribe I have met, it is but natural that I should prefer them. . . . It is in their mental characteristics that their difference from their lethargic, dying-out coast tribes is most marked. The Fang is full of fire, temper, intelligence and go.

Later in the expedition, Kingsley became the first woman to climb 13,760-foot (4,194-meter) Mount Cameroon, following a route not previously taken by any European.

Books and the Status of Women

Kingsley returned to England in 1895. As news of her accomplishments spread, she became one of the most famous English explorers of her day. She traveled around the country giving lectures spiked with anecdotes intended to spellbind her listeners. She recollected,

> Once a hippopotamus and I were on an island together, and I wanted one of us to leave. I preferred it should be myself, but the hippo was close to my canoe, and looked like staying, so I made cautious and timorous advances to him and finally scratched him behind the ear with my umbrella and we parted on good terms. But with the crocodile it was different.

In 1897, Kingsley published a book titled *Travels in West Africa,* which became a best seller, and followed it two years later with *West African Studies.* She stirred considerable controversy with statements criticizing missionaries for trying to change tribal culture. From her perspective, Africans were not inferior to Europeans, just different. Missionaries, she wrote, "have produced results which all truly interested in West Africa must deplore."

As women's rights activists unsettled English society in the late 1800s, Kingsley opposed universal suffrage, declaring that women should stick to their own spheres of interest and that politics was not one of them. Struggling with her own contradictions, she believed that women were the equal of men but lacked the talent to participate in scientific societies. She also opposed those who were crusading to open learned groups, such as the Royal Geographical Society, to women; instead, she contended, women should pursue scientific interests on their own, and their accomplishments would prompt such societies to admit them.

Kingsley proposed the formation of a society to bring together those interested in the study of Africa, but she envisioned it as a men's society. That organization, which would become the Royal African Society, was organized in 1901, a year after her death.

On the issue of imperialism, Kingsley supported the projection of British power in Africa, but she believed this should be done by developing trade rather than through colonization. According to Kingsley, this approach would help the English economy while protecting indigenous cultures.

In 1899, Kingsley volunteered to serve as a nurse in the Second Boer War. She died from typhoid at Simonstown, in Cape Colony (present-day South Africa), while taking care of prisoners of war, on June 3, 1900.

As Kingsley saw it, Africans would be served best in their relations with Europeans by the application of scientific principles, such as ethnographic studies, that would encourage Europeans to understand Africans on their own terms. "I am not Science," she once said, "but only one of her brickmakers, and I beg you to turn to her."

Further Reading

Birkett, Dea. *Mary Kingsley: Imperial Adventuress.* New York: Macmillan, 1992.

Brown, Don. *Uncommon Traveler: Mary Kingsley in Africa.* New York: Houghton Mifflin, 2000.

Frank, Katherine. *A Voyager Out: The Life of Mary Kingsley.* Boston: Houghton

Mifflin, 1986.
Myer, Valerie Grosvenor. *A Victorian Lady in Africa: The Story of Mary Kingsley*. Southampton, UK: Ashford, 1989.

L

LEAKEY FAMILY

1903: Louis Leakey is born on August 7 in Kabete, Kenya
1913: Mary Leakey is born on February 6 in London
1942: Meave Leakey is born on July 28 in London
1944: Richard Leakey is born on December 19 in Nairobi, Kenya
1948: Mary Leakey discovers *Proconsul africanus*
1959: Mary Leakey discovers *Australopithecus boisei*
1972: Louise Leakey is born in Kenya; Louis Leakey dies on October 1
1977: Richard Leakey presents a controversial thesis about the existence of hominids
1996: Mary Leakey dies on December 9
2001: A team led by Meave Leakey discovers *Kenyanthropus platyops*

Beginning with the work of Louis Leakey in the 1930s, the Leakey family has made a succession of major discoveries that have reshaped the scientific understanding of human origins and evolution.

Louis Seymour Bazett Leakey, the patriarch of three generations of anthropologists, was born on August 7, 1903, in Kabete, Kenya (near Nairobi). His father, Harry Leakey, and his mother, Mary Bazett, were British missionaries among the Kikuyu people, whose first contact with Europeans had occurred only a short time before Louis's birth.

As a boy, Louis hunted and enjoyed bird-watching. He became interested in anthropology and the question of human origins when, in 1915, he read the book *Days Before History* (1906), in which author Henry Rushton Hall discusses European Stone Age tools.

He also learned from the Kikuyu how to speak their language (he later said he did so before he spoke English) and learned about their customs and folklore. He was initiated into the tribe at age thirteen, and the tribal chief once said of him, "We call him the black man with the white face because he is more of an African than a European."

Leakey entered Cambridge University in 1922. Two years later, he took a medical leave of absence after suffering an injury while playing rugby. The mishap proved to be fortuitous, as it allowed him to participate in an archaeological expedition to Tanganyika (today Tanzania) sponsored by the British Natural History Museum and led by the prominent Canadian paleontologist W.E. Cutler. As a part of the project, Leakey learned how to collect fossils and conduct field research.

Upon returning to Cambridge, Leakey studied under the renowned professor of anthropology Albert Cort Haddon and graduated in 1926. Two years later, he married Henrietta Avern; the couple would have two children. In 1930, Leakey obtained his doctorate from Cambridge.

Louis Leakey in East Africa

From 1926 to 1936, Leakey led four expeditions to East Africa to search for fossils he believed would provide evidence about human origins. He did so at a time when most scientists considered such a hunt in Africa to be foolish; the evidence, they said, pointed to Europe and Asia as the originating point for the human species.

In northern Tanganyika, however, the Olduvai (or Oldupai) Gorge already had proved lucrative as a source for Stone Age artifacts. Leakey scaled the gorge's sloping terrain in 110-degree-Fahrenheit (43-degree Celsius) temperatures, his eyes close to the ground as he searched and found more artifacts.

In 1936, Louis Leakey, recently divorced from Henrietta, married Mary Douglas Nicol, whom he previously had hired as a scientific illustrator. He had fallen in love with Mary while he still was married to Henrietta, and the affair caused a controversy that cost him his research fellowship at Cambridge.

Kenyan-born British paleoanthropologist Louis Leakey began the work of at least three generations of family members in the search for hominid fossils and the study of human ancestry. *(Hulton Archive/Stringer/Getty Images)*

Louis found in Mary a scientific partner every bit his equal in talent and intellect. She was born in London on February 6, 1913, to Erskine Nicol, a landscape painter, and Cecilia Frere. Even as a child, Mary showed an interest in prehistory when she studied drawings made by cave dwellers in France. She audited university courses in archaeology and geology and became an accomplished scientific illustrator before she met Louis.

Mary Leakey at Lake Victoria

In 1945, Louis Leakey became the curator at Coryndon Memorial Museum in Nairobi. Three years later, as the Leakeys continued their search for fossils, Mary made an important discovery on the island of Rusinga in Lake Victoria: She found the skull of a hominid from the Miocene period (5 million to 24 million years ago).

Hominid refers to humans or their ancestors, who, as erect bipedal mammals, are more closely related to humans than to other species. In this case, the hominid, which Louis named *Proconsul africanus*, was an apelike creature who lived 14 million to 23 million years ago; it was likely a common ancestor of humans and apes. Mary later recalled the discovery:

> I was shouting for Louis as loud as I could and he was coming, running. This was a wildly exciting find which would delight human paleontologists all over the world, for the size and shape of a [hominid] skull of this age, so vital to evolutionary studies, could only hitherto be guessed at. Ours were the first eyes ever to see a *Proconsul* face.

Mary Leakey directed systematic excavations at two early hominid sites in East Africa and made numerous discoveries that shed new light on hominid evolution. She was the wife of Louis Leakey, mother of Richard Leakey, and grandmother of Louise Leakey. *(Melville B. Grosvenor/National Geographic/Getty Images)*

Louis and Mary Leakey at Olduvai Gorge

The Leakeys began their first major excavation of the Olduvai Gorge in 1952; they expanded their search in 1960 with funds from the National Geographic Society. Over time, Louis and Mary discovered more than 100 different forms of extinct animal life in the area, including a pig as large as a rhinoceros and a short-necked giraffe.

While working in the gorge on July 17, 1959, Mary discovered *Zinjanthropus boisei*, later called *Australopithecus boisei*, a primate species that lived about 1.7 million years ago. "Zinj," as Louis called it, had a brain half the size of modern human beings.

At first, Louis thought Zinj was an ancestor of human beings, but his ideas changed in 1964, when he and Mary made another discovery: a new species called *Homo habilis*, or "handy man." This creature was less apelike than *Australopithecus*, and it had a larger cranial capacity, smaller teeth, a human-like foot, and hand bones that suggested an ability to hold and manipulate objects. In all likelihood "handy man" hunted small prey; whether it acquired a language remains unclear.

OLDUVAI GORGE

When Louis and Mary Leakey began excavating at Olduvai Gorge, they penetrated a site that was millions of years old. Located in the eastern Serengeti Plains of northern Tanzania, Olduvai Gorge is a steep ravine about 30 miles long (50 kilometers) and 295 feet deep (90 meters). Deposits located in the sides of the gorge date from about 15,000 to 2.1 million years ago. In these deposits, scientists have unearthed fossils of plants, animals, hominid remains, and items from the Stone Age.

The first European to discover Olduvai Gorge was Wilhelm Kattwinkel, a German entomologist, in 1911. A few years later, German paleontologist Hans Reck discovered the remains of hundreds of extinct Pleistocene mammals in the area.

The Olduvai fossil beds formed in a lake basin between 4 and 9 miles (6.4 and 14.5 kilometers) in diameter. Fault movements, volcanic action, and water flow have combined to cut through the rock and expose the beds, while volcanic ash has helped to preserve the fossils.

There are, in all, seven primary deposits: Bed I (1.7 million to 2.1 million years old); Bed II (1.15 million to 1.7 million years old); Bed III (800,000 to 1.15 million years old); Bed IV (600,000 to 800,000 years old); the Masek Beds (400,000 to 600,000 years old); the Ndutu Beds (32,000 to 400,000 years old); and the Naisiusiu Beds (15,000 to 22,000 years old).

It was in the upper part of the 200-foot-thick (60-meter-thick) Bed I that Mary Leakey found *Zinjanthropus boisei* in July 1959. The lower third of Bed II has yielded *Homo habilis*, and Beds II and IV have yielded *Homo erectus*. In addition, the Naisiusiu Beds have yielded a *Homo sapiens* skeleton dating to about 17,000 years ago. Today, scientists continue to excavate the site for clues to the prehistoric past.

Critics claimed that *Homo habilis* failed to meet the definition of a new species, that it resembled *Australopithecus* more than any type of *Homo*. Later evidence, however, seemed to support the Leakeys.

In addition, many scientists objected when Louis said that *Homo habilis* lived contemporaneously with *Australopithecus* (which eventually became extinct), as this challenged the concept of orderly evolution from one species to another; however, Louis considered *Homo habilis* to be the true ancestor of modern human beings. Louis died of a heart attack in London on October 1, 1972.

Mary continued the research she and Louis had begun in and around Olduvai Gorge. In 1979, at a nearby site called Laetoli, she found a long trail of human footprints embedded in volcanic ash from 3.6 million years ago. The prints showed that human bipedalism (two-footed, upright movement) had begun much earlier than previously thought.

In 1983, Mary retired from fieldwork and moved to Nairobi, Kenya, where she concentrated on her writing. She died on December 9, 1996.

Richard and Meave Leakey

Richard Leakey, born to Louis and Mary Leakey on December 19, 1944, followed in his parent's footsteps. As a boy, he participated in their digs, but as he got older, he preferred to be a safari guide.

In 1967, he discovered a geologic formation called Koobi Fora, located along the shores of Lake Turkana in Kenya, which turned out to be rich in Stone Age tools and hominid fossils. From 1968 to 1989, as a field researcher for and director of the National Museums of Kenya, he coordinated several field expeditions to Koobi Fora. On one of these expeditions, a team led by the Kenyan paleoanthropologist Kamoya Kimeu discovered Stone Age tools dating to about 1.9 million years ago.

Perhaps the most important of the museum finds under Richard's direction was "Nariokotome Boy," a nearly complete skeleton of a *Homo erectus* youngster dating from 1.6 million years ago. In two books cowritten with British anthropologist Roger Lewin, *Origins* (1977) and *People of the Lake* (1978), Leakey argued that about 3 million years ago three hominid forms coexisted: *Australopithecus africanus*, *Australopithecus boisei*, and *Homo habilis*. The first two, he said, became extinct, but the last one evolved into *Homo erectus*, the direct ancestor of *Homo sapiens* (modern human beings).

Richard Leakey ended his fieldwork in 1989, when he became head of the Kenya Wildlife Service and devoted his efforts to preventing ivory poaching. In 1994, following a plane accident in which he lost both legs below the knees, he left the wildlife service to enter politics.

In 1997, he was elected to the Kenyan parliament, and, in 1999, he was appointed head of the Kenyan civil service. He retired from that post in

2001, but remained active in fighting for the protection of plant and animal species under threat from human development.

Richard's wife, born Meave Epps in London in 1942, first worked with him in 1969, when she joined the field expedition to Koobi Fora. Meave had obtained her doctorate in zoology the previous year and married Richard in 1970. She also served as head of the National Museums' Division of Paleontology from 1982 to 2001, becoming coordinator of the museums' field research at Lake Turkana in 1989. In 1994, she led a team that found a new species of *Australopithecus anamensis* that was bipedal, dating from 4.2 million years ago.

In 2001, Meave Leakey and her team discovered a new genus and species of human ancestor called *Kenyanthropus platyops*. The specimen challenged the prevailing scientific view that *Australopithecus afarensis*, a contemporary of the newfound species, was in the direct ancestral lineage of *Homo sapiens*. In 2002, Meave and her daughter, Louise, were named explorers in residence by the National Geographic Society.

Louise Leakey was born in 1972 in Kenya to Richard and Meave. Her education included a doctorate from the University of London, after which she became head of the Koobi Fora Research Project. In that capacity, she has worked to make the research camp a year-round facility and has surveyed large areas east of Lake Turkana for future fieldwork.

Further Reading

Bowman-Kruhm, Mary. *The Leakeys: A Biography*. Westport, CT: Greenwood, 2005.

Isaac, Glynn, and Elizabeth R. McCown, eds. *Human Origins: Louis Leakey and the East African Evidence*. Menlo Park, CA: W.A. Benjamin, 1976.

Leakey, L.S.B. *By the Evidence: Memoirs, 1932–1951*. New York: Harcourt, Brace, Jovanovich, 1974.

Morell, Virginia. *Ancestral Passions: The Leakey Family and the Quest for Humankind's Beginnings*. New York: Simon and Schuster, 1995.

LEWIS AND CLARK EXPEDITION (1804–1806)

1803: President Thomas Jefferson completes the Louisiana Purchase and obtains congressional funding for an exploratory expedition through the territory

1804: Meriwether Lewis, William Clark, and the other expedition members, called the Corps of Discovery, begin their journey up the Missouri River on May 14

1805: The expedition reaches the Pacific Coast at Oregon on November 20

1806: The expedition returns to St. Louis, Missouri, on September 23

1809: Lewis dies on October 11 during a trip to Washington, D.C.
1838: Clark dies on September 1 in St. Louis

From May 1804 through September 1806, American explorers Meriwether Lewis and William Clark led an expedition through the vast territory between the Mississippi River and the Pacific Coast, much of which had been acquired by the United States in the Louisiana Purchase of 1803. The expedition members came to be known as the Corps of Discovery. In completing the journey to the Pacific Ocean, the Lewis and Clark expedition gathered vast amounts of scientific information, as well as samples and drawings, about the terrain, native peoples, flora, and fauna they encountered along the way.

The idea for the Lewis and Clark expedition had originated with President Thomas Jefferson even before the Louisiana Purchase. It reflected his personal interest in natural science, his long-standing curiosity about the American West, and his fear that the British or another foreign power might gain control of the Pacific Northwest and block America's westward expansion.

Indeed, in the late 1780s and again in the early 1790s, the Scottish-Canadian explorer Alexander Mackenzie had journeyed west to the Pacific. In 1793, he reached the Strait of Georgia (in present-day northwestern Washington and southwestern British Columbia), staking a British claim to a portion of the Pacific Northwest.

Although Mackenzie had failed to find a suitable route for overland trade, his effort posed a challenge to the United States. In 1802, Jefferson read Mackenzie's *Voyages from Montreal* (1801) and decided to take action.

Planning

Jefferson began planning an expedition that would begin in Missouri, proceed across the northern Rocky Mountains to the Pacific Ocean, find the Northwest Passage, and, in the process, establish U.S. control over the future of the region. Then, on July 4, 1803, Jefferson announced the purchase of the Louisiana Territory—an area of nearly 830,000 square miles (2.15 million square kilometers)—from France. Now, the expedition would travel on American soil, at least until it reached the Pacific Northwest, and the explorers would be exerting U.S. sovereignty.

Jefferson chose Captain Meriwether Lewis, his private secretary and former neighbor, to head the expedition. Lewis was born in Charlottesville, Virginia, on August 18, 1774, the son of William and Lucy Meriwether Lewis. He served in the U.S. Army beginning in 1795 and was promoted to captain in 1800. Jefferson later explained why he chose Lewis:

> It was impossible to find [anyone else] who to a compleat science in botany, natural history, mineralogy & astronomy, joined [together] the firmness of constitution & character, prudence, habits adapted to the woods, & a familiarity with the Indian manners & character, requisite for this undertaking.

Indeed, Lewis had studied extensively in the vast library at Jefferson's home in Virginia, Monticello. He had pored over maps and learned astronomy, botany, ethnology, mineralogy, and the practical use of the sextant from Jefferson, who was an accomplished general scientist in his own right.

Jefferson's formal instructions to Lewis, issued in June 1803, emphasized scientific findings and commerce. The president wanted extensive maps drawn up so that he might trace prospective trade routes. He wrote,

> Beginning at the mouth of the Missouri you will take careful observations of latitude & longitude, at all remarkable points on the river, & especially at the mouths of rivers, at rapids, at islands, & other places & objects distinguished by such natural marks & characters of a durable kind.

In addition, Jefferson instructed Lewis to try to establish good relations with any Native Americans the expedition might encounter and to learn about their lifeways. He also wanted Lewis to study the animals, plants, dinosaur bones, soil, minerals, and volcanoes and other natural phenomena.

Captain Lewis turned to William Clark to serve as co-commander of the expedition. (Clark had been named a captain, but his promotion was never approved by the War Department. Although he remained a second lieutenant, officially below Lewis in rank, Lewis always referred to him as "captain.") The two men had become friends in the army, where Lewis had been impressed by Clark's fortitude and trustworthiness.

William Clark was born in Caroline County, Virginia, on August 1, 1770. At the age of fourteen, he moved with his family to the Kentucky frontier, where they founded a plantation. Clark served as an infantry officer in the U.S. Army under General Anthony Wayne; in 1794, he took part in the Battle of Fallen Timbers in Ohio.

Two years later, Clark undertook a dangerous scouting mission and then resigned his commission to return to the family plantation. After being

The expedition journal of Lewis and Clark provided extensive descriptions of the land, people, plants, and animals—including the sage grouse of the Western plains—in the vast, uncharted territory between the Mississippi River and Pacific Coast. *(Granger Collection, New York)*

chosen to help lead the expedition, he spent time in Philadelphia to gain as much knowledge and training as he could from naturalists and scientists, among them Charles Willson Peale and Benjamin Rush.

Into the West

Lewis and other members of the party left Pittsburgh, Pennsylvania, in August 1803, meeting Clark along the way in Indiana that October. The members of the Corps of Discovery set up winter camp at Hartford, on the Illinois side of the Mississippi River, and officially began their journey to the west the following spring.

On May 14, 1804, the party set out from Saint Charles, Missouri—just below St. Louis on the Mississippi River—and then headed west on the Missouri River. A crowd on the riverbank cheered the explorers as they departed. Their vessels, a keelboat (a long boat with a shallow draft) and two pirogues (similar to canoes), left civilization as they knew it behind and beat against the current into an uncertain future.

The original Corps of Discovery consisted of about thirty men, including French boatmen who would transport the keelboat, soldiers, and an interpreter to help communicate with Native Americans. The boatmen faced a backbreaking challenge. They sometimes used poles to move the heavy keelboat and at other times walked on the riverbanks and pulled the keelboat with ropes. On rare occasions, they were able to use a sail to take advantage of favorable winds.

On June 26, the expedition reached the Kansas River, and, on July 21, it reached the Platte River, some 640 miles (1,030 kilometers) up the Missouri. On August 18, Lewis and Clark caught ten species of fish. Along the way, they studied minerals and the lay of the land. They were the first Americans to analyze the Great Plains in detail. In his journal, Clark wrote,

> The Plains of this countrey are covered with a Leek Green Grass, well calculated for the sweetest and most nourishing hay—interspersed with [copses] of trees, Spreding their lofty branches over Pools Springs or Brook of fine water. . . . Nature appears to have exerted herself to butify the Senery by the variety of flours Delicately and highly flavered above the Grass, which Strikes & profumes the Sensation.

In November and December, the men built a log stockade they called Fort Mandan in central North Dakota near the Mandan Indian villages, and they settled in for the winter. While there, Lewis and Clark hired a French-Canadian trader, Toussaint Charbonneau, and his wife, Sacagawea, a Shoshone Indian, to serve as interpreters with the Shoshone and the Hidatsa.

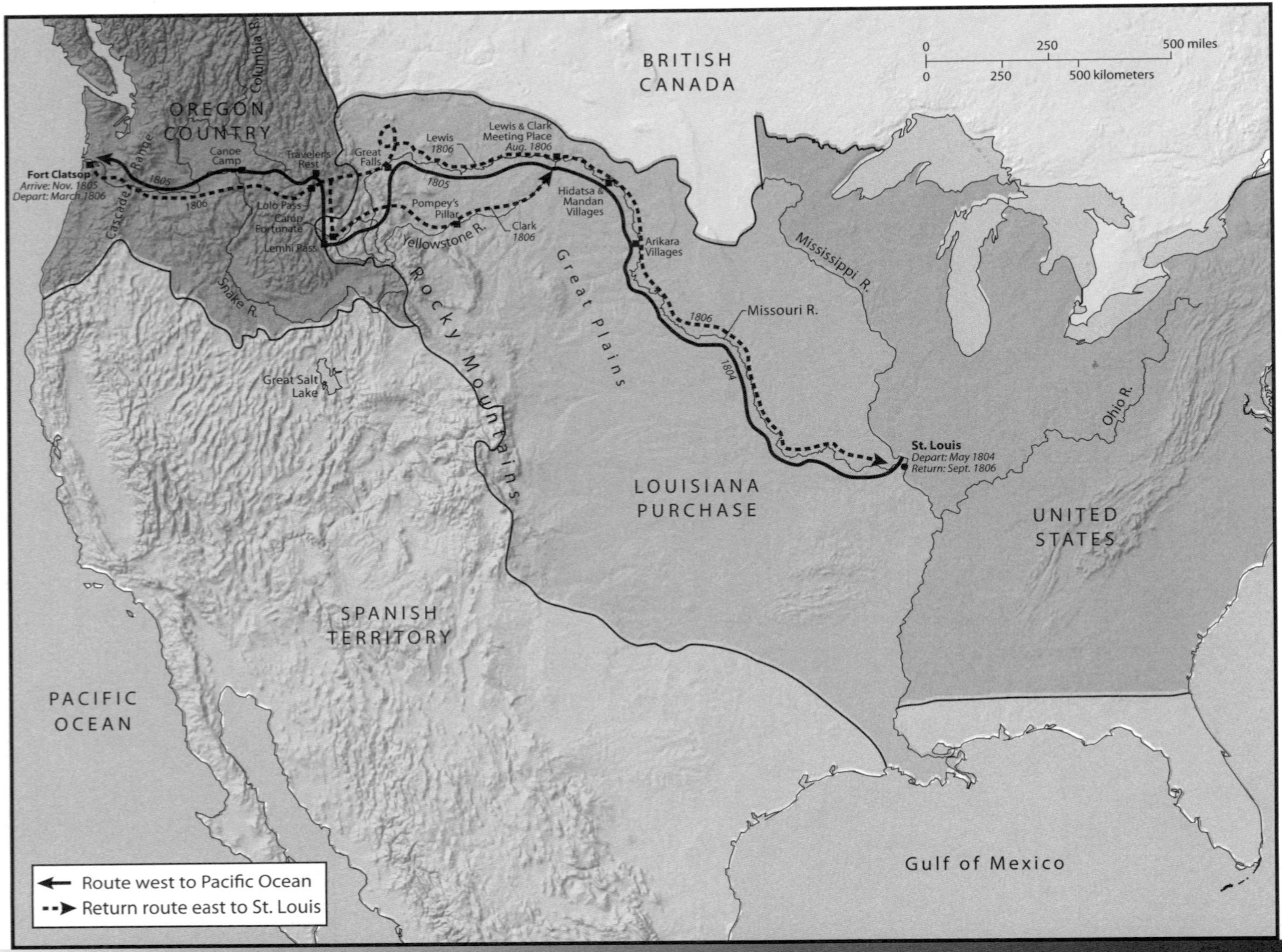

BRITISH
CANADA
0 250 500 miles
0 250 500 kilometers
OREGON
COUNTRY
Columbia R.
Fort Clatsop
Arrive: Nov. 1805
Depart: March 1806
Cascade Range
1805
1806
Canoe Camp
Travelers' Rest
Lolo Pass
Camp Fortunate
Lemhi Pass
Snake R.
Great Falls
Lewis 1806
Lewis & Clark Meeting Place Aug. 1806
1805
Pompey's Pillar
Yellowstone R.
Clark 1806
Hidatsa & Mandan Villages
Arikara Villages
Rocky Mountains
Great Plains
Great Salt Lake
Mississippi R.
Missouri R.
1806
1804
St. Louis
Depart: May 1804
Return: Sept. 1806
Ohio R.
LOUISIANA
PURCHASE
UNITED
STATES
SPANISH
TERRITORY
PACIFIC
OCEAN
Gulf of Mexico
Route west to Pacific Ocean
Return route east to St. Louis

SCIENTIFIC DISCOVERIES

In their journals, Lewis and Clark describe the many scientific discoveries and natural wonders witnessed on their expedition.

On birds, Lewis reported on September 20, 1805:

> This morning my attention was called to a species of bird [the varied thrush] which I had never seen before. It was rather larger than a robbin, tho' much it's form and action. The colours were a blueish brown on the back the wings and tale black, as wass a stripe above the croop ¾ of an inch wide in front of the neck and two others of the same colour passed from it's eyes back along the sides of the head.

On animals in the West, Lewis reported on February 15, 1806:

> The quadrupeds of this country from the Rocky Mountains to the pacific Ocean are 1st the *domestic animals,* consisting of the horse and dog only; 2cdly the *native wild animals,* consisting of the Brown white or grizzly bear . . . the black bear, the common red deer, the black tailed fallow deer, the Mule deer, Elk, the large brown wolf, the small woolf of the plains, the large wolf of the plains, the tiger cat, the common red fox, black fox or fisher, silver fox, large red fox of the plains, small fox of the plains or kit fox, Antelope, sheep, beaver, common otter, sea Otter, mink, spuck, seal, racoon, large grey squirrel, small brown squirrel, small grey squirrel, ground squirrel, swelel [mountain beaver], Braro [badger], rat, mouse, mole, Panther, hare, rabbit, and polecat or skunk.

On the Nez Perce Indians, Clark reported on October 10, 1805:

> The *Cho-pun-ish* or Pierced nose Indians are Stout likely men, handsom women. . . . Their amusements appear but fiew as their Situation requires the utmost exertion to prcure food . . . [in] the winter hunting the deer on Snow Shoes in the plains and takeing care of ther emence numbers of horsese & in the Spring cross the mountains to the Missouri to get Buffalow robes.

Until they reached the site of Fort Mandan, the Corps of Discovery had been traveling in territory that other Americans had explored. Still, Lewis and Clark had gathered much new information about Upper Louisiana (primarily Missouri and the Dakotas) based on their own observations and their questioning of Native Americans and white traders.

While at Fort Mandan, Lewis and Clark recorded their findings. They sent President Jefferson a lengthy report about the rivers and the people along their shores, the local economies, the soil, and the climate. They also sent him Native American artifacts, such as bows and robes; 108 botanical specimens intended for the American Philosophical Society, each labeled with a notation as to where and when the item had been collected and what medicinal properties it might have; sixty-eight mineral specimens, also with detailed labels; the skeletons and skins of animals; and even live animals—four magpies, a prairie dog, and a prairie grouse hen, although only one of the magpies and the prairie dog reached Jefferson alive.

Clark also sent a map he had drawn of lands west of the Mississippi River, which was highly accurate for the territory between St. Louis and Fort Mandan. All in all, they had gathered a treasure trove of scientific information, enough to make the expedition, even at this point, unprecedented in what it had learned about the American West.

To the Pacific

Lewis and Clark resumed the expedition in April 1805, with thirty-three people in the party. That September, Lewis noted in his journal several significant scientific findings, among them birds, such as the Steller's jay, green jay, black woodpecker, and blue grouse; and vegetation, such as the mountain huckleberry, Sitka alder, and western red cedar. All had been unknown to American science until that time.

On June 13, 1805, Lewis, traveling ahead, reached the Great Falls of Montana. "The grandest sight I ever beheld," he called it. He wrote,

> The rocks seem to be most happily fixed to present a sheet of the whitest beaten froath for 200 yards in length and 80 feet perpendicular. The water after descending strikes against the butment . . . and seems to reverberate and being met by the more impetuous courant they roll and swell into half formed billows of great hight which rise and again appear in an instant.

The Great Falls required the explorers to portage, carrying their canoes and supplies across rocks and cactuses. They dodged grizzly bears and rattlesnakes and endured biting insects and drenching rains.

Then, they followed the Lolo Trail from Montana into present-day Idaho, through deep snow and treacherous terrain. Along one narrow path, a horse tumbled over a cliff with valuable equipment. Deprived of food, the explorers resorted to eating some of their packhorses. Finally, in Idaho, the Corps met the Nez Perce Indians, who helped guide them west.

By following the Clearwater and Snake rivers, the expedition reached the Columbia River on October 16, 1805. Another hazardous stretch, filled with rapids and waterfalls, still awaited them, but on November 20 they finally reached the Pacific Ocean. On the coast, near present-day Astoria, Oregon, they built Fort Clatsop, where they stayed until March.

While wintering at Fort Clatsop, Lewis wrote detailed descriptions about flora and fauna and sketched animal and plant species he had seen during the trek. He also described the life of the native peoples of the Pacific region. For his part, Clark drew maps of the route west from Fort Mandan, as well as a large map, much improved over his earlier one, of the country west of the Missouri River.

The Return

The journey back from Fort Clatsop to St. Louis lasted from March to September 1806. At one point, Lewis divided the Corps of Discovery into

CHARLES WILLSON PEALE'S MUSEUM

Born and raised in Maryland, Charles Willson Peale (1741–1827) became a leading American portrait painter whose subjects included George Washington. In the early 1780s, he decided to found a museum in Philadelphia.

Initially established to house his paintings, Peale's museum came to include animal, mineral, and ethnographic specimens. Some of the items were collected by Peale, an active naturalist as well as an artist; others were donated by a variety of people interested in building a collection to reflect a national heritage and identity in the young American republic.

Thomas Jefferson donated numerous fossils to Peale's museum, which also became a repository for items from the American Philosophical Society. Peale's most famous exhibit, first displayed in 1801, was the skeleton of a giant "mammoth" or mastodon that had been discovered in the Hudson River Valley in New York State. Peale also became an expert taxidermist at a time when the craft was relatively primitive; some of his bird mountings still can be seen in museums.

At the time of the 1801 exhibition, Peale's museum—sometimes called the American Museum, or just the Museum—occupied three rooms in Independence Hall. The Quadruped Room displayed ninety specimens of mammals; in the Long Room, 700 bird specimens and 4,000 insects were on display in glass cases. A third room housed ethnographic specimens that had been gathered by the Lewis and Clark expedition.

The collections on display in Peale's museum had an enduring influence on American naturalists and their work for decades to come.

In an 1822 self-portrait, painter, naturalist, and collector Charles Willson Peale raises the curtain on his natural history museum in Philadelphia—the first of its kind in the United States. *(Granger Collection, New York)*

two smaller parties. Clark led one to explore the Yellowstone River; Lewis led the other to north-central Montana.

Lewis explored the Marias River from July 17 to July 28, 1806, and, near the Canadian border, established Camp Disappointment, where he stayed from July 21 to July 26. He was disappointed that the Marius failed to flow farther north, which would have provided a more extensive trade route and perhaps would have extended U.S. claims.

Given the small sizes of the two parties, and the possibility of encountering hostile Native Americans, splitting the Corps was risky, but it was important to gather as much information as possible. In August, the members of the Corps of Discovery reunited along the Missouri River. The expedition arrived in St. Louis on September 23, 1806.

Jefferson was ecstatic over the outcome. The expedition had discovered 122 animal species and subspecies previously unknown to science, including the grizzly bear, the California condor, and the pronghorn. In addition, it had found 178 new plant species, developed maps for the region, and opened contacts with several Native American tribes. Lewis, however, considered himself a failure for not having found an overland water route connecting the Missouri and Columbia rivers.

As for the zoological and ethnological specimens, nearly all were turned over to Charles Willson Peale's Museum at Independence Hall in Philadelphia, the only public natural history museum in the country at the time. Most were later destroyed in a fire at P.T. Barnum's American Museum in New York, to which they had been transferred.

Lewis gave the plant specimens from the expedition to the botanist Frederick Pursh, and they now are housed at the Academy of Natural Sciences in Philadelphia. The expedition's collection of birds and mammals provided a major impetus to the study of zoology in America.

The Lewis and Clark journals appeared in paraphrased form in *The History of the Expedition Under the Command of Captains Lewis and Clark*, which was published in 1814. In 1904, the Wisconsin Historical Society published the complete journals, in eight volumes.

Meriwether Lewis went on to become governor of the Louisiana Territory in 1807. He died on October 11, 1809, while on a trip from St. Louis to Washington, D.C. Evidence indicates that, in a state of depression, he committed suicide.

As for William Clark, when Missouri became a state in 1821, he ran for governor but lost. He died in St. Louis on September 1, 1838.

Further Reading

Ambrose, Stephen E. *Undaunted Courage: Meriwether Lewis, Thomas Jefferson, and the Opening of the American West.* New York: Simon and Schuster, 1996.

Curtright, Paul Russell. *Lewis and Clark: Pioneering Naturalists.* Lincoln: University of Nebraska Press, 1989.

Lavender, David Sievert. *The Way to the Sea: Lewis and Clark Across the Continent.* New York: Harper and Row, 1988.

Moulton, Gary E., ed. *The Lewis and Clark Journals: An American Epic of Discovery.* Lincoln: University of Nebraska Press, 2003.

LIVINGSTONE, DAVID (1813–1873), AND HENRY MORTON STANLEY (1841–1904)

1813: David Livingstone is born in Blantyre, Scotland, on March 19
1841: Henry Morton Stanley is born in Denbigh, Wales, on January 28
1849: Livingstone crosses the Kalahari Desert in southwestern Africa and finds Lake Ngami
1854: Livingstone reaches Luanda on Africa's west coast
1855: Livingstone journeys down the Zambezi River to the east coast of Africa
1859: Stanley immigrates to the United States
1866: Livingstone begins searching for the source of the Nile River
1871: Stanley meets Livingstone in Africa near Lake Tanganyika
1873: Livingstone dies at Chitambo in Africa on May 1
1875: Stanley shows that Lake Victoria is the source for the Nile River
1887: Stanley leads an expedition to rescue Emin Pasha, governor of Equatoria in Egyptian Sudan
1904: Stanley dies in London on May 10

The careers of Scottish explorer and missionary David Livingstone and of British-American explorer Henry Morton Stanley have been fixed in popular history by the meeting of the two men in Africa in 1871, when Stanley is said to have asked, "Dr. Livingstone, I presume?" Yet each man made important contributions in his own right to the scientific study of Africa that far exceed that meeting or a single expedition.

David Livingstone was born on March 19, 1813, in Blantyre, Scotland, to Neil Livingstone, a traveling tea salesman, and Mary Hunter Livingstone. The elder Livingstone preferred distributing Christian religious tracts to selling tea, and the family struggled to make ends meet. David began working in a cotton mill at age ten, but still attended school and read widely.

After working in the cotton mill into his twenties, Livingstone obtained a medical degree from the University of Glasgow in 1840. That same year, he was ordained as a minister in the Congregationalist Church and became a medical missionary under the London Missionary Society, serving in southern Africa.

Most English missionaries believed that Christianity alone could civilize Africa, but Livingstone thought differently: He believed it would take Christianity combined with commerce to change the continent, particularly to end what he called the "despicable" slave trade. Unless Africans learned to sell goods to Europeans for a profit, he maintained, they would be forever addicted to trafficking in human beings (trafficking that earlier had been encouraged by Europeans).

Livingstone thought it was his responsibility to open the interior of sub-Saharan Africa to European culture, and it was this commitment that led him to exploration. In 1845, he was married to Mary Moffat, the daughter of Scottish missionaries, and the couple lived with their five children in Africa for extended periods.

Livingstone in Africa

On June 1, 1849, Livingstone left Kolobeng in Bechuanaland (present-day Botswana) and traveled northwest to reach the Makololo tribe, with whom he intended to engage in missionary work. The journey made Livingstone and the two friends who accompanied him the first Europeans to cross the Kalahari Desert (in southwestern Africa) and find Lake Ngami (in northwestern Botswana), which he described as "shimmering."

In 1851, Livingstone again crossed the Kalahari and reached the upper Zambezi River. He began to think of the river as a waterway to commerce, an artery for the ready and profitable exchange of goods between Europeans and central Africans.

On his next journey, accompanied by twenty-seven Makololo warriors, Livingstone traveled northwest through Portuguese Angola to Luanda on the Atlantic Coast, which he reached in May 1854. By this time, he was taking a more scientific approach to his exploration, tracking altitudes, latitudes, and longitudes as he went, measuring rainfall, and noting geographical features. In doing so, he provided Europeans with valuable information about central and southern Africa.

In 1855, Livingstone headed a large expedition—with more than 100 porters—down the Zambezi River toward the east coast of Africa. During that journey, he became the first white person to see what the tribal people called "the smoke that thunders," which he named Victoria Falls.

Continuing east, he left the Zambezi on a side excursion and failed to discover the Kebrabasa Rapids. Had he done so, he would have learned what he failed to understand until years later: With its treacherous features, the Zambezi could not serve as a viable water route for trade.

Nevertheless, Livingstone reached the Indian Ocean at the mouth of the Zambezi in May 1856. Combined with his trip to Luanda, this made him the first European to cross the width of southern Africa.

With this expedition completed, Livingstone returned to England a hero. The Royal Geographical Society honored him with a medal, Queen Victoria granted him a private audience, and crowds mobbed him on the streets. In 1857, Livingstone published an account of his exploits, *Missionary Travels and Researches in South Africa,* which sold 70,000 copies and made him wealthy.

In an expedition from 1858 to 1863 sponsored by the British government, Livingstone next explored the Zambezi, Shire, and Ruvuma rivers, along with Lake Malawi in southeast Africa. He subsequently obtained private funding to explore the watersheds of the Zambezi and to find the source of the White Nile. At that time, the origin of the White Nile was being debated by two other prominent British explorers, Richard Burton and John Hanning Speke.

Beginning in 1866, Livingstone explored lakes Malawi, Mweru, and Bangweulu. In 1871, he became the first European to reach the Lualaba River, which he thought might be the headwaters of the Nile. (In fact, it was the headwaters of the Congo River.)

Henry Morton Stanley

It was during the latter expedition that Livingstone met Henry Morton Stanley, an American journalist-explorer working as a special correspondent for the *New York Herald.*

Stanley was born John Rowlands on January 28, 1841, in Denbigh, Wales, the illegitimate son of Elizabeth Parry. His mother abandoned him while he was a baby, and he was raised by his maternal grandfather for the first years of his life.

Taken to a workhouse in 1847, he obtained a basic education before sailing for the United States as a cabin boy aboard the *Windermere.* Arriving in New Orleans in 1859, he is said to have taken the name Stanley from a wealthy American merchant who took him in and found him a job.

Stanley fought for the Confederacy in the American Civil War and was captured in the Battle of Shiloh in April 1862. After his release, he joined a Federal artillery regiment and then served in the U.S. Navy as a merchant marine. Traveling west after the war, he took up writing and became a newspaper reporter in 1867, first for the *Missouri Democrat* in St. Louis and, later, for the *New York Herald.*

When and where Stanley came up with the idea of searching for David Livingstone—little heard from after years in the African interior—is not known for certain. Stanley once said that the idea originated with the publisher of the *Herald,* James Gordon Bennett, Jr. Evidence suggests that it was Stanley's idea. In fact, as early as 1866, he had expressed an interest in traveling to Africa to find the famous Scottish explorer.

The Meeting

The heart of Scottish explorer David Livingstone was buried near Lake Bangweulu in present-day Zambia, south of his 1871 meeting place with Henry Morton Stanley. The inscribed section of the tree is now housed at the Royal Geographical Society in London. *(Hulton Archive/Stringer/Getty Images)*

In 1868, Stanley traveled to Africa on an assignment to cover a showdown between British and Ethiopian troops. Two years later, Bennett agreed to send Stanley to search for Livingstone, whose last communication had been in the form of a letter the previous year from Ujiji on Lake Tanganyika. Bennett wanted a series of articles that would help to sell newspapers; Stanley wanted fame.

After arriving in Zanzibar in January 1871, Stanley departed Bagamoyo on the east coast of Africa on March 21. He rode a thoroughbred stallion and was accompanied by a phalanx of porters and soldiers carrying an American flag and singing as they went.

In November, Stanley finally made contact with an ailing David Livingstone near Lake Tanganyika. Perhaps he uttered the famous words "Dr. Livingstone, I presume?" Or perhaps Stanley fabricated the phrase later to reflect what he thought was a proper greeting given the formalities of English society, at least as he perceived them. In any event, the statement first appeared in public in the *New York Herald* on July 2, 1872, in a story about the meeting between the two explorers.

Whatever words were spoken, Livingstone was overjoyed to see Stanley. In his search for the source of the White Nile, the Scotsman had returned to Ujiji suffering from dysentery and ulcerated feet. Moreover, the supplies he had left there, including medicine he needed, had been plundered. Stanley's replenishments were thus welcome, and Livingstone was pleased with the opportunity to tell his stories in the *Herald.*

Stanley stayed with Livingstone in central Africa for four months. In his dispatches to the *Herald,* he portrayed the Scotsman as a benevolent, self-sacrificing missionary.

When his health returned, Livingstone invited Stanley to join him in exploring the northern coast of Lake Tanganyika, which they reached on November 28, 1871. In doing so, they discovered that the Rusizé River could not be the source of the Nile, because the Rusizé flowed into the lake. Livingstone had been hoping that Lake Tanganyika might be more important to the Nile than Lake Albert or Lake Victoria.

Stanley the Explorer

Stanley's visit with Livingstone transformed him from a reporter into an African explorer. When Livingstone died at Chitambo on May 1, 1873, Stanley vowed to find the source of the Nile.

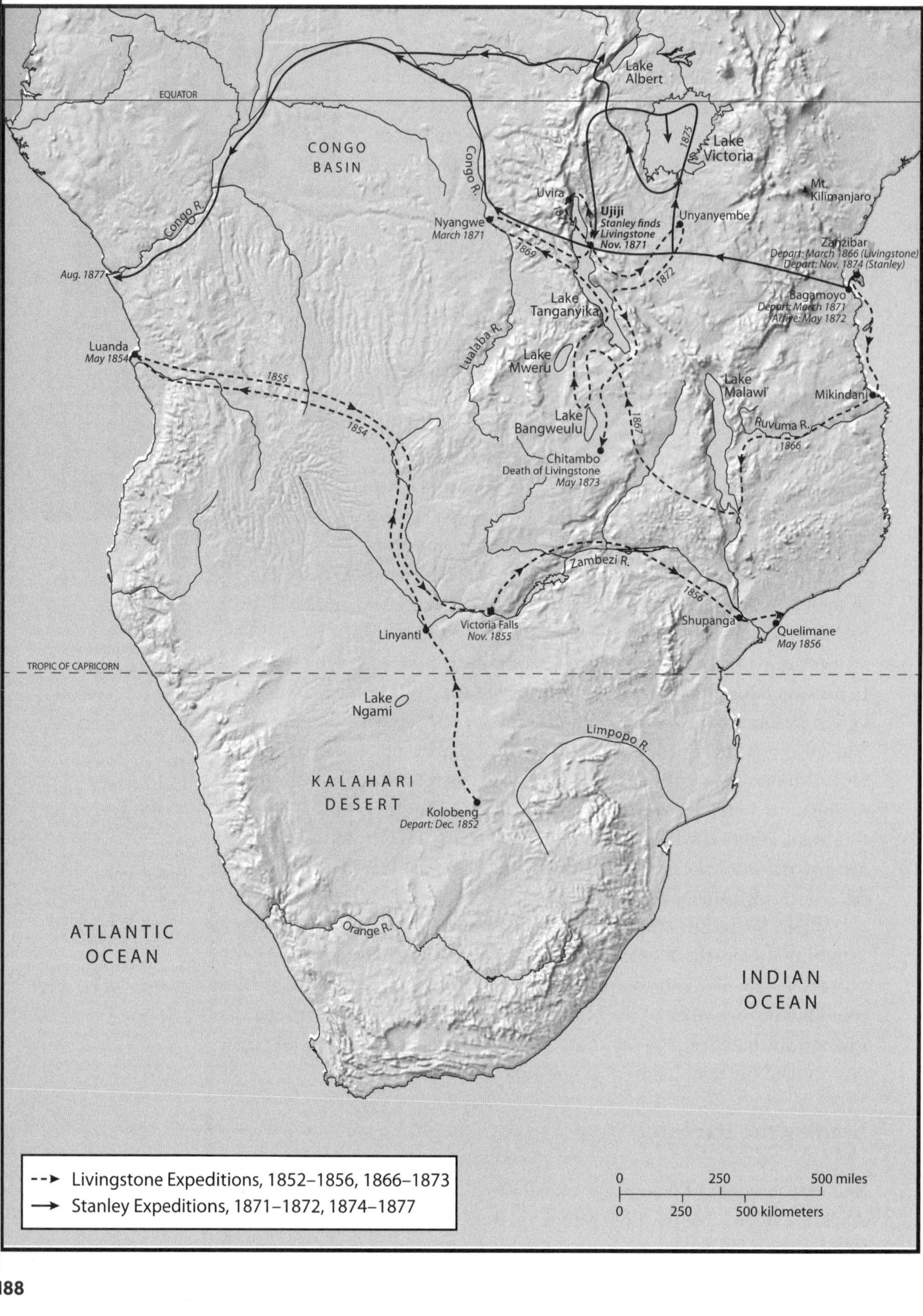
Lake Albert
EQUATOR
CONGO BASIN
Congo R.
Lake Victoria
1875
Mt. Kilimanjaro
Uvira
Ujiji
Stanley finds Livingstone Nov. 1871
Unyanyembe
Nyangwe
March 1871
1869
1872
Zanzibar
Depart: March 1866 (Livingstone)
Depart: Nov. 1874 (Stanley)
Congo R.
Aug. 1877
Lake Tanganyika
Bagamoyo
Depart: March 1871
Arrive: May 1872
Lualaba R.
Luanda
May 1854
1855
1854
Lake Mweru
Lake Malawi
Mikindani
Lake Bangweulu
1867
Ruvuma R.
1866
Chitambo
Death of Livingstone
May 1873
Zambezi R.
1856
Shupanga
Quelimane
May 1856
Linyanti
Victoria Falls
Nov. 1855
TROPIC OF CAPRICORN
Lake Ngami
Limpopo R.
KALAHARI DESERT
Kolobeng
Depart: Dec. 1852
ATLANTIC OCEAN
Orange R.
INDIAN OCEAN
Livingstone Expeditions, 1852–1856, 1866–1873
Stanley Expeditions, 1871–1872, 1874–1877
0 250 500 miles
0 250 500 kilometers

In 1875, Stanley spent eight months sailing on Lake Victoria and then circumnavigating it. Lake Victoria turned out to be one big body of water rather than a series of smaller ones, as many had assumed. Notably, its waters were found to flow toward the north, thereby confirming John Hanning Speke's argument that Lake Victoria was the source of the White Nile.

From Lake Victoria, Stanley journeyed to Lake Tanganyika, which he also circumnavigated. From there, he traveled up the Lualaba River and discovered that it fed the Congo River, which he followed to the Atlantic Coast.

In 1887, Stanley returned to Africa, when he led an expedition to rescue Emin Pasha, whom the British had appointed governor of Equatoria in southern Egypt (now Sudan). Emin—in reality a Prussian physician and con man named Eduard Schnitzer—was under assault by Islamic revolutionaries under the Mahdi (a self-proclaimed Islamic redeemer). Stanley led the successful relief expedition, in the course of which he made notable contributions to exploration and endured great hardship.

On assignment for the *New York Herald*, Henry Morton Stanley traveled to central Africa in search of missing explorer David Livingstone. After the encounter, Stanley continued his own jungle exploration and made several major discoveries. *(London Stereoscopic Company/Stringer/Hulton Archive/Getty Images)*

With the Sudanese who accompanied him, Stanley became the first white man to cross the Ituri forest. There, he was attacked by natives with poisoned arrows and battled starvation; several of his men were reduced to mere skin and bones. He also explored the Ruwenzori Mountains, found that the Semliki River emptied into Lake Albert, and discovered and named Lake Edward, which he confirmed as the source of the Semliki.

Stanley supported colonialism of a benevolent kind, saying in his latter years, "What we want now is to develop the country, not so much for the white man, but for the natives themselves." He had wanted Britain to rule the Congo, but King Leopold II of Belgium gained control during the 1880s. Leopold intended to rule the region as a private estate, not as a colony of Belgium. Under Leopold, Belgian settlers committed numerous atrocities—such as cutting off the hands of reluctant workers—in extracting rubber from the land.

Unwittingly, Stanley had opened the door to harsh Belgian rule when, in 1879, he had undertaken the construction of a highway near the Congo River at King Leopold's behest; he also established river stations, a small railway, and a steamboat operation. Indeed, he even had persuaded local chieftains to grant sovereignty over their land to Leopold.

When, in the 1890s, Stanley heard of the Belgian atrocities, he refused to believe them. As the evidence mounted, however, he became critical of the developments and tried to persuade Leopold to permit an international

STANLEY'S AFRICAN OBSERVATIONS

Henry Morton Stanley's writings about Africa display the mixture of science and adventure he experienced on the continent. His two-volume *Through the Dark Continent* (1878) included maps, drawings, and ethnographic descriptions such as the following:

> The Waguha, among whose country we had voyaged since leaving Tembwé, are an unusually ceremonious people. . . . The art of the coiffeur is better known here than in any portion of Africa east of Lake Tanganyika. The "waterfall" and "back-hair" styles are superb, and the constructions are fastened with carved wooden or iron pins. Full dress includes a semicircle of finely plaited hair over the forehead painted red, ears well ochred, the rest of the hair drawn up taut at the back of the head, overlaid and secured by a cross-shaped flat board, or with skeleton crown of iron; the head is then covered with a neatly tasseled and plaited grass cloth, like a lady's breakfast-cap, to protect it from dust. In order to protect such an elaborate construction from being disordered, they carry a small head-rest of wood stuck in the girdle.

> They greeted each other in the following manner:

> A man appears before a party seated; he bends, takes up a handful of earth or sand with his right hand, and throws a little into his left—the left hand rubs the sand or earth over the right elbow and the right side of the stomach, while the right hand performs the same operation for the left parts of the body, the mouth meanwhile uttering rapidly words of salutation.

investigation—a proposal the monarch flatly rejected. (The Congo came under the direct control of Belgium in 1908 after Leopold suffered financial setbacks.)

A naturalized U.S. citizen, Stanley became a British subject again in 1892. He served in Parliament from 1895 to 1900, and was knighted in 1899. He wrote several books on his African expeditions, including *How I Found Livingstone in Central Africa* (1872), *Through the Dark Continent* (1878), and *The Congo and the Founding of Its Free State* (1885). He died on May 10, 1904, in London, following an attack of pleurisy.

Interestingly, Stanley had helped create the image of a "saintly" Livingstone, which made the Scotsman more esteemed than Stanley. Despite his accomplishments and intentions, Stanley was more often associated with the brutal exploitation of the Congo. Whatever their real virtues and flaws, both men provided Europeans with previously unknown knowledge about the geography, people, and climate of central and southern Africa.

Further Reading

Dugard, Martin. *Into Africa: The Epic Adventures of Stanley and Livingstone.* New York: Doubleday, 2003.

Jeal, Tim. *Stanley: The Impossible Life of Africa's Greatest Explorer.* New Haven, CT: Yale University Press, 2007.

Newman, James L. *Imperial Footprints: Henry Morton Stanley's African Journeys.* Washington, DC: Brassey's, 2004.

See also: Burton, Richard Francis; Speke, John Hanning.